# Urban Governance
# and Minorities

edited by
**Herrington J. Bryce**

Published in cooperation with the
Joint Center for Political Studies

The Praeger Special Studies program—
utilizing the most modern and efficient book
production techniques and a selective
worldwide distribution network—makes
available to the academic, government, and
business communities significant, timely
research in U.S. and international economic, social, and political development.

# Urban Governance and Minorities

PRAEGER SPECIAL STUDIES IN U.S. ECONOMIC, SOCIAL, AND POLITICAL ISSUES

**Praeger Publishers**    New York   Washington   London

29260

Library of Congress Cataloging in Publication Data
Main entry under title:

Urban governance and minorities.

(Praeger special studies in U.S. economic, social, and
political issues)
   Includes bibliographical references.
   1. Municipal government—United States—Addresses,
essays, lectures.   2. Political participation—United States—
Addresses, essays, lectures.   3. Afro-Americans—Politics
and suffrage—Addresses, essays, lectures.   I. Bryce,
Herrington J.
JS341.U72              352'.008'0973        75-44875
ISBN 0-275-23500-9

PRAEGER PUBLISHERS
111 Fourth Avenue, New York, N.Y. 10003, U.S.A.

Published in the United States of America in 1976
by Praeger Publishers, Inc.

Printed in the United States of America

This publication is an outgrowth of the Joint Center's continuing probe for knowledge and understanding in areas of immediate concern to minority group citizens. It is based on the deliberations of black and white scholars, politicians and other professionals at a one-day Public Policy Forum on Urban Governance, which was held in Washington, D.C. in the spring of 1975.

Except for the challenges inherent in international politics, urban growth is one of the most volatile problems confronting America today. Our cities are dynamic entities, and they are constantly changing. Some changes provide solutions to old problems, some exacerbate existing ones, while others give rise to new concerns. Inevitably, each increment of growth and every kind of change ushers in new challenges which require decisions and actions by those responsible for making our cities more livable.

These are some of the reasons why research and debate on urban growth and change are necessary and why the Joint Center decided to sponsor the Forum on Urban Governance. Furthermore, urban centers are not just the sum of the individuals who reside in them. They are also centers of employment, trade, education, government, and culture. They provide amenities not only to their residents, but to their suburban neighbors and to the nation as a whole. Regardless of how we may choose to define the function of cities and in spite of the serious trouble in which many find themselves today, they continue to play vital roles in our way of life.

Black Americans have a special stake in the governance and survival of the cities. Nearly 60 percent of all blacks live in central cities—more than twice the percentage of white city residents. As the urban black population continues to grow, the future of black Americans becomes increasingly entertwined with the future of cities.

The views and ideas presented in this book make a substantial contribution to the continuing search for solutions to our urban problems. We are indebted to the authors for sharing them with us.

The rise of blacks in the last decade to the mayoral offices across the country is a landmark event in the governance of our cities. This phenomenon is closely related to the urbanization of blacks. Part I of this volume begins with this background, and proceeds with a paper by Thomas Pettigrew that describes some of the pioneering campaigns and the strategies best suited for black ascendancy to the mayoral office. His paper is followed by my own, which assesses the socioeconomic quality of cities in which blacks have become mayors and the legal powers conferred on these mayors.

Part II focuses on the economy and the responsibility of mayors. Certainly, the most trying and difficult responsibility of many mayors relates to the budget. Roy Bahl and Alan Campbell relate budgetary expenditures to the racial composition of cities. Seymour Sacks outlines the changing employment functions of cities. Kenneth Gibson, mayor of Newark, describes the process he follows and ultimate decisions he as a mayor has to make in preparing the budget for a city that is in crisis. The last chapter in the section, by Howard Lee, mayor of Chapel Hill, North Carolina, describes the management and governance problems of a small city and offers some recommendations for improvement.

It is felt by many observers that as blacks became mayors, the center of power shifted to other levels of government. Part III of this book deals with that subject. David Walker describes the forces behind the shift of power to county, regional, and state levels of government. Lee Calhoun raises the question, "Is this shift good for blacks? How has at least one black mayor responded?" A countervailing force to the shift of decision making to a wider body is the rise of neighborhood governments. Melvin Kotler argues the case for this development. Harvey Garn and Nancy Tevis bring the argument full circle by pointing to some of the strengths and weaknesses of Kotler's argument; at the same time, they suggest that what is really needed is a form of government consistent with the goals of urban growth. This, they suggest, is a metropolitan state.

Part IV deals with another aspect of the shift of power—the shift of power to citizens. Ricardo Millett draws upon empirical data to evaluate the experience of the Model Cities experiment with citizen participation. Charles Hamilton concludes that blacks opted for the wrong prizes and, consequently, citizen participation led to very little of the sensible type of long-term benefits for blacks as a group. Ira Katznelson describes the experience of other ethnic groups with citizen participation in New York. What did they opt for? Paul Peterson sees very little future for citizen participation—at least as expressed by maximum feasible participation. Clarence Stone disagrees and suggests that citizen participation might be the essential cornerstone of the new ruling coalition in our cities.

There is little doubt that a major problem facing our urban citizens is crime. The incidence of victimization and the rate at which blacks commit crime are both alarmingly high and result in very large expenditures by cities. Hence, it would be an error to have a conference on governance that did not look at the problem of crime. Lee Brown, a Ph.D. turned sheriff, traces the causes, trends, and proposed areas of reform in the criminal justice system. George Crockett, a judge, emphasizes that one area of the justice system that is in need of greater scrutiny is the discretion which judges exercise.

Gerald Caplan offers an extensive discussion as to the role of citizens in decreasing the crime rate. The section closes with two respondents. Jerry Wilson, the former chief of police in Washington, D.C., responds to one of the popular recommendations—the professionalization of police, which he opposes. Leroy Clark argues for work reform as a means of reducing recidivism.

The book concludes with a paper by Woody and Mann stating that the integration of planning and governance is the trend of the future.

This book is an outgrowth of the Public Policy Fellows Program at the Joint Center for Political Studies, funded by the Ford Foundation. It grew out of a one-day conference that represented the Joint Center's continuing effort to address major problems facing the nation and minorities within it. Barbara Buhl had the chief responsibility of coordinating the conference and assisted in obtaining data for Chapter 3 of the text. She was assisted by Vernease Herron, who also helped with Chapter 3, and Emily Kay. Beverly Gaustad Bryce, Eric Martin, Milton Morris, and Robert McGuire were helpful in conceptualizing the project and Edgar Russell and Eleanor Farrar were always helpful in getting over the bottlenecks. The publication effort has been managed by Dolores Wainwright with Barbara Crawford and Deena Akhavan. The arduous task of editing the manuscripts down from a total of 550 pages to this book's present size was aided by Daniel Gottlieb and Janet King of D.W. Gottlieb and Associates. These individuals, however, bear no responsibility for the remaining errors.

Finally, we want to thank Jewel Lafontant, deputy solicitor general of the United States; Marguerite Barnett, assistant professor of political science at Princeton; Harry Wheeler, director of manpower for the city of Newark, and Charles Harris, chairman, department of political science, Howard University for their participation as chairpersons of the conference.

# CONTENTS

## PART VI: CONCLUSION

# LIST OF TABLES AND FIGURES

# I

# THE RISE TO
# MAYORAL POWER

# 1

## MINORITIES AND THE FUTURE OF CITIES

Herrington J. Bryce
Ernest Erber
Phillip Clay

It is now apparent that most blacks will continue to live in large cities for a very long time to come. True, there will be increasing numbers of blacks moving to inner and older suburbs, and a few with relatively high incomes will move out of center city enclaves, which are predominantly black, into enclaves in the suburbs that are predominantly white. But the black population will continue to be urban and concentrated in the central city. Thus, urban governance and minorities will continue a close tie.

## BACKGROUND

The year 1970 marked a turning point in black settlement patterns and in the impetus for social change that opened residential opportunities to blacks. This was the end of a decade (the 1960s) when the struggle for civil rights was at its peak and when governmental and private action was mobilized against discrimination in education, housing, voting rights, and employment.

By 1970, the impetus came to an end. "Benign neglect" had displaced much of the active concern in the 1960s over the status of minorities and the poor in all sectors of our national life. Federal funding of categorical programs in the cities was being replaced with revenue sharing and there was a lessening of federal directives and new emphasis on local government decision making. There also was good reason for concern that national policy was moving toward retreat on efforts to open up our society to blacks.

The geographic mobility of blacks was in response to the expansion of job opportunities in the North, the urbanization of the South, the expectation that racial equality might be realized, and the rapid development of suburban areas for whites, which opened new residential opportunities for blacks in northern

3

cities. Almost 1.5 million blacks left the South during the 1960s and the percentage of blacks living in the South declined from 60 percent in 1960 (it had been 68 percent in 1950) to 53 percent by 1970. Consequently, almost 40 percent of all blacks living in the North in 1970 had been born in the South.[1]

By 1970, blacks also had made a massive shift from rural to urban areas. Those living within metropolitan areas increased by 31.6 percent between 1960 and 1970. Most of this shift was into central cities. Blacks increased as a percentage of central city populations from 16.4 percent to 20.5 percent from 1960 to 1970. For central cities whose metropolitan areas had a population of one million or more, the percentage of blacks increased from 18.8 percent to 25.2 percent from 1960 to 1970.[2]

Today, 43 percent of the U.S. black population is concentrated in the 26 cities that have more than 100,000 blacks. The 26 cities are New York, Chicago, Detroit, Philadelphia, Washington, Los Angeles, Baltimore, Houston, Cleveland, New Orleans, Atlanta, St. Louis, Memphis, Dallas, Newark, Indianapolis, Birmingham, Cincinnati, Oakland, Jacksonville, Kansas City (Missouri), Milwaukee, Pittsburgh, Richmond, Boston, and Columbus (Ohio). While these cities are located in all parts of the country, most of them are outside the South and in areas where a pattern of black concentration began in 1950s. These cities received the largest migration from the South during the 1960s. By 1970, Washington, D.C., Atlanta, Georgia, and Newark, New Jersey had black majorities and four other cities—Baltimore, Detroit, New Orleans, and St. Louis—were more than 40 percent black.

There was another great change in the shifting populations: by 1970, blacks became more urban than whites. The percentage of blacks living in an urban setting (in Standard Metropolitan Statistical Areas or SMSAs) was 74 percent, while 68 percent of whites lived in these areas (see Table 1.1). Most of the blacks were concentrated in the central city, while a growing majority of urban whites lived in suburbs. In other words, the trend has been one of increasing concentration of the black population in the inner core of metropolitan areas. The percentage increase in the proportion of blacks in the inner city in the early 1970s has been increasing at about 1 percent a year, and the percentage of the black population in rural areas has been showing a comparable decline of about 1 percent a year.[3] But it was not by their moves alone that blacks became a larger proportion of the central city population; it was also because whites have continued to leave the central cities. It appears from these data that while whites have ceased to concentrate and even show some small deconcentration, blacks are continuing to concentrate both in center cities and within the largest metropolitan areas as a whole. The Annual Housing Survey (1973) shows that among recent movers (almost all white), there was a net out-migration from metropolitan areas to nonmetropolitan areas of 3.5 percent.[4]

But the outstanding feature of the central city in the 1960s and 1970s has been the structural change in the function of the city compared to other parts of

## TABLE 1.1

### Population Distribution and Change Inside and Outside Metropolitan Areas, 1960 and 1970
### (numbers in thousands)

| Area | Black | | White | |
|------|-------|------|-------|------|
| | 1960 | 1970 | 1960 | 1970 |
| United States | 18,872 | 22,580 | 158,832 | 177,749 |
| Metropolitan areas | 12,741 | 16,771 | 105,829 | 120,579 |
| Inside central cities | 9,874 | 13,140 | 49,415 | 49,430 |
| Outside central cities | 2,866 | 3,630 | 56,414 | 71,148 |
| Nonmetropolitan areas | 6,131 | 5,810 | 53,003 | 57,170 |
| Percent Distribution | | | | |
| United States | 100 | 100 | 100 | 100 |
| Metropolitan areas | 68 | 74 | 67 | 68 |
| Inside central cities | 52 | 58 | 31 | 28 |
| Outside central cities | 15 | 16 | 36 | 40 |
| Nonmetropolitan areas | 32 | 26 | 33 | 32 |

Source: U.S. Department of Commerce, Bureau of the Census, *The Social and Economic Status of the Black Population in the United States*, 1974, Table 4.

the metropolitan area. As suburbs developed, the city was forced to give up its domination of the metropolis. The suburbs captured jobs in the central city and generated new jobs in the suburbs as well. Over the years, the process gathered momentum to the point where suburbs began to dominate the metropolis, state legislatures, and regional decision-making bodies.[5] In Chapter 8 of this volume, David Walker presents ample evidence of this fiscal-political shift.

The out-migration of whites from the central city did open up some housing opportunities in the city for blacks. Blacks entered the neighborhoods that whites left, and many of the former black neighborhoods were then taken over by new immigrants (Puerto Ricans or blacks from the South). When this was not the case, neighborhoods fell into abandonment (as described by Alexis in Chapter 11 of this book).

Not all blacks, however, flowed into the central city. More than 800,000 joined the 2.7 million blacks who were already in suburbia, many of them in traditional black population pockets. The percentage of the black metropolitan population living in the suburbs increased from 11 percent in 1960 to 16 percent in 1970. The suburbanization of blacks was limited to the largest metropolitan areas, with most of this movement occurring in less than a dozen of these areas. In suburban neighborhoods in 1970, 40 percent of the blacks were in neighborhoods where the majority of persons were black, while only 29 percent of blacks were in neighborhoods that were 15 percent black or less. In all metropolitan areas where there has been substantial black suburbanization, blacks have moved into only a fraction of the suburban neighborhoods. Even more significantly, they have settled in the oldest suburban areas, or those nearest to black inner-city ghettos.

But the spirit of the 1960s led to some of the progress of blacks in obtaining better homes and probably to less concentration in the core of the central cities, has been subdued. What can we expect now?

## FACTORS THAT WILL AFFECT BLACK CONCENTRATION

Blacks choose their place of residence for reasons that do not differ essentially from those of whites. "When the most important housing advantages of whites are compared to those most important for Negroes, it becomes apparent that both races base their housing choices on substantially the same criteria."[6] The answers produced by the classic study *Why Families Move*[7] are applicable to both races. Intersectional moves, such as those from South to North, are almost always in pursuit of a higher standard of living and, above all, improved employment opportunities. Movement within the same urban area is largely influenced by job location, though other factors, such as neighborhood environment, quality schools, better air, and the like, are important considerations in the decision-making process.[8]

Although sharing with whites the same criteria for deciding where to live, blacks obviously locate in a pattern distinctly different from that of whites. Is the explanation economic? The facts do not suggest so.

A study by Hermalin and Farley of black underrepresentation in the suburbs is particularly insightful on this point.[9] Using 1970 census data, the authors found that if income were the sole determinant, many more blacks would live in the suburbs and fewer would live in central cities. In the Los Angeles, Houston, Seattle, San Diego, Kansas City, Indianapolis, San Jose, Portland, Providence, and Washington, D.C. metropolitan areas, over 55 percent of the blacks would have been living in the suburbs if distributed on the basis of income comparable to that of whites in the suburbs. Instead, according to the 1970 census, only 17 percent of blacks lived in these suburbs.

The authors also analyzed the city/suburb distribution by race on the basis of what each race paid for housing in 1970. By this gauge, a far higher percentage of blacks would have lived in the suburbs given their expenditures for housing. The proportion of blacks living in suburbs of the nation's 29 largest cities would have been 43 percent rather than 16 percent, and much closer to the 57 percent of whites who lived in these suburbs.

A look at the overall distribution of races by income and place of residence in metropolitan areas leads to two inescapable conclusions: less income, and the consequent lower ability to pay for housing, accounts for some of the difference in residential patterns of the races, but the difference between the 43 percent of blacks who could afford to live in the suburbs and the 16 percent who actually lived there in 1970 is a strong indication of noneconomic causes. Hermalin and Farley came to a similar conclusion: "Evidence strongly indicates that residential segregation in central cities in 1970 is far in excess of what would be expected on economic grounds alone."[10] This confirms similar findings by Taeuber and Taeuber in their classic 1965 study based on the 1960 census.[11]

Since economic factors only partially account for the distribution of blacks in our metropolitan areas, it is necessary to identify noneconomic ones. Two noneconomic causes are important: the desire of blacks to live in areas of black population concentration, and the prevention of blacks from living where they want and can afford to live by discriminatory practices in the sale or rental of housing.

Opinion polls shows that the percentage of blacks who choose to live in all-black neighborhoods is between 8 to 13 percent of those polled; the rest prefer an interracial environment. Depending on how the question is phrased, varying proportions of blacks express preferences for racial ratios in acceptable neighborhoods from "mostly black" to "makes no difference," with the largest number preferring a 50 percent black, 50 percent white neighborhood.[12] Thus, it clearly is not a black desire for separatism that creates a balkanization of races; instead, it is discriminatory practices that prevent blacks from realizing their preferences. An examination of these discriminatory practices and an assessment of their continuing strength is essential to projecting where blacks will live in the future.

Among the discriminatory attitudes of whites toward blacks that are most likely to lead to hostile practices, those that relate to residential proximity probably are most powerful. Residential proximity of the races could pose for whites a threat that touches upon almost everything that they have striven to achieve. But if they are homeowners, they see a threat to their investment, almost always the major part of their assets.

Accordingly, those institutions that relate to the buying or renting of residential property are intensely aware of the racial implications of their operations. The result has been the development of policies and an intricate network of "standard" procedures that have a consistent racial effect.

The real estate industry, for example, gatekeeper to housing, has long been organized along racial lines, with a dual racial market as its most flagrant characteristic. The introduction into a neighborhood of a person of another race was once listed as grounds for disciplinary action by the rules governing the National

Association of Realtors (NAR).[13] Though such objectives are no longer avowed, the practice is still in vogue.

Real estate brokers have always considered it part of their professional role to guide buyers and tenants into settings in which they are likely to be compatible with their new neighbors. The key to neighborly compatibility, in the broker's lexicon, was similarity. Real estate advertisements once featured the sales theme of "live among people of your own kind." At that time, this was not an emphasis on racial homogeneity, since this form of homogeneity was assumed and readers could not have imagined things being otherwise. "Your own kind" referred mainly to income, occupation, and life-style. By implication, finding the right neighborhood and your own kind was not likely to happen unless the broker "steered" the homeseeker.

Steering has been made an illegal practice by fair housing laws, but it continues to be practiced. It is still an instinctive standard operating procedure for many brokers to steer blacks to neighborhoods that already have black residents or to steer them to a black broker with listings in the black neighborhoods. Whites, in turn, are steered away from these neighborhoods.

A case was filed against steering on March 8, 1976 in the U.S. District Court of New Jersey by the Fair Housing Council of Bergen County, Inc., the city of Englewood, a municipal corporation of the state of New Jersey, and other individuals against some of the realtors operating in Bergen County. The outcome of this case will have an important impact on "steering" in the future.

Given the limited areas of interracial housing, the practice of steering blacks into these areas and whites away from them leads to further concentration of blacks. This process is accelerated when brokers, including those who are black, resort to "blockbusting"; that is, spreading rumors of an impending large-scale influx of black households, wholesale white flight, and a resulting glut of homes on the market that will cause prices to tumble. Steering, with or without blockbusting, results ultimately in the formation and maintenance of racial concentration.

## THE FUTURE DISTRIBUTION OF BLACKS

Recent trends affecting constraints upon the ability of blacks to live in the area of their choice show little evidence of significant national change that is likely to produce a markedly different distribution of the black population in the next several years.

Economic constraints affecting black residential choice have tightened since 1970 with deepening unemployment and declining real wages. The median income of all black families dropped from 61 percent of white family income in 1969 to 58 percent in 1973.

Employment for blacks is not likely to improve unless overall employment improves, and it is even questionable whether most blacks will be able to resume making advances once the recession has ended. Lost footholds may not be easily regained in the face of long-range factors affecting the U.S. economy, such as increased energy costs, environmental costs, and structural changes in employment. Further, a considerable body of expert opinion holds that the rate of economic growth in the United States is leveling off to a lower plateau for the foreseeable future. Many economists see no significant decline in current unemployment rates through most of the remaining 1970s.

Steeply rising unemployment and declining real wages for blacks are accompanied by sharply rising housing costs as housing starts plunged downward in 1973 and continued down through 1975. Meanwhile, the cost of construction materials, labor, and mortgage interest rates has continued to rise, pushing up the average cost of newly constructed dwelling units in the Northeast, for example, more than 40 percent between 1970 and 1975. At the same time, the federal government's housing subsidy programs for low and moderate-income families were abruptly terminated in 1973, bringing the flow of subsidized units into the market to a virtual halt. It is still an open question how well the new 235 housing subsidy program will work to help blacks spread out of the inner city, since the income and down payment requirements are higher. Housing assistance programs inaugurated by the Housing and Community Development Act of 1974, principally Section 8 (a form of rent subsidy), are lagging badly and there is no indication that they will provide enough dwelling units to appreciably increase the housing opportunities of blacks, especially outside of the central city.

The passage of laws against discrimination in housing has, beyond any doubt, increased housing opportunities for blacks and will probably lessen the tendency toward concentration; but the effects are considerably limited because of the problem of enforcement.

Title 8 requires the secretary of the Department of Housing and Urban Development to act affirmatively in carrying out the purposes of the Civil Rights Act. Usually, this is interpreted to mean going beyond measures to prevent discrimination against a person of a minority race who has undertaken to buy or rent housing. Going beyond: mere prevention of discrimination requires the establishment of goals for minority occupancy in communities throughout each metropolitan area in order to overcome the effects of past discrimination. The planned allocation of subsidized housing for an entire housing market area, often referred to as a "fair share plan," is a major component of such affirmative action. Supplemented by an affirmative marketing plan that establishes minority racial occupancy targets and devises systematic advertising and selling procedures to attract minority homeseekers, housing allocation plans can open and are opening residential opportunities for blacks in areas long considered closed to them by virtue of economic and racial constraints, but the process is slow and many suburbs still have zoning barriers of various types.[14]

The real estate industry is making slow but steady progress in adapting itself to the existence of fair housing laws. The recently concluded fair marketing agreement between the U.S. Department of Housing and Urban Development (HUD) and the National Association of Realtors, even if largely limited to an agreement to observe fair housing laws, marks a milestone in the transformation of the "gatekeepers." This formal document, reluctantly accepted by the NAR, offers good possibilities for further positive evolution favorably affecting the "steering" practices of brokers. Agreement to obey the law can be considered as progress only when measured against past performance. For an appraisal of the shortcomings of this and other voluntary marketing agreements, see Robert C. Weaver's testimony before the House Subcommittee on Civil and Constitutional Rights, chaired by Rep. Don Edwards (D-Cal.), March 9, 1976. Real estate licensing boards in a number of states also have proven effective in alerting brokers to fair housing law observance and have made them exceedingly conscious of the possible suspension or loss of license that will result from violations. Those brokers who in the past have chafed under the irrationality of doing business in a dual racial market find fair housing laws a powerful public rationale for doing what they have always believed to be morally right and a protection against those of their discriminating peers who otherwise might penalize them.

Since 1950, litigation on behalf of the rights of racial minorities to equal opportunity in housing has led to a substantial body of case law that interprets federal and state constitutions and statutes to give increased protection against discrimination.[15] In federal courts, including the Supreme Court, setbacks against discrimination have outnumbered advances since 1971. In a recent federal court decision, however, "redlining"—the practice by financial institutions of denying mortgages on properties in inner city and interracial neighborhoods—has been declared a violation of federal law by a federal district court in Cincinnati, marking a break in the civil rights losing streak in federal courts. A number of state court systems, however, have acted against exclusionary zoning by suburbs, even if only on the basis of equality of access without regard to income, and only indirectly affecting equal access with regard to race.[16]

Furthermore, the authority of suburban governments to exclude housing within the means of low and moderate-income households, and indirectly to exclude racial minorities, is increasingly threatened by trends toward regional decision making. Most metropolitan areas now have regional councils of government and regional planning agencies that, though largely advisory, establish regional norms and standards by which suburban "home rule" measures can be judged. Embattled and financially drained central cities look towards regional solutions to pass part of the urban burden onto their suburbs; their reception is not always positive.

Thus, Hartford, Connecticut sued its suburbs and HUD for allocating community development block grant funds to the suburban jurisdictions in the absence of a housing assistance plan that meets the statutory requirements of the Housing and Community Development Act of 1974. A federal district court recently decided in favor of Hartford and permanently enjoined the federal funds until the suburbs assume their share of housing for low and moderate-income households.

## IMPLICATIONS

The continued concentration of blacks in central cities is not without its consequences for urban governance. Clearly, blacks, as citizens, should maintain and foster self determination. But whites need not fear. As the Taeubers have demonstrated, however, even when blacks are concentrated in large cities, as is currently the trend, the number of such cities in which they could have a majority is limited because a black population of only 24 million people is simply too small. Thus, the fear of black takeover of all large cities is unwarranted.

Furthermore, it is questionable that being an overwhelming majority in cities is advantageous to black political success. Pettigrew, in Chapter 2 of this volume, gives the keys to success. A large majority is simply not necessary for the growth and exercise of black political power. The fact is, as Bryce and Martin show in Chapter 3, most of the small and medium-size cities with black mayors have a minority black population, and most black mayors of cities (as opposed to small towns) could not be elected to these positions without white support.

The concentration of black voting power may be at the cost of distributing that power over a wider area. There are no accurate guidelines on the critical mass of blacks needed to assure victory in political races. Data from the Joint Center for Political Studies, for example, show several jurisdictions with a population that is at least 50 percent black that have no black elected officials on the governing board. For example, there are nearly 70 counties with a black population of at least 50 percent with no blacks elected to the governing board.[17]

Though it is likely that urban blacks will continue to be concentrated in central cities, there will be continuing changes in the areas of the city they will occupy. The coming energy crisis, the rising cost of development outside the city, the preference of many young whites for inner-city locations and proximity to jobs and cultural activities, and the increased value of inner-city real estate as long-range investment will create competition for inner-city space. As a result, in a number of cities, areas that were traditionally black now are undergoing white resettlement and blacks are being displaced. The entry of whites into the inner city, bringing a higher tax base and prospects of interracial neighborhoods, increases the hope that the cities will be revitalized and reverse the process

Alexis describes in Chapter 11. It also, however, presents an equity problem. What will be done for those blacks who are being displaced? Would they be helped by neighborhood government, as outlined by Kotler, in Chapter 10, or other neighborhood organizations as described by Garn and Tevis in Chapter 12?

## NOTES

1. U.S. Department of Commerce, Bureau of the Census, *The Social and Economic Status of the Black Population in the United States*, Current Population Reports, series P-23, no. 42 (Washington, D.C.: Government Printing Office, 1972), Table 2.

2. Ibid., 1973, Table 4, and 1974, Table 5.

3. U.S. Department of Commerce, Bureau of Census, op. cit., 1973, Table 4.

4. See U.S., Department of Commerce, Bureau of the Census, *Housing Characteristics of Recent Movers for the United States and Regions, Current Population Reports,* series H-150-73D (Washington, D.C.: U.S. Government Printing Office, 1975), p. xvii. See also *Current Population Reports*, series P-20, no. 262 (March 1974) and no. 273 (December 1974).

5. For a discussion of this trend see, generally, David Birch, *The Economic Future of the City and the Suburb* (New York: Committee for Economic Development, 1970). Also see Ernest Erber, "The Inner City in the Post-Industrial Era: A Study of its Changing Social Fabric and Economic Function," in *The Inner City*, eds. Declan Kennedy and Margrit Kennedy (New York: Halsted Press, 1974).

6. Norman M. Bradburn, Seymour Sudman and Galen L. Gockel, *Racial Integration in American Neighborhoods: A Comparative Survey* (Chicago: National Opinion Research Center, 1970), p. 262.

7. Peter H. Rossi, *Why Families Move: A Study in the Social Psychology of Urban Residential Mobility* (Glencoe, Ill.: Free Press, 1955).

8. Bradburn, op. cit., Table 9.8.

9. Arthur I. Hermalin and Reynolds Farley, "The Potential for Residential Integration in Cities and Suburbs: Implications for the Busing Controversy," *American Sociological Review* 38 (October 1973): 595-610.

10. Ibid., p. 601.

11. Karl E. Taeuber and Alma F. Taeuber, *Negroes in Cities: Residential Segregation and Neighborhood Change* (Chicago: Aldine Publishing Company, 1965).

12. Angus Campbell and Howard Schuman, *Racial Attitudes in 15 American Cities* (Ann Arbor, Mich.: Institute for Social Research, 1968), Tables IIa and IIb.

13. Quoted in Rose Helper, *Racial Policies and Practices of Real Estate Brokers* (Minneapolis: University of Minnesota Press, 1969), p. 201. At that time, the name of NAR was the National Association of Real Estate Boards.

14. Ernest Erber and John P. Prior, *Housing Allocation Planning: An Annotated Bibliography* (Monticello, Ill.: Council of Planning Librarians Exchange Bibliography, March 1974), no. 547.

15. Martin E. Sloane and the legal staff of National Committee Against Discrimination in Housing (NCDH), *Fair Housing and Exclusionary Land Use* (Washington, D.C.: NCDH and the Urban Land Institute, 1974).

16. Herbert M. Franklin, David Falk, and Arthur J. Levin, *In-Zoning: A Guide for Policy-Makers on Inclusionary Land Use Programs* (Washington, D.C.: The Potomac Institute, 1974).

17. Joint Center for Political Studies, *Black Political Participation: A Look at the Numbers* (Washington, D.C.: Joint Center for Political Studies, 1975), Section 3, 1-15.

# 2

## BLACK MAYORAL
## CAMPAIGNS
Thomas F. Pettigrew

Tuesday, November 7, 1967 has been called the last good day in American race relations. In Boston on that date Mrs. Louise Day Hicks, one of the North's leading white opponents of interracial education, lost decisively in the mayoral election. More important, the mayoralty victories of Richard Hatcher in Gary and Carl Stokes in Cleveland ushered in a new era in American politics. Since that fateful day, significant black entry into the political decision making of urban America has accelerated, with successful mayoralty races in major cities as diverse as Atlanta, Detroit, Los Angeles, Raleigh, and Washington.

The mass media typically interpret these mayoralty elections in exclusively racial terms and pay little attention to the many other dynamics involved. Race, to be sure, has been a dominant factor in all of these elections and we shall focus on it in this chapter; but we shall delineate in more detail just how the racial factor actually influences elections and how it interacts with other political phenomena.

This discussion will draw on data collected by my research project in four of these cities—Cleveland (1969), Gary (in 1968 and 1971), Newark (in 1970) and Los Angeles (in 1969 and 1973).[1] Typically, the project has analyzed voting data and surveyed probability samples of both blacks and whites who are registered to vote.

First, we shall discuss a number of phenomena that have occurred repeatedly in these cities when a black candidate has run for mayor. From these phenomena, we can derive a few crude rules of thumb about how race operates as a factor in these elections. Second, we shall discuss briefly a number of strategies for the black mayoralty candidate seeking the support of white as well as black voters.

## RECURRENT PHENOMENA

The four cities under review—Cleveland, Gary, Los Angeles, and Newark— are dissimilar in many ways. They vary widely in political structure, size, prosperity and composition of their populations. Cleveland and Gary hold partisan mayoralty elections; Los Angeles and Newark hold nonpartisan elections. Moreover, the candidates of both races in these contests differed in style and personality.

Nonetheless, there are numerous uniformities that appear across these cities and elections. One is race. Many blacks view the mayoralty contests as the sine qua non to representation in city government. Many whites feel strongly threatened by the prospect of a black mayor. In short, many blacks and whites perceive these contests in largely racial terms.

This effect is heightened by the fact that these are mayoralty elections. The office of mayor, like those of governor and president, is a high executive post. This contrasts with the offices to which a disproportionate share of blacks have been elected so far—city council member, legislator, and lower executive posts. A black's running for mayor is more likely to elicit both racial fears and racial hopes.

The uniformities that arise from this racial effect can be organized as follows: (1) voter turnout; (2) the role of partisanship; (3) the loyal black electorate; (4) the importance of candidate image; (5) the role of relative deprivation; and (6) common nonracial perceptions of blacks and whites. Let us consider each phenomenon in turn.

### Voter Turnout

Our first rule of thumb can be stated as follows: The first time a black candidate runs for mayor with a good chance of winning, the voter turnout of both blacks and whites is heavy.* Indeed, the total turnout will often set a local record for mayoralty elections.

Thus, in Cleveland and in Gary in November 1967, 80 percent of each race's registrants voted, while in Los Angeles in June 1967 the figure was better

---

*Two of the candidates under discussion (Stokes in 1965, Gibson in 1966) had run earlier for mayor, but neither of them was perceived (correctly) as having a good chance to win. Stokes was running as an independent in a partisan election; and Gibson was late in entering the race. Similar situations have arisen in New Haven, Connecticut and in Houston, Texas. Hence the qualification in the rule of thumb concerning "a good chance of winning." This qualification also covers the ill-fated Baltimore mayoralty primary of 1971, when there was only a 43 percent turnout of black registrants.

than 70 percent—a record for mayoralty elections in that city. Turnout in Newark in June 1970 was 76 percent, though the black turnout of about 74 percent was slightly below that of whites. Other cities seem to have had the same experience. Heavy turnouts of both races were recorded, for example, in Richard Austin's unsuccessful bid in Detroit in 1969 and Maynard Jackson's successful bid in Atlanta in 1973.

This initially heavy turnout is at best a mixed blessing for the black challenger. The high turnout of blacks, of course, is essential for victory, but the high turnout of whites generally includes many racially threatened whites who usually do not vote. This phenomenon is consistent with vast political science research on nonvoters, who are repeatedly found to be more conservative, authoritarian, and antiblack as a group than voters.[2]

This recurrent phenomenon of a heavy turnout of both races affects black candidates differently in cities of varying racial proportions. When blacks approach almost half of those registered, as in Newark in 1970, the effect is obviously minimal, but when white registrants vastly outnumbered black registrants, the effect can be catastrophic. In Los Angeles in 1969, where only about one-sixth of those registered were black, the record turnout in the runoff against incumbent mayor Samuel Yorty cost Bradley the election (52.1 to 47.9 percent), even after he had led Yorty by 42 to 28 percent in the initial race.

Our second rule of thumb, involving a somewhat different turnout phenomenon, can be stated as follows: The second time a black candidate runs for mayor with a good chance of winning, the voter turnout of blacks declines somewhat and the turnout of whites declines substantially. The total effect is to improve the probability of victory for the black candidate.

A black mayor's first-term performance usually dampens some of the black community's aspirations as to what he realistically can be expected to achieve. Even more, however, the mayor's performance reassures whites that their worst fears were simply not realized.

These racial fears also recede when a competent black candidate establishes himself in an initial race and begins to receive the type of media coverage that white political figures typically receive. Such was the case with Bradley in Los Angeles between his losing bid in 1969 and his victory in 1973.

Lowered white turnout in the second election generally means that fewer of the most racist whites have gone to the polls; thus, the percentage of white votes for a black mayoralty candidate will increase. When Stokes first ran as an independent in 1965, only about 11 percent of Cleveland's white voters supported him, compared to 19 percent in 1967 and 22 percent in 1969.* Hatcher's

---

*The slight rise in Stokes' white voter percentage from 19 to 22 percent between 1967 and 1969 may seem insignificant; but Penn Kimball demonstrates how this modest increase made the crucial difference in an election won by only 3,753 votes.[3]

percentage of the white vote rose slightly from roughly 15 percent to 18 percent between 1967 and 1971.* Bradley's percentage of "Anglo" white (excluding Chicano) voters increased dramatically, from roughly 36 percent to 49 percent between his 1969 and 1973 runoff races, and gave him the victory he had missed initially. These increases in white voting percentages are due to two separate processes: (1) the significant decline in white turnout in the second election (which accounts for Hatcher's modest increase and much of Stokes's increases); and (2) as in Bradley's case, the conversion of some white voters.

## The Role of Partisanship†

We now turn to our third rule of thumb: While the racial factor is much more important, partisanship does influence white voting when a black candidate runs for mayor—in nonpartisan as well as partisan elections.

Let us consider the November 1967 results from Cleveland and Gary, two cities with partisan elections. Even though the whites of both cities were registered overwhelmingly Democratic and Stokes and Hatcher ran as the Democratic nominees, fewer than one in five whites voted for them. Indeed, in both cities, over three-quarters of the registered white Democrats who went to the polls cast their ballots for the white Republican over the black Democratic candidate. To be sure, the white-dominated county Democratic committees were hostile to their own black nominees. Under those conditions, partisanship appears to play no role at all for white voters, even in these supposedly partisan mayoralty campaigns.

Nevertheless, a more careful analysis places this conclusion in doubt. Table 2.1 provides a summary of our 1969 survey data from a probability sample of 388 of Cleveland's registered whites. For each of the seven self-rated categories of partisanship, two percentages are shown for the 1969 vote for Stokes against Republican Ralph Perk. The first percentage is the predicted vote based solely on responses to 18 racial attitude questions asked five months prior to the

*The estimation of voting by race from election returns alone is difficult and speculative at best because of precincts that are racially mixed. Nelson cites the 1971 Gary election in which 25 percent of the white voters supported Hatcher.[4] The author previously cited the figure as 22 percent,[5] but on recalculation for this paper it now appears that the most likely estimate is only about 17 to 18 percent.

†Much of this discussion leans heavily upon the analyses by Robert Riley in his recently submitted dissertation for the Ph.D. degree in social psychology at Harvard University. I wish to thank him for use of his material in this paper.

## TABLE 2.1

### Racially Predicted and Reported 1969 Stokes White Vote by Partisanship

| | Voting Percentages | | |
| --- | --- | --- | --- |
| Self-Reported Partisanship | Racially Predicted* | Post-Election Report | Discrepancy |
| Strong Democrats | 23.1 | 34.8 | +11.7 |
| Weak Democrats | 26.8 | 24.2 | −2.6 |
| Independents, leaning toward Democrats | 23.9 | 24.0 | +0.1 |
| Independents | 23.4 | 18.7 | −4.7 |
| Independents, leaning toward Republicans | 14.6 | 12.5 | −2.1 |
| Weak Republicans | 28.0 | 6.0 | −22.0 |
| Strong Republicans | 27.8 | 11.0 | −16.8 |

*Derived from regression equations utilizing responses to 18 racial attitude questions administered to a probability sample of 388 registered whites in May and June of 1969. See footnote on p. 23 for examples of these questions.

*Source*: Adapted from Table 16 of a Ph.D. dissertation submitted by Robert Riley to the Psychology and Social Relations Department, Harvard University, April 1975.

election.* The second percentage is the actual vote for Stokes these same respondents reported in a follow-up survey after the election.†

---

*The 18 questions divided into three conceptually different and largely independent subscales. The best vote predictor was the *Competitive Racism Scale*. It contained such items as: "Over the past few years, Negroes have got more than they deserve"; "Poverty programs promote laziness and not hard work"; and "Negroes have been favored too much for city jobs lately." The next vote predictor was the *Neighborhood Threat Scale*, typified by the item: "How likely do you think it is that the Negroes will bring violence to this neighborhood—very likely, somewhat likely, or very unlikely." Least predictive was the more standard *Contact Racism Scale*, typified by the item: "Do you think white students and Negro students should go to the same schools or to separate schools?"

†The reported vote was apparently quite accurate with no discernible bandwagon effect toward the winner. Our sample's reported vote closely corresponded with the official voting results for the city as a whole as well as for the individual precincts sampled.

Table 2.1 shows that partisanship did have an effect on the vote beyond that of racial attitudes. Republicans, weak and strong, all voted for Democrat Stokes far less than predicted by their responses to the racial questions. Independents of all varieties and weak Democrats cast their ballots in the aggregate just about as predicted by the simple racial attitude model. But strong Democrats, who constituted 26 percent of our white sample, voted more for their party's nominee than predicted on the basis of their racial opinions. Since there were roughly twice as many strong Democrats among Cleveland whites in 1969 as there were weak and strong Republicans combined (according to our sample estimates), it appears that Carl Stokes actually had a small net gain in white votes from the fact he was a highly identified Democrat. Given the fact that Cleveland's black voters, like the vast majority of the nation's black electorate, are Democrats, the mayor's Democratic Party identification probably helped him marginally with his black support. Admittedly, these are small effects, but in an election won by less than 4,000 votes out of about 240,000 cast, these small partisanship effects probably made a significant difference.

This partisanship effect is not, however, found only in mayoralty elections that are explicitly structured along partisan lines. In Los Angeles the 1969 Bradley versus Yorty runoff race, both men were Democrats in a formally non-partisan election. Bradley, though, was already a nationally identified liberal Democrat, supported by many of the late Robert Kennedy's backers; and Yorty was a maverick, often conservative Democrat who had frequently favored Republican candidates and sought Republican votes. The results of our post-election survey shows that this partisanship distinction was reflected among the white electorate. Table 2.2 provides the 1969 Bradley runoff voting percentages of non-Jewish "Anglo" whites by age and education as well as partisanship.* Jewish and Chicano voters are excluded because of their heavy Democratic identification and higher support of Bradley. Indeed, a black mayoralty candidate is likely to find his strongest white following among young, college-educated, Jewish voters and his weakest among older, poorly educated, Christian voters. Note the powerful age and education effects evident in Table 2.2, especially among Democrats.

But even when we exclude Jewish and Chicano sample members and roughly control for age and education in Table 2.2, the partisanship effect appears in all four comparisons. It is strongest among those most supportive of Bradley (the college-educated young) and weakest among those least supportive (the non-college-educated old).

---

*Only in sprawling Los Angeles did we not draw a probability sample of the registered whites. These data refer to probability samples of two contrasting white areas—the heavily-Jewish Beverly-Fairfax area and a predominantly working-class area in the northern part of the San Fernando Valley.

## TABLE 2.2

### Whites Voting for Bradley, Los Angeles, June 1969*
### (percent)

| Education | Democratic | | Republican | |
|---|---|---|---|---|
| | 21-39 Years Old | 40+ Years Old | 21-39 Years Old | 40+ Years Old |
| College | 79 | 49 | 35 | 17 |
| High school or less | 44 | 19 | 28 | 15 |

*These data exclude both Jewish and Chicano sample members from data gathered in probability samples of the Beverly-Fairfax and northern San Fernando Valley areas. See the text for a fuller description.

*Source*: T. F. Pettigrew and R. T. Riley, "The Bradley-Yorty Elections of 1969 and 1973," paper in preparation.

## The Loyal Black Electorate

The loyal black electorate is described in our fourth rule of thumb. The black electorate typically provides a high turnout and considerable loyalty and discipline for mayoralty elections when the strategy is clear and straightforward and the black candidate has good winning chances. It will not easily expand, however, with new registrants; nor is its loyalty and discipline blind.

This high turnout and level of discipline is exemplified by the black turnout percentages of the four cities already cited—all of them above 70 percent. Save for the 1967 elections in Cleveland and Gary, these turnouts were achieved without the type of political organization and effort traditionally associated with high turnouts in nonpresidential elections.

Moreover, in each case the black turnout approximately equaled or even surpassed the white turnout, despite the educational differences between the two groups, the wider experience of the white electorate, harassment of blacks by white officials in Cleveland and Gary, and a far greater distrust of the political system among blacks. This last point deserves special emphasis, for the high black turnout is occurring while black political estrangement is actually increasing.[6] According to national survey data reported by the University of Michigan's Institute for Social Research, the trust in government among black Americans registered +50 in 1958 on a 200-point index that ranges from +100 (most trusting) to −100 (least trusting). It rose to +60 in 1964 but declined precipitously to +40 in 1968 and −40 in 1972. White trust in government also declined, but far more gradually—from +50 in 1958 to +40 in 1964, +22 in 1968, and +10 in 1972. Consistent with these plunging indices, both black and white turnout percentages for presidential elections have been declining since 1960; yet the black registrants went to the polls in these mayoralty contests.

Loyalty and discipline have also characterized black voters once they get to the ballot box. When Hatcher campaigned in 1971 without the large volunteer effort of 1967 and against a well-known black opponent, Gary's black voters surprised most political pundits and supported the mayor at a ratio better than eleven to one. Much the same phenomenon occurred again in Gary in its 1975 mayoralty election.

Discipline has been evident in races where two black candidates, together with white candidates, vied in mayoralty primaries. Gibson, in the May 12, 1970 primary in Newark, received almost ten black votes for each one cast for George Richardson. Likewise, even in the confused, heated, and ill-fated 1971 mayoralty Democratic primary in Baltimore, George Russell received about nine black ballots for each one cast for Clarence Mitchell, III.[7]

Mention of Baltimore recalls a number of unsuccessful black efforts to win mayoralty posts that challenge this view of a responsive black electorate. Why, for example, was the Baltimore black turnout such a disappointing 43 percent? Why, too, was Stokes unable to swing the black electorate of Cleveland behind his former campaign director, Arnold Pinckney, in the Cleveland race in November of 1971? These failures are worth examining, because they point out the limitations of the amazing performance of black voters in other elections.

The basic answer to both of the 1971 debacles is simply that these political efforts were ill-timed and generally bungled. Political organization in the black community of Baltimore was not extensive, in spite of Russell's expensive $408,000 campaign.[8] Even had Mitchell not been in the race, it seems unlikely that Russell could have won in 1971. Only 37 percent of the registered voters were black; Baltimore did not provide Russell with the same chance to attract white voters that Los Angeles had for Bradley; and the leading white candidate was appealing to precisely the white voters who would otherwise have been most likely to support Russell.

The 1971 Cleveland race was similarly confused. Stokes supported a white liberal for the Democratic Party nomination, then asked black voters to shift to Pinckney running as an independent in November. This late entry and switch tactic might have looked attractive on paper (a potentially split white vote against a solid black plurality), but it required many of Cleveland's black voters, and Pinckney did not generally look like a winner. Even at that, about 77 percent of the black votes went to Pinckney and 21 percent to the white Democrat, James Carney. However, black turnout fell below that of whites for the first time in three elections.[9]

Increasing the black registration percentage is a realm where even the successful mayoralty campaigns have generally failed. The celebrated case of Cleveland's all-out effort in 1967 to lift black registration is all too typical. The local branch of the Congress on Racial Equality, armed with a Ford Foundation grant, tried leaflets, intensive community coverage, and transportation to the registration office. The late Dr. Martin Luther King, Jr. and his staff visited the city and campaigned. Yet in the three target black wards, the net gain in black registrants over 1966 was only 1,147.[10]

## The Importance of Candidate Image

The importance of candidate image is at the center of our fifth rule of thumb: A positive candidate image is a necessary ingredient in a black candidate's campaign for black and white voters alike, but it is especially critical for white voters, since it can mediate and modify the effects of their racial attitudes on their voting.

We measured two parts of a candidate's image: his performance image and his personal image. In Gary in 1971 there was general agreement that Mayor Hatcher was intelligent and honest. Supporters and detractors differed in their views of his effectiveness and sincerity, with white fears of reverse discrimination most evident.

This candidate profile takes on even greater importance, however, when we see how it alters the effect of racial attitudes on white voting. Measuring racial attitudes in Cleveland with the 18 questions described earlier, we expected a direct effect of prejudice leading to white opposition to Stokes.* To our surprise, the relationship does appear but virtually vanishes when candidate image is entered into the equation.

Put in causal sequence terms, the racial bigotry of white voters in Cleveland had formed solidly before any thought of Stokes running for mayor had arisen. Next, an impression of Stokes was developed once he announced himself as a serious candidate. Here racial attitudes played their crucial role. Those whites whose initial opinions of black Americans and civil rights were more favorable tended to form positive views of Stokes; those whites whose racial opinions were more unfavorable tended to form negative views of Stokes.

But other important factors besides racial views influenced the whites' image of Stokes. These factors included his personal style and campaign, particularly as reported by the mass media, and partisanship; for, as already discussed, strong Democrats were more motivated to develop a positive image of their party's nominee than Republicans. The next step in the sequence is for candi-

---

*This analysis, too, is contained in Riley's Ph.D. dissertation cited above.

date image to heavily influence the final vote of whites. We were surprised to learn that racial attitudes did not play a direct role in this final step except as mediated by candidate image. Put differently, racist attitudes of white voters are not in a psychological vacuum beyond reach and influence; they can be countered by other factors that influence candidate image. We shall return to this crucial point in the closing section of this chapter.

## The Role of Relative Deprivation[11]

We have already noted that Jewish voters and the young, college-educated voters identified as liberal Democrats are consistently, across the four cities, the most willing in the white community to support a black's candidacy. On the other hand, we found major opposition to black candidates among the lower middle class. In Gary in 1968, for example, those earning between $6,000 and $12,000 annual family income were the most negative to Hatcher and most positive to Governor George Wallace of Alabama.*

Why the lower middle class? At least part of the answer lies in the difficult position of the lower middle class in industrial societies. Caught insecurely between the prosperous and the poor, it is doing well enough to aspire to the life of the prosperous while it constantly fears a fall back to the status of the poor. This explanation implies that lower-middle-class prejudice might be in part a result of "relative deprivation."[12] Relative deprivation, a major theoretical tool in social psychology, refers to a principal fact of social motivation beyond the basic physiological requirements, much of human behavior is motivated more by relative than absolute standards. You may in an absolute sense be making more money than ever before, but if you have shifted your standards of comparison upward or perceive others moving up in income even faster than you, this may cause you to feel relatively deprived.

The relative deprivation that our research has found significant involves group comparisons. White voters who feel that black Americans as a group have been making recent economic gains faster than those of white Americans as a group are by far the most hostile to the black candidate in every election we have studied. Recall that these findings date from studies conducted from 1968 to 1973, before the worst of double-digit inflation hit the nation. The misconception apparently derives from publicity given the "war on poverty" of the

---

*This relationship is best expressed statistically as a quadratic function centered around $9,000 as follows: ($9,000 − reported family income)$^2$, where the larger this squared discrepancy, the larger the reported 1967 Hatcher vote and the smaller the intended 1968 Wallace vote.

1960s, publicity that was often misconstrued by white workers as the federal government giving "lazy blacks" what the whites had attained by hard work. This sense of racial relative deprivation was most commonly found among lower-middle-class respondents in each of the four cities studied.

Thus, our sixth rule of thumb: Black mayoralty candidates find their strongest white support among voters who are Jewish, young, college educated, or liberal Democrats. Their strongest white opposition is centered in the lower middle class, many of whom feel a strong sense of racial relative deprivation.

## Common Nonracial Perceptions of Blacks and Whites

There is little that a black candidate can do to counter directly the keen sense of relative deprivation experienced by many lower-middle-class whites. A promising possibility, however, and one that has been successfully applied by many black candidates in a variety of cities, is to address the immediate civic concerns of threatened whites without reference to race. This forthright strategy is made possible by the typically large degree of agreement between white and black communities as to the most critical problems facing the city.

Table 2.3 presents the relevant data for Gary in 1971. The percentages refer to the proportions of the black and white respondents who freely mentioned the listed problem areas in response to the open-ended questions. Given the sharp racial cleavage in Gary, the close agreement between the races on the basic problems facing the city may come as a surprise. Yet both blacks and whites overwhelmingly agreed that the most immediate and burning issue was crime and its control. Other issues trailed far behind in concern, though again there was cross-racial consensus that sanitation, street repair, and recreational issues were of pressing importance. The differentiation on such directly racial issues as school desegregation, however, underscores the limits of cross-racial perceptions of civic problems. When a city is in the midst of tense racial conflict over school desegregation and similar issues, the ability of political leaders, black and white, to find common ground is severely limited.

We are now ready to propose the seventh and final rule of thumb: Except during times of tense racial conflict, there is often considerable cross-racial agreement as to the city's major problems. This situation allows the black candidate to appeal for both black and white voters with a common platform. We turn now to a wider consideration of mayoralty campaign strategy based on these seven rules of thumb.

## TABLE 2.3

### Perception of Basic Problems Facing Gary, 1971a

| Category | Percentage of Total Black Sample Responding (N = 118) | Percentage of Total White Sample Responding (N = 226) |
|---|---|---|
| Crime | | |
| Juvenile delinquency, poor police protection, break-ins, young people killing and raping, unsafe to walk on streets, and so forth | 70* | 43 |
| Sanitation | | |
| Better garbage collection needed, streets are filthy, new sewers needed, and so forth | 17 | 13 |
| Street repair | | |
| Streets and alleys need paving, roads never get fixed, and so forth | 14 | 12 |
| Recreational facilities | | |
| More playgrounds needed, where are the parks? and so forth | 14 | 8 |
| Housing and urban renewal | | |
| Not enough housing, housing is too expensive, over-crowding in apartments, tear down the slums and old buildings, and so forth | 14 | 4 |
| Street lights | | |
| More street lights needed here in this neighborhood, and so forth | 7 | 6 |

(Continued)

(Table 2.3 continued)

| Category | Percentage of Total Black Sample Responding (N = 118) | Percentage of Total White Sample Responding (N = 226) |
|---|---|---|
| Racial issues | | |
| More equality, desegregation needed, less polarization, and so forth | 3 | 1 |
| Too much desegregation, control blacks' behavior, and so forth | 0 | 11 |
| Public schools | | |
| Not enough schools, poor schools, fighting in schools, serve hot lunches in school, and so forth | 6 | 5 |
| Economic | | |
| Stop inflation, taxes are too high, and so forth | 10 | 1 |
| Traffic | | |
| Lower speed limits, more traffic lights, too much traffic in neighborhood, traffic through city should be rerouted, and so forth | 2 | 4 |
| Pollution | | |
| Air and water pollution plus general "beautification" | 2 | 3 |
| Miscellaneous | | |
| Stray dogs, nothing could help Gary, corruption in government, problems of youth, reduce welfare, increase welfare, too many poolrooms and liquor stores, and so forth | 14 | 10 |

aNote that a category is scored for the respondent if it is included in the responses to any one of the three questions posed. Consequently, the percentages add up to more than 100, since a single respondent could have mentioned more than one topic.

Source: The data reported in this table derive from the responses to the following open-ended questions: "What do you think is the most important problem facing Gary today?" "Of all the things in this neighborhood that you would like to see improved and that the city can do something about, what one thing do you think the city should do first?" "What could . . . Richard Hatcher do as Mayor now that might convince you to vote for him in the future?" Only the black sample was asked the first of these three queries, and only non-Hatcher supporters were asked the third

26

## BLACK MAYORAL STRATEGIES

With full recognition of their tentativeness, the above findings can be utilized to formulate a few suggestions for political strategy of future black mayoralty aspirants.

Race is the dominant factor in these elections. Three variables are critical in formulating this first strategic consideration: the candidate's percentage of black votes, his percentage of white votes, and the black percentage of total votes cast. The particular election will determine the relative importance of each variable toward assuring victory. In some cases, first priority should be given to registering eligible blacks and ensuring a high black turnout at the polls, while in others the candidate's proportion of the white vote can be the crucial variable. In general, obtaining a higher proportion of the white votes than is lost from the black votes is the desired aim, though how much higher this proportion must be is, of course, a function of the black percentage of the total electorate.

Many of our rules of thumb suggest possible means by which black mayoralty aspirants may seek white voters. Thus, the fact that partisanship remains a factor, even in nonpartisan elections dominated by race, implies that black candidates should emphasize their party affiliations when campaigning in white areas. Mass media exposure of ties with the national party organization is one method of publicizing party affiliation.

The candidate's image plays a critical role in mediating and often modifying harsh racial attitudes of some white Americans. We have found a small—but critically important—number of white voters in each of our four cities who are racial bigots in every sense of that pejorative term, yet support the black candidate. They often like his style, share his political party affiliation, and have friends who support him. The opportunities for utilizing a positive image are, however, extremely limited in communities where threatened lower-middle-class whites predominate. Considering the strong sense of racial relative deprivation of most lower-middle-class whites, the black candidate should be careful not to exacerbate needlessly their fears and sensitivities.

Given the narrow social spectrum predisposed to favor a black candidacy, attention is best focused on upper-status Jewish voters (appearances at social action forums of synagogues and temples); highly educated voters (visits to college areas, speeches to faculty and students, League of Women Voters, and so forth);* young voters (addresses to young married groups and similar organizations); and the strongly identified white members of the candidate's political party.

---

*This is to be distinguished from high income areas, for high income is not a good indication of support for black candidates. Indeed, high income and relatively low education is a classic example of status inconsistency that tends toward extreme conservatism.

Note that the success of this focused strategy depends upon the character of the opposing white candidate. If the white candidate is conservative and even openly antiblack, the hope of gaining a large proportion of the Jewish, college-educated, and young voters is obviously enhanced. But if the white opponent is reasonably liberal and conspicuously careful to run a clean, nonracial campaign, then the focused strategy is in trouble. The very whites most predisposed to black leadership comprise the basic constituency of the white opponent; and this makes such an opponent generally harder to defeat.

Finally, basing one's campaign largely on the issues that both races agree are the most critical for the city is an obvious but important tactic. Media advertising on these issues, with specific examples drawn from both black and white neighborhoods, should be effective. Together with these broad citywide issues, specific neighborhood concerns might also be addressed in such a way as to emphasize the commonality of interests between the black and white areas and to reassure threatened white voters about their projected fear that they and their areas will be discriminated against in reverse.

## NOTES

1. Earlier results of this project have appeared in a number of publications: T. F. Pettigrew and R. T. Riley, "The Social Psychology of the Wallace Phenomenon," in *Racially Separate or Together?*, ed. T. F. Pettigrew, Chapter 10 (New York: McGraw-Hill, 1971); T. F. Pettigrew, R. T. Riley, and R. D. Vanneman, "George Wallace's Constituents," *Psychology Today* 92 (February 1972): 47-49; T. F. Pettigrew, "When a Black Candidate Runs for Mayor: Race and Voting Behavior," in *Urban Affairs Annual Review, 1972*, ed. H. Hahn, pp. 95-117 (Beverly Hills, Calif.: Sage, 1972); T. F. Pettigrew, "Racism and the Mental Health of White Americans," in *Racism and Mental Health*, eds. C. Willey, B. Kramer, and B. Brown, pp. 269-98 (Pittsburgh: University of Pittsburgh Press, 1973); and R. D. Vanneman and T. F. Pettigrew, "Race and Relative Deprivation in the Urban United States," *Race* 13, no. 4 (April 1972): 461-86.

2. Among the many studies indicating that nonvoters are typically more apathetic, alienated, authoritarian, prejudiced, and uninformed than voters are the following: G. M. Connelly and H. H. Field, "The Non-voter—Who He Is, What He Thinks," *Public Opinion Quarterly* 8 (1944): 175-87; P. K. Hastings, "The Non-voter in 1952: A Study of Pittsfield, Mass.," *Journal of Psychology* 38 (1954): 301-12; P.K. Hastings, "The Voter and the Non-voter," *American Journal of Sociology* 62 (1956): 302-307; H. H. Hyman and P. B. Sheatsley, "Some Reasons Why Information Campaigns Fail," *Public Opinion Quarterly* 11 (1947): 412-23; M. Janowitz and D. Marvick, "Authoritarianism and Political Behavior," *Public Opinion Quarterly* 17 (1953): 185-201; Penn Kimball, *The Disconnected* (New York: Columbia University Press, 1972); S. M. Lipset, *Political Man* (Garden City, N.Y.: Doubleday, 1960), pp. 79-103; F. H. Sanford, *Authoritarianism and Leadership* (Philadelphia: Institute for Research in Human Relations, 1950), p. 168; and S. A. Stouffer, *Communism, Conformity, and Civil Liberties* (Garden City, N.Y.: Doubleday, 1955).

3. Op. cit., pp. 150-52.

4. W. E. Nelson, Jr. *Black Politics in Gary: Problems and Prospects* (Washington, D.C.: Joint Center for Political Studies, March 1972), p. 33.

5. T. F. Pettigrew, "When a Black Candidate Runs for Mayor: Race and Voting Behavior," in *Urban Affairs Annual Review, 1972*, ed. H. Hahn, p. 106 (Beverly Hills, Calif.: Sage, 1972).

6. Institute for Social Research, "Blacks' Trust in Government Falls Sharply," in *Racial Discrimination in the United States*, ed. T. F. Pettigrew, pp. 329-33 (New York: Harper and Row, 1975).

7. G. J. Fleming, *Baltimore's Failure to Elect a Black Mayor in 1971* (Washington, D.C.: Joint Center for Political Studies, 1972), p. 25.

8. Ibid., p. 26.

9. Kimball, op. cit., pp. 156-57.

10. Ibid., p. 148.

11. An earlier and more detailed treatment of this section is contained in Vanneman and Pettigrew, op. cit.

12. For an application of this same relative deprivation to black Americans, see T. F. Pettigrew, *Racially Separate or Together?* (New York: McGraw-Hill, 1971), Chapter 7.

# 3

## THE QUALITY OF
## CITIES WITH
## BLACK MAYORS
Herrington J. Bryce
Eric Martin

In 1967, black Americans made their debut into the mayoral offices of two major American cities—Gary, Indiana and Cleveland, Ohio. The stories behind these two landmark events are described by Thomas Pettigrew in Chapter 2 of this volume.[1] Since 1967, the number of black mayors of American cities has increased steadily. As of November 1975, there were 150. The rise of blacks to these offices raises several questions: Is the ascendance to the mayor's office a hollow prize?[2] Have black mayors inherited some of the nation's worst cities? Are black mayors unusually weak in constitutional authority and thereby limited in their power? This chapter represents the first systematic attempt to answer these questions.

## SOCIOECONOMIC CONDITIONS IN CITIES
## WITH BLACK MAYORS

As of 1974, there were 26 cities with black mayors and populations of at least 25,000. Most of these cities are located in the North, although 54 percent of all black elected officials are in the South. Many of the cities are important centers of industry, education, and culture. United States Steel is located in Gary, Indiana; the automobile industry is concentrated in Detroit; major universities are located in Los Angeles, Atlanta, Berkeley, College Park (Maryland), Boulder (Colorado), Chapel Hill (North Carolina), and New Brunswick (New Jersey). To top it off, the nation's capital, Washington, D.C., is headed by a black mayor.

## Population

Large populations place severe pressures on public budgets. The larger the population, the more public goods and services a city must provide—and the higher the cost, since costs tend to rise with population size.

Large populations also test the political and managerial skills of mayors. Large cities are centers of trade, culture, education, and government. At the same time, they are besieged by environmental and social problems and severe budget limitations. Aware of this fact, many cities are attempting to control growth, while at the same time recognizing that a very slow growth rate or population decline is viewed as a sign of decay.

Nine of the 26 cities with black mayors ranks among the 100 largest in the country (see Table 3.1). Three of these cities—Los Angeles, Detroit, and Washington—are among the 15 largest.

These 26 cities also rank high in their respective states. Although its national rank is 799, College Park is the seventh largest of over 150 Maryland cities and towns.

Nevertheless, nearly half of the cities with black mayors suffered a sharp population decline during the last decade while the overall urban population of the nation rose by 19 percent. East St. Louis, Illinois, which lost 14 percent of its population, was one of the 50 greatest population losers in the country. Prichard, Alabama lost about 12 percent of its population, placing it among the 60 great population losers.

The population decline began well before the arrival of the current black mayors. Between 1950 and 1960, Detroit lost about 10 percent of its population; Highland Park, Michigan about 17 percent; East Orange, New Jersey about 2 percent; Newark, New Jersey about 7 percent. Prichard, Dayton, and Inkster (Michigan) did not elect their black mayors until 1970—after the decline had been registered.

## Racial Composition

While the general population in many of these cities has declined, or at least slackened in growth, the black population has increased sharply. In Boulder, Colorado the black population has increased by nearly 300 percent; in Chapel Hill, East Orange, and Highland Park, by over 100 percent.

Interestingly enough, though, most of the larger cities with black mayors are not predominantly black. In fact, only three cities have a decisive black majority—Compton (California), East St. Louis (Illinois), and Washington, D.C.

With few exceptions, the cities with black mayors have the greatest concentration of blacks in their respective states, but most do not have a majority black population.

# TABLE 3.1

## Population Characteristics, 1970

| City/State | Size of Population | | | Population Change (1960-70) | | |
| | Number | Rank[a] | | | Rank | |
| | | U.S.[b] | State[c] | Percent | U.S. | State |
|---|---|---|---|---|---|---|
| Prichard, Ala. | 41,644 | 468 | 7 | -12.2 | 787 | 14 |
| Berkeley, Calif. | 116,689 | 124 | 15 | 4.9 | 524 | 112 |
| Compton, Calif. | 78,493 | 219 | 35 | 9.4 | 446 | 105 |
| Los Angeles, Calif. | 2,816,111 | 3 | 1 | 13.3 | 401 | 95 |
| Boulder, Colo. | 66,870 | 278 | 6 | 77.3 | 84 | 4 |
| Gainesville, Fla. | 64,510 | 289 | 11 | 117.2 | 44 | 7 |
| Atlanta, Ga. | 497,024 | 27 | 1 | 2.0 | 579 | 9 |
| East St. Louis, Ill. | 69,947 | 258 | 9 | -14.3 | 802 | 58 |
| Gary, Ind. | 175,249 | 75 | 3 | -1.6 | 641 | 14 |
| College Park, Md. | 26,357 | 799 | 7 | 41.5 | 172 | 3 |
| Detroit, Mich. | 1,411,336 | 5 | 1 | -9.4 | 768 | 37 |
| Grand Rapids, Mich. | 197,534 | 65 | 2 | 11.5 | 415 | 16 |
| Highland Park, Mich. | 35,444 | 573 | 36 | -6.9 | 734 | 34 |
| Inkster, Mich. | 38,548 | 523 | 33 | -1.3 | 634 | 27 |
| Pontiac, Mich. | 85,339 | 200 | 14 | 3.7 | 547 | 22 |
| Ypsilanti, Mich. | 29,502 | 708 | 41 | 40.9 | 175 | 8 |
| East Orange, N.J. | 75,467 | 227 | 8 | -2.3 | 657 | 32 |
| New Brunswick, N.J. | 41,855 | 459 | 20 | 4.3 | 531 | 19 |
| Newark, N.J. | 382,377 | 35 | 1 | -5.7 | 716 | 33 |
| Chapel Hill, N.C. | 25,541 | 822 | 16 | 103.1 | 59 | 1 |
| Raleigh, N.C. | 121,128 | 116 | 4 | 31.8 | 224 | 2 |
| Cincinnati, Ohio | 452,550 | 29 | 3 | -10.2 | 773 | 43 |
| Dayton, Ohio | 243,459 | 59 | 6 | -7.4 | 743 | 42 |
| Waco, Texas | 95, 326 | 167 | 13 | -2.5 | 660 | 38 |
| Charlottesville, Va. | 38,880 | 521 | 12 | 32.1 | 220 | 3 |
| Washington, D.C. | 756,510 | 9 | 1 | -1.0 | 628 | 1 |

| Change in Black Population (1960-70) | | | Percent of Total Population Black | | | Density | | |
|---|---|---|---|---|---|---|---|---|
| | Rank | | | Rank | | Persons per | Rank | |
| Percent | U.S. | State | Percent | U.S. | State | Square Mile | U.S. | State |
| −6.0 | 515 | 11 | 50.4 | 13 | 2 | 1,631 | 756 | 9 |
| 25.6 | 310 | 52 | 23.5 | 123 | 4 | 11,011 | 51 | 4 |
| 98.6 | 92 | 33 | 71.5 | 1 | 1 | 8,268 | 96 | 17 |
| 50.3 | 207 | 45 | 17.9 | 167 | 6 | 6,060 | 189 | 42 |
| 264.8 | 42 | 1 | 0.7 | 557 | 5 | 5,144 | 257 | 4 |
| 75.2 | 134 | 4 | 18.7 | 159 | 14 | 2,472 | 627 | 20 |
| 36.3 | 253 | 3 | 51.1 | 12 | 1 | 3,783 | 417 | 3 |
| 32.9 | 271 | 24 | 69.1 | 3 | 1 | 5,036 | 268 | 29 |
| 34.2 | 265 | 10 | 53.0 | 9 | 1 | 4,177 | 360 | 7 |
| 14.7 | 376 | 5 | 3.3 | 422 | 5 | 5,129 | 259 | 3 |
| 37.0 | 249 | 10 | 43.7 | 26 | 3 | 10,968 | 53 | 3 |
| 55.7 | 185 | 9 | 11.2 | 248 | 12 | 4,402 | 328 | 27 |
| 146.7 | 54 | 2 | 55.3 | 5 | 1 | 11,815 | 41 | 2 |
| 27.2 | 307 | 12 | 44.5 | 24 | 2 | 6,126 | 188 | 15 |
| 65.2 | 160 | 6 | 26.7 | 100 | 5 | 4,329 | 339 | 28 |
| 22.9 | 318 | 14 | 19.5 | 155 | 8 | 7,204 | 135 | 10 |
| 108.7 | 82 | 4 | 53.1 | 8 | 2 | 19,352 | 10 | 5 |
| 53.6 | 190 | 13 | 22.7 | 129 | 10 | 7,479 | 122 | 25 |
| 50.2 | 203 | 15 | 54.2 | 7 | 1 | 16,252 | 16 | 9 |
| 102.6 | 88 | 1 | 10.2 | 266 | 16 | 3,274 | 496 | 2 |
| 25.2 | 312 | 6 | 22.7 | 129 | 11 | 2,757 | 570 | 6 |
| 14.9 | 373 | 20 | 27.6 | 95 | 4 | 5,780 | 204 | 12 |
| 29.5 | 291 | 13 | 30.5 | 77 | 3 | 6,342 | 178 | 16 |
| 5.2 | 440 | 24 | 19.8 | 152 | 11 | 1,624 | 758 | 34 |
| 2.6 | 455 | 11 | 14.7 | 196 | 11 | 3,738 | 421 | 6 |
| 30.6 | 285 | 1 | 71.1 | 2 | 1 | 12,321 | 36 | 1 |

[a]Ranking is such that 1 indicates highest. All ranking in this survey covers those cities with at least 25,000 residents.

[b]Calculations are based on ranking of 845 cities with populations of at least 25,000.

[c]For the number of cities over 25,000 and total number of incorporated cities by state, see Appendix Table 3.A.

*Source*: Calculations in this and other tables in this chapter are based on data taken from Department of Commerce, Bureau of the Census, *County and City Data Book, 1972* (U.S. Government Printing Office, 1973). William Lindamood wrote the computer program for all calculations.

## Overcrowding

Overcrowding is one of the major problems of cities. The migration from city to suburb has frequently been explained in terms of the need to escape the congestion of cities—the need for space. Social scientists have repeatedly found a significant correlation between the congestion of a city and such urban maladies as crime and pollution. Even the overall cost of government rises with density. As a matter of fact, there are many urbanologists who argue that density is the key to city problems.

The data in Table 3.1 reveal that half the cities with black mayors rank in the upper 25 percent of the nation's most densely populated cities. Even Los Angeles, the epitome of urban sprawl, ranks among the 200 densest cities in the country. In some cities, like East Orange, the Table 3.2 figures may actually understate the problem. Every city has its schools, business districts, and other nonresidential areas, and East Orange Mayor William S. Hart, Sr. estimates that most of his 35,000 constituents live on 4 percent of the land.

## Age of Housing

When a high proportion of a city's housing is old, abandonment and the migration from inner city to suburb are more likely; and old housing increases the need for reinvestment and construction if the city is to remain a viable place to live.

Cities with black mayors contain some of the oldest structures in the country (see Table 3.2). Nearly half of these cities have an exceptionally high percentage of housing units built prior to 1950. Niney-six percent of the units in Highland Park, for instance, were built before 1950, giving it the second oldest housing in the nation.

In five cities with black mayors the actual number of housing units declined between 1960 and 1970. On the other hand, Chapel Hill had one of the fastest increases in the country—146 percent. But, in general, the growth rate of new housing in cities with black mayors has been low.

## Poverty

High poverty rates place cities under severe pressures to provide social services and welfare assistance ranging from hospitals to cash payments. City revenues are restricted, since poor families pay little in taxes.

The poverty rates in many cities with black mayors are both high and deep (see Table 3.3). That is to say, a high percentage of the poor are not borderline cases. Income maintenance or other poverty-relieving policies need to be sizeable.

# TABLE 3.2

## Housing, 1970, Year-Round

| City/State | Units in Structures Built Prior to 1950 | | | | Percent Change in Number of Units 1960-70 |
| | Percent of All Units | Rank | | | |
| | | U.S. | State | City Size Class* | |
|---|---|---|---|---|---|
| Prichard, Ala. | 59.6 | 336 | 6 | 167 | -1.6 |
| Berkeley, Calif. | 71.5 | 187 | 2 | 23 | 14.2 |
| Compton, Calif. | 49.5 | 465 | 23 | 130 | 2.4 |
| Los Angeles, Calif. | 51.7 | 431 | 19 | 5 | 15.3 |
| Boulder, Colo. | 29.3 | 669 | 7 | 176 | 88.5 |
| Gainesville, Fla. | 28.5 | 679 | 12 | 179 | 117.2 |
| Atlanta, Ga. | 48.5 | 475 | 5 | 21 | 11.2 |
| East St. Louis, Ill. | 75.2 | 149 | 8 | 46 | -8.8 |
| Gary, Ind. | 65.1 | 268 | 12 | 33 | 4.2 |
| College Park, Md. | 40.1 | 571 | 5 | 297 | 28.4 |
| Detroit, Mich. | 84.3 | 57 | 4 | 1 | -4.2 |
| Grand Rapids, Mich. | 73.0 | 167 | 11 | 21 | 15.5 |
| Highland Park, Mich. | 96.0 | 2 | 2 | 2 | -10.8 |
| Inkster, Mich. | 26.6 | 691 | 28 | 367 | 11.6 |
| Pontiac, Mich. | 63.4 | 289 | 16 | 82 | 8.4 |
| Ypsilanti, Mich. | 57.7 | 357 | 19 | 180 | 26.4 |
| East Orange, N.J. | 79.3 | 104 | 14 | 33 | 4.1 |
| New Brunswick, N.J. | 72.8 | 170 | 21 | 79 | 5.2 |
| Newark, N.J. | 81.3 | 88 | 10 | 4 | -5.5 |
| Chapel Hill, N.C. | 33.4 | 636 | 16 | 332 | 146.1 |
| Raleigh, N.C. | 40.7 | 565 | 12 | 69 | 40.3 |
| Cincinnati, Ohio | 72.2 | 176 | 17 | 7 | 0.8 |
| Dayton, Ohio | 70.5 | 199 | 18 | 25 | 1.9 |
| Waco, Texas | 51.7 | 431 | 6 | 120 | -2.5 |
| Charlottesville, Va. | 48.3 | 479 | 8 | 245 | 32.1 |
| Washington, D.C. | 67.9 | 234 | 1 | 8 | 6.1 |

*For the number and distribution of cities by size, see Appendix Table 3.B.
*Source*: See Table 3.1.

## TABLE 3.3

### Poverty, 1970

| City/State | Rate | | | | Mean Income Deficit* | | | |
|---|---|---|---|---|---|---|---|---|
| | Percent of All Below Poverty Level Families | Rank | | | Amount (dollars) | Rank | | |
| | | U.S. | State | City Size Class | | U.S. | State | City Size Class |
| Prichard, Ala. | 25.3 | 9 | 2 | 6 | 1,878 | 47 | 1 | 34 |
| Berkeley, Calif. | 10.6 | 227 | 15 | 36 | 1,425 | 603 | 106 | 82 |
| Compton, Calif. | 17.1 | 56 | 1 | 13 | 1,854 | 62 | 17 | 14 |
| Los Angeles, Calif. | 9.9 | 262 | 23 | 6 | 1,606 | 319 | 65 | 6 |
| Boulder, Colo. | 5.2 | 607 | 7 | 55 | 1,365 | 683 | 12 | 192 |
| Gainesville, Fla. | 14.0 | 119 | 11 | 31 | 1,549 | 413 | 13 | 106 |
| Atlanta, Ga. | 15.9 | 79 | 7 | 6 | 1,710 | 178 | 1 | 2 |
| East St. Louis, Ill. | 28.3 | 6 | 1 | 3 | 1,852 | 64 | 9 | 16 |
| Gary, Ind. | 12.3 | 160 | 1 | 27 | 1,835 | 72 | 1 | 5 |
| College Park, Md. | 2.9 | 771 | 6 | 400 | 1,480 | 519 | 5 | 257 |
| Detroit, Mich. | 11.3 | 185 | 3 | 5 | 1,698 | 192 | 20 | 5 |
| Grand Rapids, Mich. | 8.9 | 328 | 10 | 52 | 1,590 | 355 | 28 | 48 |
| Highland Park, Mich. | 14.5 | 111 | 1 | 53 | 1,786 | 102 | 12 | 62 |
| Inkster, Mich. | 8.4 | 360 | 13 | 171 | 1,952 | 30 | 5 | 21 |
| Pontiac, Mich. | 10.1 | 248 | 5 | 58 | 1,769 | 120 | 14 | 29 |
| Ypsilanti, Mich. | 8.6 | 350 | 12 | 165 | 1,857 | 61 | 8 | 44 |
| East Orange, N.J. | 8.1 | 385 | 17 | 95 | 1,556 | 403 | 20 | 105 |
| New Brunswick, N.J. | 9.6 | 280 | 11 | 131 | 1,521 | 458 | 22 | 220 |
| Newark, N.J. | 18.4 | 38 | 1 | 1 | 1,600 | 360 | 15 | 12 |
| Chapel Hill. N.C. | 8.1 | 385 | 15 | 180 | 1,300 | 738 | 16 | 378 |
| Raleigh, N.C. | 10.3 | 241 | 13 | 38 | 1,523 | 453 | 8 | 65 |
| Cincinnati, Ohio | 14.8 | 148 | 4 | 9 | 1,580 | 377 | 30 | 18 |
| Dayton, Ohio | 10.6 | 227 | 8 | 36 | 1,601 | 328 | 21 | 42 |
| Waco, Texas | 15.7 | 87 | 10 | 19 | 1,423 | 610 | 37 | 168 |
| Charlottesville, Va. | 9.0 | 318 | 11 | 153 | 1,286 | 755 | 12 | 391 |
| Washington, D.C. | 12.7 | 152 | 1 | 8 | 1,830 | 77 | 1 | 4 |

*Deficit is difference between total income of families below the poverty level and their respective low income thresholds. (The income level that separates poor from nonpoor is based upon size of family and urban or rural residence.)

Source: See Table 3.1.

In most of these cities it would take nearly $2,000 to raise the average poor family above the poverty line.

Sixteen of the 26 cities rank in the upper third of all U.S. cities in terms of poverty. Five—Prichard, Compton, Atlanta, East St. Louis, and Newark—are among the 100 with the highest rates of poverty, and nearly all these cities have high poverty rates for their respective states.

## Fiscal Capacity

A city's fiscal capacity is usually measured by per capita income. This gives some indication of the amount of money a mayor can raise, by taxes or fees, to conduct the affairs of government.

The actual amount available depends upon the tax system and the level and distribution of wealth. The amount of goods and services the city supplies depends upon the costs of providing goods and services, the amount demanded by citizens, the requirements of city and state laws, and the quality of goods and services provided.

In general, however, the larger a city's per capita income and general revenues, the more public goods and services it can provide.

Since factors such as the cost of goods and services are related to the size and location of a city, and because some of the kinds of goods and services a city is required to provide are determined by state laws, it is important that we compare cities with black mayors not simply with all cities in the country, but with cities of similar size and also cities in the same state.

Of the cities served by black mayors, Los Angeles has the largest per capita income (see Table 3.4), followed closely by Berkeley, East Orange, and Washington, D.C. Eight of the 26 cities rank in the lowest half of all cities in terms of per capita income. Prichard and East St. Louis are among the five lowest per capita income cities in the country.

Half of the 26 cities are among the lowest per capita income places in their respective states, and are therefore less able to raise the funds for comparably priced goods and services.

Thus, while we may conclude that there are several vibrant and nondecaying cities with black mayors, in general, cities with black mayors rank unfavorably with respect to poverty, density, housing, and other key socioeconomic indicators.

In many of the cities with black mayors, unemployment is a severe problem and the white flight from the cities has been considerable—at least in the past. Yet, most of the jobs in these cities belong to nonresidents. In Compton, California, a city which ranks in poverty and which has an unemployment rate of 9.8 percent, over 80 percent of the jobs are held by people who do not live in the city. Even though the decline of Newark is well advertised, over 60 percent of the jobs in that city are held by people who do not live there. This fiscal drain

## TABLE 3.4

### Fiscal Capacity (Per Capita Income), 1970

| City/State | Per Capita Income (dollars) | U.S. | Rank State | City Size Class |
|---|---|---|---|---|
| Prichard, Ala. | 1,796 | 843 | 14 | 455 |
| Berkeley, Calif. | 3,945 | 124 | 35 | 10 |
| Compton, Calif. | 2,259 | 829 | 126 | 227 |
| Los Angeles, Calif. | 3,951 | 123 | 34 | 1 |
| Boulder, Colo. | 3,375 | 313 | 5 | 96 |
| Gainesville, Fla. | 2,745 | 706 | 24 | 204 |
| Atlanta, Ga. | 3,156 | 437 | 3 | 18 |
| East St. Louis, Ill. | 1,963 | 841 | 58 | 229 |
| Gary, Ind. | 2,814 | 668 | 18 | 79 |
| College Park, Md. | 3,095 | 469 | 4 | 245 |
| Detroit, Mich. | 3,200 | 417 | 32 | 5 |
| Grand Rapids, Mich. | 3,172 | 426 | 33 | 46 |
| Highland Park, Mich. | 3,011 | 522 | 39 | 277 |
| Inkster, Mich. | 3,054 | 493 | 36 | 257 |
| Pontiac, Mich. | 2,843 | 647 | 49 | 188 |
| Ypsilanti, Mich. | 2,943 | 574 | 42 | 301 |
| East Orange, N.J. | 3,877 | 134 | 13 | 42 |
| New Brunswick, N.J. | 3,028 | 509 | 31 | 268 |
| Newark, N.J. | 2,492 | 791 | 38 | 30 |
| Chapel Hill, N.C. | 3,311 | 347 | 3 | 184 |
| Raleigh, N.C. | 3,241 | 386 | 5 | 39 |
| Cincinnati, Ohio | 3,132 | 448 | 27 | 19 |
| Dayton, Ohio | 3,078 | 478 | 30 | 59 |
| Waco, Texas | 2,625 | 746 | 33 | 209 |
| Charlottesville, Va. | 3,185 | 420 | 2 | 218 |
| Washington, D.C. | 3,842 | 139 | 1 | 3 |

Source: See Table 3.1.

on cities will be dampened by laws which require residency; or by laws which permit commuter taxes.

## STATUTORY POWERS OF MAYORS

Are black mayors sufficiently powerful to make an impact on their communities? Several factors determine the power of any mayor. Some are objective, others are subjective.

The objective factors are spelled out in the city charter. City charters specify the mayor's appointive powers, the term of office, the method of election, the powers over the budget, and the veto power. All of these factors are independent of his or her less tangible personal virtues.*

Only 10 of the 26 black mayors have real statutory powers and responsibilities. The other 16 black mayors have minimal statutory powers. They must exercise influence through personal talent, through membership on the city council, and through appeal to a citywide constituency. They have no significant powers of appointment, budget control, or veto of ordinances and resolutions.

The weak position of black mayors relates to the size of the cities they serve. Weak mayoral forms are common in cities with a population of 25,000 to 250,000,[4] and two-thirds of the black mayors serve in cities of this size.

There is no evidence that white minorities are deliberately electing blacks to weak mayoral governments. Most black mayors are not elected to positions that have short terms. The majority are elected to four-year terms and all may succeed themselves. In addition, most are elected by popular vote in communities with a predominantly white voting-age population.

Table 3.5 shows graphically the dilemma that a black mayor can face in these cities. Most of the voters are white, but a large and disproportionate share of the poor are black—a fact that few if any black mayors can ignore. Yet, as we shall see, only 10 of these 26 mayors are in a statutorily strong position to do anything as mayor to reduce this poverty—black or white. The others must exercise this power as well-placed members of the city council.

## HOW MAYORS ARE CHOSEN

Clearly, the method by which a mayor is selected is an important determinant of his powers. Mayors elected by popular vote are generally stronger than those elected by city council. Mayors elected by popular vote have an independent constituency and some voter approval for their programs. Table 3.5 shows that among the 26 black mayors, 21 are elected by the public. This is important since three cities—Compton, East St. Louis, and Washington—have a black voting-age population in the clear majority. In Chapel Hill, College Park, Grand Rapids (Michigan), and Boulder, blacks account for less than 10 percent of the voting-age population. As a rule, then, the appeal and the programs of the black mayor must be broadly based; they cannot be solely oriented to blacks.

---

*The assessment of the powers of mayors has been an intriguing exercise and it will be observed that the procedures used here are a little more "quantitative" than some others and also more extensive.[3]

## TABLE 3.5

## Distribution of Families by Race and Poverty

| City and State | Percentage of All Families Who Are Black | Percentage of Poor Families Who Are Black |
|---|---|---|
| Prichard, Ala. | 44 | 70 |
| Berkeley, Calif. | 28 | 42 |
| Compton, Calif. | 68 | 72 |
| Los Angeles, Calif. | 17 | 37 |
| Boulder, Colo. | * | 2 |
| Gainesville, Fla. | 19 | 28 |
| Atlanta, Ga. | 48 | 75 |
| East St. Louis, Ill. | 66 | 87 |
| Gary, Ind. | 49 | 75 |
| College Park, Md. | 2 | 11 |
| Detroit, Mich. | 40 | 69 |
| Grand Rapids, Mich. | 10 | 32 |
| Highland Park, Mich. | 54 | 72 |
| Inkster, Mich. | 43 | 75 |
| Pontiac, Mich. | 31 | 45 |
| Ypsilanti, Mich. | 23 | 49 |
| East Orange, N.J. | 52 | 73 |
| New Brunswick, N.J. | 24 | 42 |
| Newark, N.J. | 52 | 66 |
| Chapel Hill, N.C. | 11 | 37 |
| Raleigh, N.C. | 20 | 51 |
| Cincinnati, Ohio | 26 | 54 |
| Dayton, Ohio | 28 | 50 |
| Waco, Texas | 20 | 37 |
| Charlottesville, Va. | 16 | 25 |
| Washington, D.C. | 74 | 90 |

*Less than 1 percent.
*Source*: See Table 3.1.

## Term of Office

Short terms generally restrict the impact of any mayor on a city and his ability to develop a bureaucracy, constituency, or program. In many cities, mayors are elected or appointed to terms as short as one or two years. Table 3.6 shows that in 16 of the 26 cities, black mayors are elected to four-year terms. In all 26, the mayors may succeed themselves.

## Form of Government

City governments generally take one of three forms: council-manager, commission, or council-mayor.

In the council-manager form of government, a professional city adminis- trator is the chief executive officer. This person prepares and administers the

### TABLE 3.6

### Method of Election, Voting-Age Population, and Term of Office

| City and State | Election by Popular Vote | Election by Council Vote | Total Voting-Age Population Number | Total Voting-Age Population Percent Black[a] | Term of Office (years) |
|---|---|---|---|---|---|
| Prichard, Ala. | X | | 24,549 | 46 | 4 |
| Berkeley, Calif. | X | | 93,022 | 20 | 4 |
| Compton, Calif. | X | | 42,517 | 65 | 4 |
| Los Angeles, Calif. | X | | 1,966,855 | 16 | 4 |
| Boulder, Colo. | X | | 48,433 | b | 2 |
| Gainesville, Fla. | | X | 49,423 | 14 | 1 |
| Atlanta, Ga. | X | | 337,438 | 46 | 4 |
| East St. Louis, Ill. | X | | 41,848 | 63 | 4 |
| Gary, Ind. | X | | 107,425 | 48 | 4 |
| College Park, Md. | X | | 20,293 | 3 | 2 |
| Detroit, Mich. | X | | 1,017,608 | 37 | 4 |
| Grand Rapids, Mich. | X | | 130,727 | 9 | 4 |
| Highland Park, Mich. | X | | 23,897 | 46 | 4 |
| Inkster, Mich. | X | | 22,538 | 44 | 4 |
| Pontiac, Mich. | | X | 53,472 | 23 | 2 |
| Ypsilanti, Mich. | X | | 23,567 | 16 | 2 |
| East Orange, N.J. | X | | 55,898 | 46 | 4 |
| New Brunswick, N.J. | X | | 31,515 | 17 | 4 |
| Newark, N.J. | X | | 240,033 | 48 | 4 |
| Chapel Hill, N.C. | X | | 20,157 | 8 | 2 |
| Raleigh, N.C. | X | | 88,857 | 20 | 2 |
| Cincinnati, Ohio | | X | 312,055 | 24 | 2 |
| Dayton, Ohio | X | | 166,849 | 27 | 4 |
| Waco, Texas | | X | 66,850 | 17 | 1 |
| Charlottesville, Va. | | X | 28,009 | 15 | 2 |
| Washington, D.C. | X | | 532,404 | 64 | 4 |

[a]Calculations based on data taken from U.S. Census of Population, 1970.
[b]Less than 1 percent.
*Source*: See Table 3.1.

# TABLE 3.7

## Form of City Government

| Size Class and City | Mayor-Council | Mayor-Council with Chief Administrative Officer | Council-Manager | Commission |
|---|---|---|---|---|
| 25,000-49,999 | | | | |
| Prichard, Ala. | X | | | |
| College Park, Md. | | | X | |
| Highland Park, Mich. | X | | | |
| Inkster, Mich. | | | X | |
| Ypsilanti, Mich. | | | X | |
| New Brunswick, N.J. | | X | | |
| Chapel Hill, N.C. | | | X | |
| Charlottesville, Va. | | | X | |
| 50,000-99,999 | | | | |
| Compton, Calif. | | | X | |
| Boulder, Colo. | | | X | |
| Gainesville, Fla. | | | X | * |
| East St. Louis, Ill. | | | | X |
| Pontiac, Mich. | | | X | |
| East Orange, N.J. | X | | | |
| Waco, Texas | | | X | |
| 100,000-249,999 | | | | |
| Berkeley, Calif. | | | X | |
| Gary, Ind. | | X | | |
| Grand Rapids, Mich. | | | X | |
| Raleigh, N.C. | | | X | |
| Dayton, Ohio | | | X | |
| 250,000-499,999 | | | | |
| Atlanta, Ga. | | X | | |
| Newark, N.J. | | X | | |
| Cincinnati, Ohio | | | X | |
| 500,000-999,999 | | | | |
| Washington, D.C. | | X | | |
| 1 million or more | | | | |
| Los Angeles, Calif. | | X | | |
| Detroit, Mich. | X | | | |

*In 1975, East St. Louis changed to a mayor-council form of government.

budget, makes all appointments of department heads, enforces ordinances, and assumes responsibility for the management and supervision of departments. A principal reason for having a city manager is to put the government in the hands of professionals. The mayor's power in this form of government is derived largely through manipulation, personal association with the manager, and from being a highly placed voting member of the city council. The mayor has no veto power. Only in emergencies does such a mayor have the power to act as the "preserver of the peace" and command law enforcement officers.

Table 3.7 shows that more than half of the cities with black mayors have a council-manager form of government, since nearly 77 percent of cities with black mayors fall into the size range (25,000 to 250,000) in which that form of government is common.

The council-manager form of government can pose a severe problem for the black mayor. The city manager is appointed by the council while the mayor is frequently elected by the populace, presumably on the strength of his or her platform of programs and promises. The manager has no responsibility to discharge the mayor's programs and the mayor has no official power or machinery to implement them.

There may be less of a problem in cities where the incumbent black mayor has a direct and important role in selecting the city manager. A definite problem does arise, however, in cities where the mayor is elected at large (as opposed to being chosen by peers in the council) and does not appoint the city manager. In such a case, the mayor is not assured of the allegiance of either the council or the city manager.

Some persons contend that the council-manager form of government exists to protect the white minority against the black majority by putting the reins of government in the hands of a nonelected official not subject to political pressures of blacks; but of the cities with high black voting-age populations (45 percent or more) only two—Compton and Inkster, Michigan—have a council-manager form of government.

In the commission form of government, each commissioner serves as both an elected member of the city council and a department head independent of the mayor. This weakens the mayor, since he shares his or her administrative and executive powers with other elected commissioners. In East St. Louis, the only city with a black mayor that has this form, there are five commissioners. The mayor is a commissioner and heads the police department.

The mayor is usually most powerful in the mayor-council form of government. In that form, the mayor has appointive, administrative, budgetary, and veto powers over legislation. Moreover, the mayor may appoint a chief administrator who is responsible to the mayor and whose role is to free the mayor of day-to-day administrative tasks. In addition, the mayor or an appointee of the mayor is usually responsible for the long-range planning for the city.

Among cities served by black mayors, ten have a mayor-council form of government, and six of these have chief administrative officers appointed by the mayor. Mayors in the mayor-council form of government are not, however, equally powerful. For this reason, we must look at some of the other determinants of power.

## Budget Control

Without substantial control over the city budget, the mayor is unable to implement the programs he or she desires. Budget control comes in various forms: (1) the power to appoint a person or commission to prepare and submit the budget; (2) an item veto over specific line items in the budget; (3) the general authority to approve the budget, or (4) the ability to vote on the budget. The most meaningful, of course, are the powers to submit and the power to veto budget items.

Generally, in cities with a council-manager form of government, the mayor's power over the budget comes through his or her vote on the council. The mayor has no veto power. This is the case in the 15 cities where blacks are mayors in a council-manager structure. In the one city with a commission form of government, East St. Louis, each commissioner prepares his own budget. The mayor submits his and, working as a council, the members resolve budgetary differences.

Table 3.8 shows that in the ten cities with a mayor-council form of government the mayor has some responsibility for the budget. The styles, however, differ. In Highland Park, for example, the mayor submits a budget to the council through his appointed finance director. Unless the council acts within a specified period of time, the budget stands as submitted. The mayor can veto a budgetary act of the council.

In Prichard state laws give the council a very active role in budget determination, although the mayor is in name the budget officer. The mayor's veto powers over budgetary matters are weak. It is the council that is responsible for the final budget. The mayor may veto salaries, but a majority vote by the council can override the veto.

In Atlanta, the mayor controls the budget by serving on two bodies: the budget commission, with four other members, and the appropriations committee, which consists of the mayor, three members of the council appointed by the mayor, the chairman of the council's finance committee, the chief administrative officer, and the director of finance. They prepare the budget that the mayor submits to the council. Hence the mayor has abundant control over the budget.

In Washington, D.C., the mayor prepares a balanced budget for submission to the city council and to Congress. Congress maintains line-item approval of the total district budget and can affect budget priorities. The mayor can cast a

## TABLE 3.8

### Mayor's Budget Responsibility

| City and State | Preparation and Submission* | Vote on Council | Veto |
|---|---|---|---|
| Prichard, Ala. | see text | see text | see text |
| Berkeley, Calif. | | X | |
| Compton, Calif. | | X | |
| Los Angeles, Calif. | X | | X |
| Boulder, Colo. | | X | |
| Gainesville, Fla. | | X | |
| Atlanta, Ga. | X | | X |
| East St. Louis, Ill. | see text | X | |
| Gary, Ind. | X | | X |
| College Park, Md. | | X | |
| Detroit, Mich. | X | | X |
| Grand Rapids, Mich. | | X | |
| Highland, Park, Mich. | X | | X |
| Inkster, Mich. | | X | |
| Pontiac, Mich. | | X | |
| Ypsilanti, Mich. | | X | |
| East Orange, N.J. | X | | see text |
| New Brunswick, N.J. | X | | see text |
| Newark, N.J. | X | | see text |
| Chapel Hill, N.C. | | X | |
| Raleigh, N.C. | | X | |
| Cincinnati, Ohio | | X | |
| Dayton, Ohio | | X | |
| Waco, Texas | | X | |
| Charlottesville, Va. | | X | |
| Washington, D.C. | X | | X |

*Some member of the executive branch may be responsible to the mayor to submit the budget.

*Source*: See Table 3.1.

line-item veto over the budget, subject to an override by two-thirds of the city council.

The power of Congress over the district budget is not so alarming as it might appear. City budgets are generally constrained by a higher level government unit—a county, or the state ʾacting as final government authority. In the case of the District of Columbia, the federal government acts as the state.

In the three New Jersey cities, budget items are passed in the form of resolutions that the mayor, according to state law, cannot veto. The councils may increase budget items by a two-thirds vote and decrease them by a majority vote.

## Veto Powers

The power to veto ordinances and resolutions is obviously significant, but it is also affected by the size of the vote necessary to override it. The higher the vote necessary to override, the greater the veto power. Many city councils are small, and a two-thirds requirement means that the balance of power rests with two or three persons. In a city like Los Angeles, however, there are 15 council members, so opponents of the mayor must have the support of 10 members. This has enabled Mayor Thomas Bradley to successfully veto budget items.

In all ten cities with mayor-council forms of government, the black mayor has a veto power. Most exercise it within ten days after receipt of the proposed ordinance or resolution (see Table 3.9).

## Appointive Powers

In the past, many city mayors had the power to appoint and remove city officials at will, without the consent of the council. Such mayors could more easily steer their city administrations in the direction required to get their programs through. At the same time, they could reward loyal supporters through patronage.

Cities across the nation have trimmed these powers. Now, most mayors can make few appointments without council consent. Furthermore, civil service rules govern many appointments. As a consequence, city civil servants develop their own constituencies, and many departments have their own personnel and promotion systems—all of which make them less subject to the command of the mayor. Many mayors must deal with key officials who were in office before they took over and who will be there after their terms are over. This situation has caused controversy in Atlanta, where the current black mayor, Maynard Jackson, is at odds with a police chief appointed by the previous mayor to a ten-year term.

The mayor's appointive powers often are further restricted by ethnic claims. In the view of some observers, blacks have inherited the city after other ethnic groups have become well entrenched—in the police force, the sanitation department, and education and welfare bureaucracies.

In the council-manager form of government, the city manager is responsible for appointments. Black mayors under this form of government have influence over appointments primarily as voting members of the council. They themselves have no appointive powers.

# TABLE 3.9

## Veto Powers over Ordinances and/or Resolutions

| City and State | Power to Veto | Number or Proportion of Council Votes Needed to Override | Size of Council | Length of Time To Exercise Veto | Length of Time For Council Override |
|---|---|---|---|---|---|
| Prichard, Ala. | Yes | 2/3 | 5 | 10 days | 2 weeks* |
| Berkeley, Calif. | No | – | – | – | – |
| Compton, Calif. | No | – | – | – | – |
| Los Angeles, Calif. | Yes | 2/3 | 15 | 10 days | 60 days |
| Boulder, Colo. | No | – | – | – | – |
| Gainesville, Fla. | No | – | 5 | – | – |
| Atlanta, Ga. | Yes | 2/3 | 18 | 8 days | 2 weeks |
| East St. Louis, Ill. | No | – | – | – | – |
| Gary, Ind. | Yes | 2/3 | 9 | 10 days | 2 weeks |
| College Park, Md. | No | – | – | – | – |
| Detroit, Mich. | Yes | 2/3 | 9 | 7 days | 7 days |
| Grand Rapids, Mich. | No | – | – | – | – |
| Highland, Park, Mich. | Yes | 4 | 5 | 2 days | 2 weeks |
| Inkster, Mich. | No | – | – | – | – |
| Pontiac, Mich. | No | – | – | – | – |
| Ypsilanti, Mich. | No | – | – | – | – |
| East Orange, N.J. | Yes | 2/3 | 10 | 10 days | 2 weeks |
| New Brunswick, N.J. | Yes | 2/3 | 5 | 10 days | 3 days |
| Newark, N.J. | Yes | 2/3 | 9 | 5 days | 2 weeks |
| Chapel Hill, N.C. | No | – | – | – | – |
| Raleigh, N.C. | No | – | – | – | – |
| Cincinnati, Ohio | No | – | – | – | – |
| Dayton, Ohio | No | – | – | – | – |
| Waco, Texas | No | – | 6 | – | – |
| Charlottesville, Va. | No | – | 5 | – | – |
| Washington, D.C. | Yes | 2/3 | 13 | 10 days | 30 days |

*Law requires council meetings twice a month. Council must act on veto at first regular meeting after veto.

*Source*: See Table 3.1.

The black mayor of East St. Louis (a commission form of government) has a slightly different kind of appointive power. He can appoint members of the police board, which he oversees. The commissioners of other departments make their own appointments. In Alabama, state law gives councils in cities with a population of 12,000 or more, including Prichard, power to assign themselves the sole power of appointment of all the standard city officials—even some lower-echelon employees. The mayor might legally remove some of these appointees, but he would need a majority vote of the council to sustain his action. In fact, as in law, the council makes these appointments through its own initiative and as it sees fit. The mayor may make appointments not specifically called for by law, such as special boards and commissions.

Most of the black mayors under the mayor-council form of government can appoint boards, commissions (usually without council consent) and many department heads.

## TABLE 3.10

### Number of Cities with 25,000 or More Residents and Total Number of Cities in Selected States

| States | Number of Cities 25,000 or More | Total Number of Cities in State |
|--------|-------------------------------|-------------------------------|
| Alabama | 14 | 390 |
| California | 126 | 404 |
| Colorado | 13 | 262 |
| Florida | 21 | 389 |
| Georgia | 12 | 573 |
| Illinois | 58 | 1,262 |
| Indiana | 20 | 543 |
| Maryland | 7 | 151 |
| Michigan | 44 | 528 |
| New Jersey | 39 | 335 |
| North Carolina | 16 | 470 |
| Ohio | 48 | 926 |
| Texas | 35 | 940 |
| Virginia | 7 | 233 |

Source: U.S. Department of Commerce, Bureau of the Census.

## TABLE 3.11

Size-Class Distribution of Cities in the United States with
Populations of at Least 25,000 and Classification of Cities
with Black Mayors According to Population Size

| Population Size | Number of Cities in U.S. | Cities with Black Mayors |
|---|---|---|
| 25,000-49,999 | 455 | Prichard, Alabama<br>College Park, Maryland<br>Highland Park, Michigan<br>Inkster, Michigan<br>Ypsilanti, Michigan<br>New Brunswick, New Jersey<br>Chapel Hill, North Carolina<br>Charlottesville, Virginia |
| 50,000-99,999 | 232 | Compton, California<br>Boulder, Colorado<br>Gainesville, Florida<br>East St. Louis, Illinois<br>Pontiac, Michigan<br>East Orange, New Jersey<br>Waco, Texas |
| 100,000-249,999 | 97 | Berkeley, California<br>Gary, Indiana<br>Grand Rapids, Michigan<br>Raleigh, North Carolina<br>Dayton, Ohio |
| 250,000-499,000 | 30 | Atlanta, Georgia<br>Newark, New Jersey<br>Cincinnati, Ohio |
| 500,000-999,999 | 20 | Washington, D.C. |
| 1 million or more | 6 | Los Angeles, California<br>Detroit, Michigan |

*Source*: U.S. Department of Commerce, Bureau of the Census.

## TABLE 3.12

### Percent of Jobs in Selected Cities with Black Mayors which are Held by Non-Residents

| City | Percent of Total Workers Living Outside City | Unemployment Rate, 1970 (percent) |
|------|------|------|
| Population 250,000 and over | | |
| Atlanta, Georgia | 55.2 | 4 |
| Cincinnati, Ohio | 53.1 | 4.8 |
| Detroit, Michigan | 41.8 | 7.2 |
| Los Angeles, California | 38.0 | 7.0 |
| Newark, New Jersey | 63.7 | 6.5 |
| Washington, D.C. | 57.5 | 3.8 |
| Population 100,000-250,000 | | |
| Berkeley, California | 58.9 | 8.3 |
| Dayton, Ohio | 62.4 | 5.2 |
| Gary, Indiana | 45.3 | 5.5 |
| Population 50,000-100,000 | | |
| Boulder, Colorado | 34.9 | 4.7 |
| Compton, California | 85.9 | 9.8 |
| East Orange, New Jersey | 71.3 | 3.9 |
| East St. Louis, Illinois | 69.2 | 10.3 |
| Pontiac, Michigan | 66.4 | 12.2 |

*Source*: U.S. Bureau of Census, Department of Commerce, *Journey to Work, 1970* (Washington, D.C.: Government Printing Office, 1973).

## CONCLUSION

It has been said that America's mayors do not govern. They are facilitators, conciliators, and even magicians.[5] Black mayors of medium and large cities are no exception to this general rule. Nearly half of all black mayors of medium and large cities are in statutorily weak positions, where their power is based almost exclusively on personality and the respect of fellow legislators. The rise of blacks to mayoral offices in many cities where a little more than a decade ago many could not vote is no small achievement; contrary to popular belief, though, most of them do not serve predominantly black populations.

Furthermore, there is little question that the cities they serve tend to be the most severely troubled, but their ability to resolve the problems of these cities is affected by factors outside the control of any mayor, black or white. The demand for public goods and services is rapidly outstripping the ability of cities to raise revenues. Inflation has pushed up the cost of running cities, and recession has severely reduced the ability to raise revenues.

# NOTES

1. Thomas F. Pettigrew, *The Racial Factor in Black Mayoralty Campaigns*, prepared at Harvard University for presentation to the Public Policy Forum, April 10, 1975, Washington, D.C. (see, Chapter 2 of this volume).

2. For more on the hollow-prize thesis, see Frances Fox Piven and Richard A. Cloward, "Black Control of Cities I: Heading It Off By Metropolitan Government," *New Republic*, September 30, 1967, pp. 11-16; and Frances Fox Piven and Richard A. Cloward, "Black Control of Cities II; How the Negro Will Lose," *New Republic*, October 7, 1967, pp. 15-19.

3. See: Edward Banfield and James Q. Wilson, *City Politics* (Cambridge, Mass.: Harvard University Press, 1963); Robert A. Dahl, *Who Governs?* (New Haven: Yale University Press, 1961), pp. 225-27, 308; Edward Banfield, *Political Influence* (New York: Free Press, 1961), Chapter 8 and pp. 17, 309, 312-21; Aaron Wildavsky, *Leadership in a Small Town* (Totowa, N.J.: Bedminster Press, 1964), pp. 244-45, 248; H. H. Gerth and C. Wright Mills, *From Max Weber* (New York: Oxford University Press, 1946), p. 109; Andrew S. McFarland, *Power and Leadership in Pluralist Systems* (Stanford, California: Stanford University Press, 1969), pp. 153-219; and Jeffrey L. Pressman, "Preconditions of Mayoral Leadership," *American Political Science Review* 66 (1972): 511-24.

4. Leonard A. Cole, "Electing Blacks to Municipal Office (Structural and Social Determinants)," *Urban Affairs Quarterly* 10, no. 1 (September 1974): 17-39.

5. Scott Greer, *Governing the Metropolis* (New York: John Wiley & Sons, 1962), p. 80.

# THE ECONOMY
# OF THE CITY
# AND THE MAYOR

# 4

## CITY BUDGETS
## AND THE BLACK
## CONSTITUENCY
### Roy W. Bahl
### Alan Campbell

The fiscal crisis of American cities is related to the existence of a relatively large black population. To examine this issue, as well as others, a sample has been selected from the 37 largest central cities and divided into two groups: one composed of cities with a majority or near-majority black population; the other overwhelmingly white in its ethnic composition.* Certain social and economic characteristics of both sets of cities are then related to the magnitude of their public expenditures and the characteristics of the resource base from which part of the resources must be drawn to support these expenditure levels.

## SOCIOECONOMIC FACTORS AND FISCAL CHARACTERISTICS

Population in cities with large black populations is generally declining both absolutely and relative to surrounding metropolitan areas. Of the eight minority cities, seven have experienced absolute declines in population (only Atlanta has grown and this is primarily due to annexation), but all eight are located in metropolitan areas whose populations have increased. On the other hand, five of

---

*Data used in this analysis are drawn from the Census of Governments, the Census of Population, and from a body of research on metropolitan fiscal disparities, primarily for the Advisory Commission on Intergovernmental Relations, carried out by Sacks and Callahan.[1] The eight cities in the first group, referred to hereafter as minority cities, have a percentage of nonwhite population ranging from 39 percent (Cleveland) to 72.3 percent (Washington, D.C.). The nine cities in the second group, referred to as "white" cities, have nonwhite percentages that range from 6 percent (Minneapolis) to 15.6 percent (Milwaukee). (See column 1 of Table 4.1.)

# TABLE 4.1

Socioeconomic Characteristics: Cities with Relatively Large and Relatively Small Nonwhite Populations, 1970

| | Percent of City Population Nonwhite | Ratio of City to Suburban Median Family Income | Percent Increase in City Population 1960-70 | Percent Increase in SMSA Population 1960-70 |
|---|---|---|---|---|
| *Cities with Large Proportions of Nonwhite Population* | | | | |
| Washington, D.C. | 72.3 | .74 | − .7 | 42.9 |
| Baltimore, Md. | 47.0 | .83 | − 3.5 | 19.9 |
| Newark, N.J. | 56.0 | .65 | − 5.6 | 9.9 |
| Detroit, Mich. | 44.5 | .83 | − 9.5 | 11.6 |
| St. Louis, Mo. | 41.3 | .78 | −17.0 | 14.7 |
| Cleveland, Ohio | 39.0 | .80 | −14.2 | 14.9 |
| Atlanta, Ga. | 51.5 | .79 | 2.0 | 36.6 |
| New Orleans, La. | 45.5 | .86 | − 5.4 | 20.5 |
| *Cities without Large Proportions of Nonwhite Population* | | | | |
| Providence, R.I. | 9.5 | .85 | −13.5 | 11.6 |
| Minneapolis, Minn. | 6.0 | .85 | − 9.9 | 22.4 |
| Milwaukee, Wisc. | 15.6 | .91 | − 3.2 | 17.5 |
| San Antonio, Texas | 8.5 | .97 | 11.4 | 25.7 |
| San Bernardino, Calif. | 15.4 | .93 | 14.2 | 41.2 |
| San Diego, Calif. | 11.0 | 1.00 | 21.6 | 34.0 |
| Denver, Colo. | 10.9 | .90 | 4.4 | 32.1 |
| Portland, Oregon | 7.8 | .94 | 2.9 | 22.8 |
| Seattle, Wash. | 11.9 | .95 | − 4.8 | 28.4 |
| Averages Eight Minority Cities | 49.64 | .79 | − 6.74 | 21.38 |
| Nine White Cities | 10.73 | .92 | 2.57 | 26.19 |

| Central City Median Family Income | Central City Minority Median Family Income | Ratio of Minority to Total Median Family Income | Percent of Families Below Poverty Line | Percent of SMSA Population Living in Central City |
|---|---|---|---|---|
| 9583 | 8488 | .89 | 12.7 | 26.5 |
| 8815 | 7289 | .83 | 14.0 | 43.7 |
| 7735 | 6742 | .87 | 18.4 | 20.6 |
| 10045 | 8645 | .86 | 11.3 | 36.0 |
| 8182 | 6534 | .80 | 14.3 | 26.3 |
| 9107 | 7617 | .84 | 13.4 | 36.4 |
| 8399 | 6451 | .77 | 15.9 | 35.8 |
| 7435 | 4745 | .64 | 21.6 | 56.7 |
| 8430 | 5627 | .67 | 13.3 | 19.6 |
| 9960 | 7353 | .74 | 7.2 | 23.9 |
| 10262 | 7491 | .73 | 8.1 | 51.1 |
| 7734 | 5374 | .69 | 17.5 | 75.7 |
| 8658 | 6164 | .71 | 12.8 | 9.1 |
| 10166 | 7408 | .73 | 9.3 | 50.3 |
| 9654 | 7287 | .75 | 9.4 | 41.9 |
| 9799 | 6844 | .70 | 8.1 | 38.0 |
| 11037 | 8460 | .77 | 6.0 | 37.3 |
| 8663 | 7064 | .81 | 15.2 | 35.3 |
| 9522 | 6890 | .72 | 10.2 | 38.5 |

*Source*: U.S. Bureau of Census, *Census of Population and Housing, 1970*, Series PHC(2), *General Demographic Trends for Metropolitan Areas*, 1960-70; and Advisory Commission on Intergovernmental Relations, *City Government Financial Emergencies* (Washington, D.C.: ACIR, July 1973), A-42, Appendix B.

TABLE 4.2

Fiscal Characteristics: Cities with Relatively Large and Relatively Small Nonwhite Populations, 1970

| | Ratio of City to Suburban Per Capita Expenditures | | Ratio of City to Suburban Per Capita State and Federal Aids | | Total Taxes as a Percent of Median Family Income | Per Capita State and Federal Aid to the Overlapping Central City Governments | |
|---|---|---|---|---|---|---|---|
| | Total | Education | Total | Education | Income | Total | Education |
| *Cities with Large Proportions of Nonwhite Population* | | | | | | | |
| Washington, D.C. | 2.37 | 1.07 | 303 | 59 | 0.6 | 358 | 49 |
| Baltimore, Md. | 1.83 | 1.03 | 259 | 93 | 9.2 | 329 | 75 |
| Newark, N.J. | 1.67 | 1.05 | 271 | 215 | 9.3 | 276 | 84 |
| Detroit, Mich. | 1.03 | .68 | 144 | 107 | 4.9 | 189 | 95 |
| St. Louis, Mo. | 1.59 | .94 | 119 | 71 | 6.8 | 99 | 52 |
| Cleveland, Ohio | 1.39 | 1.08 | 132 | 109 | 3.5 | 87 | 36 |
| Atlanta, Ga. | 1.76 | 1.14 | 102 | 87 | 3.5 | 97 | 69 |
| New Orleans, La. | 1.03 | 1.02 | 86 | 79 | 2.8 | 100 | 59 |
| *Cities without Large Proportions of Nonwhite Population* | | | | | | | |
| Providence, R.I. | 1.48 | 0.95 | 156 | 82 | 6.9 | 111 | 37 |
| Minneapolis, Minn. | 1.04 | 0.54 | 78[a] | 43[a] | 3.1 | 177[a] | 51[a] |
| Milwaukee, Wis. | 1.16 | 0.73 | 89 | 70 | 3.5 | 199 | 40 |
| San Antonio, Texas | .98 | 0.62 | 93 | 90 | 2.2 | 89 | 77 |
| San Bernardino, Calif. | 1.22 | 1.15 | 129 | 97 | 3.0 | 278 | 111 |
| San Diego, Calif. | 1.03 | 0.82 | 96 | 102 | 2.3 | 194 | 88 |
| Denver, Colo. | 1.64 | 0.87 | 159 | 73 | 4.9 | 149 | 49 |
| Portland, Ore. | 1.48 | 0.88 | 123 | 88 | 2.7 | 125 | 61 |
| Seattle, Wash. | 1.11 | 0.55 | 85[b] | 43[b] | 2.8 | 137[b] | 60[b] |
| Averages | | | | | | | |
| Eight Minority Cities | 1.58 | 1.00 | 177.00 | 102.50 | 5.1 | 191.88 | 64.88 |
| Nine White Cities | 1.24 | .79 | 112.00 | 76.44 | 3.5 | 162.11 | 63.78 |

| | Property Taxes as a Percent of Total Revenues | Per Capita Expenditures | | Per Student Education Expenditures | Per Student Education State Aid |
|---|---|---|---|---|---|
| | | Total | Education | | |
| *Cities with Large Proportions of Non-white Population* | | | | | |
| Washington, D.C. | 50.8 | 1006 | 261 | 843 | 251 |
| Baltimore, Md. | 73.9 | 638 | 222 | 822 | 337 |
| Newark, N.J. | 82.9 | 735 | 216 | 937 | 393 |
| Detroit, Mich. | 56.5 | 474 | 177 | 898 | 511 |
| St. Louis, Mo. | 29.7 | 463 | 176 | 709 | 219 |
| Cleveland, Ohio | 48.4 | 512 | 210 | 896 | 179 |
| Atlanta, Ga. | 66.1 | 554 | 218 | 804 | 281 |
| New Orleans, La. | 38.7 | 334 | 126 | 560 | 308 |
| *Cities without Large Proportions of Non-white Population* | | | | | |
| Providence, R.I. | 98.8 | 392 | 139 | 867 | 208 |
| Minneapolis, Minn. | 88.0 | 540 | 154 | 927 | 324 |
| Milwaukee, Wis. | 96.9 | 562 | 183 | 857 | 214 |
| San Antonio, Texas | 68.3 | 252 | 123 | 458 | 302 |
| San Bernardino, Calif. | 34.7 | 635 | 267 | 740 | 429 |
| San Diego, Calif. | 53.8 | 484 | 186 | 624 | 318 |
| Denver, Colo. | 41.1 | 502 | 170 | 836 | 225 |
| Portland, Ore. | 78.5 | 486 | 188 | 832 | 299 |
| Seattle, Wash. | 43.6 | 524 | 150 | 848 | 347 |
| Averages | | | | | |
| Eight Minority Cities | 67.1 | 631 | 217 | 879 | 348 |
| Nine White Cities | 55.8 | 545 | 190 | 871 | 335 |

aIncludes St. Paul.
bIncludes Everett.
*Source:* Advisory Commission on Intergovernmental Relations, *City Financial Emergencies: The Intergovernmental Dimensions* (Washington, D.C., ACIR, July 1973), Appendix B.

the nine white cities are undergoing population increases, while the population of the white city Standard Metropolitan Statistical Areas (SMSAs) is growing significantly faster than that of the minority city SMSAs.

Resident incomes average about 79 percent of the metropolitan area income level in black cities, while they average 92 percent in the white cities, indicating a significant disparity. Further, as may be seen from Table 4.1, the overall level of income is 10 percent less in the minority cities than in the white cities. The median income of blacks is slightly higher in the minority than in the white cities (80 percent of the citywide median compared to 72 percent). Thus, blacks would appear to have higher incomes if they reside in a predominantly minority city. As might be expected, minority cities show a substantially greater percent of families with incomes below the poverty line than do the white cities.

If the literature describing the impact of unfavorable population mix on central city finances[2] has any validity, then the fiscal position of the minority cities should be markedly worse than that of the white cities. Moreover, there is every reason to expect these characteristics to be reinforced in the black city group over the next decade.

The literature describes blacks as higher-cost citizens, since the poor require more services; for example, poor children may require special preschool training and hot lunch programs, crime rates are higher, fire incidence is greater, and so forth. The revenue base generated by a lower-income population is smaller, however, and this characteristic leads to irreversible fiscal deterioration. The "minority" city, with a smaller tax base but greater service requirements, must tax at a higher rate than its white suburbs, but still provides a lower level of service. Suburban flight of higher-income (white) residents results, resources decline even further, the city's minority proportion increases, tax burdens must rise even higher, and so it goes.

Thus the result will be—or is—higher expenditure levels, population decline, decreased tax revenues, heavy concentration of the poor, and a declining city core relative to the balance of the metropolitan area. The data in Table 4.1 show this pattern.

Table 4.2 shows, as expected, that the minority cities display a quantitatively different fiscal structure than the white cities and, particularly, higher levels of expenditures. The data on the finances of overlapping governments show both per capita total expenditures and per capita education expenditures to be greater in minority than in white cities.

This results from the fact that tax effort in the minority cities is over 60 percent higher (the difference rises to 75 percent if Washington, D.C. is excluded) and that state and federal aid to minority city governments is 18 percent higher. For education, however, the minority and white cities receive an approximately equal per capita aid amount.

These data (summarized in Table 4.3) show that among the 37 largest central cities, total and education expenditures, as well as tax effort, are higher where the nonwhite percentage is greater, and where per capita grants are higher.

## TABLE 4.3

### Simple Correlation among Selected Central City Socioeconomic and Fiscal Characteristics, 1970
#### (37 largest central cities)

| | Per Capita Total Expenditures | Per Capita Education Expenditures | Per Capita State and Federal Aid | Median Family Income | Percent of Families Below Poverty Line | Tax Effort |
|---|---|---|---|---|---|---|
| Percent nonwhite | .39 | .33 | .27 | -.25 | .51 | .51 |
| Per capita total expenditures | 1.00 | .75 | .86 | .17 | -.07 | .82 |
| Per capita education expenditures | .75 | 1.00 | .52 | -.07 | .10 | .81 |
| Per capita state and federal aid | .86 | .52 | 1.00 | .11 | .00 | .48 |
| Median family income | .17 | -.07 | .11 | 1.00 | -.89 | -.19 |
| Percent of families below poverty line | -.07 | .10 | .00 | -.89 | 1.00 | .22 |
| Tax effort | .82 | .81 | .48 | -.19 | .22 | 1.00 |

*Source:* Data compiled by author.

## METROPOLITAN FISCAL DISPARITIES

The disparities between cities and suburbs in service levels, aid flows, and tax effort[3] would suggest a pattern of more pronounced socioeconomic and fiscal disparities for minority cities suffering suburban flight than that for white cities. While this is clearly true for income and population growth rate variables (Table 4.1), it is not observed for fiscal variables: the minority city governments spend 58 percent more in total than do their suburbs, while the white city governments spend only 24 percent more than their suburbs. For education, reflecting the impact of aid and higher level of tax effort, the minority cities spend about the same as their suburbs while the white cities spend about 25 percent less.

As may be seen in Table 4.4, the 37 largest SMSAs show a significant positive correlation between the city-suburb ration of per capita expenditures and the percentage of nonwhites living in the central city.

## PUBLIC EMPLOYMENT CHARACTERISTICS

There are compelling reasons to study the differential local government compensation and employment patterns in minority and white cities. Studies of the determinants of public expenditures shows that jurisdictions with greater proportions of nonwhites spend more per person for police, fire, and sanitation,

## TABLE 4.4

### Simple Correlations among Selected Socioeconomic Characteristics and Indicators of City-Suburb Fiscal Disparity

|  | Per Capita Expenditure Disparity | Per Capita Education Expenditure Disparity | Tax Effort Disparity | Per Capita State and Federal Aid Disparity |
|---|---|---|---|---|
| Percent nonwhite | 0.45 | 0.26 | – | 0.27 |
| Per capita expenditure disparity | 1.00 | 0.80 | – | – |
| Per capita education education expenditure disparity | – | 1.00 | – | – |
| Tax effort disparity | – | – | 1.00 | – |
| Per capita state and federal aid disparity | – | – | – | 1.00 |

*Source*: Data compiled by author.

## TABLE 4.5

**Public Employment Characteristics: Cities with Relatively Large and Relatively Small Nonwhite Populations**

| | Total Local Government Employment Population Ratio | | | Total Local Government Employment Population Ratio (Education) | | | City Government Employees in the Common Functions per 10,000 Population |
|---|---|---|---|---|---|---|---|
| | CC* | OCC† | CC/OCC | CC | OCC | CC/OCC | |
| *Cities with Large Proportions of Nonwhite Population* | | | | | | | |
| Washington, D.C. | 64.15 | 30.03 | 2.14 | 19.57 | 20.60 | 0.95 | 216.54 |
| Baltimore | 48.31 | 18.30 | 2.64 | 20.00 | 13.23 | 1.51 | 159.91 |
| Newark | 44.48 | 30.52 | 1.46 | 19.89 | 16.06 | 1.24 | 325.10 |
| Detroit | 23.81 | 33.84 | 0.70 | 4.71 | 23.49 | 0.20 | 114.77 |
| St. Louis | 18.63 | 30.90 | 0.60 | 11.51 | 17.44 | 0.66 | 125.90 |
| Cleveland | 31.27 | 35.00 | 0.89 | 5.67 | 21.82 | 0.26 | 114.65 |
| Atlanta | 22.30 | 39.46 | 0.57 | 5.98 | 23.62 | 0.25 | 135.92 |
| New Orleans | 23.74 | 34.87 | 0.68 | 7.21 | 21.92 | 0.33 | 132.68 |
| *Cities without Large Proportions of Nonwhite Population* | | | | | | | |
| Providence | 26.07 | 18.18 | 1.43 | 11.54 | 11.88 | 0.97 | 262.12 |
| Minneapolis | 14.12 | 33.63 | 0.42 | n.a. | 22.30 | n.a. | 109.01 |
| Milwaukee | 26.04 | 38.82 | 0.67 | 5.94 | 23.26 | 0.26 | 103.81 |
| San Antonio | 20.05 | 56.42 | 0.36 | 5.89 | 41.75 | 0.14 | 67.34 |
| San Bernardino | 16.00 | 35.11 | 0.46 | n.a. | 20.30 | n.a. | 115.00 |
| San Diego | 22.48 | 38.69 | 0.58 | 7.97 | 26.11 | 0.31 | 76.38 |
| Denver | 23.63 | 32.43 | 0.73 | 6.37 | 25.07 | 0.25 | 122.91 |
| Portland | 21.78 | 33.70 | 0.65 | 6.83 | 23.95 | 0.29 | 106.01 |
| Seattle | 26.38 | 34.17 | 0.77 | 5.21 | 25.24 | 0.21 | 103.36 |
| Averages | | | | | | | |
| Eight minority cities | 34.59 | 31.61 | 1.21 | 11.82 | 19.77 | 0.68 | 165.68 |
| Nine white cities | 21.84 | 35.68 | 0.67 | 5.53 | 24.43 | 0.27 | 118.44 |

*Central Cities.

†Outside Central Cities.

*Note:* n.a. — data not available.

*Source:* U.S. Bureau of the Census, *Local Government Employment in Selected Metropolitan Areas and Large Counties, 1970,* Series GE 70, no. 3 (Washington, D.C.: U.S. Government Printing Office, 1971).

and that the sensitivity of expenditures to larger nonwhite percentages is of considerable size. John Weicher, for example,[4] found that a difference of 1 percent in the nonwhite proportion is associated with a $0.18 per capita higher level of police expenditures. On the other hand, larger proportions of nonwhite population tend to be associated with lower per capita expenditures for education.

While there is consensus about the statistical significance of the minority effect on per capita expenditure level, there is little agreement over the interpretation of this relationship. Some have argued that the nonwhite variable is a convenient proxy for a myriad of poverty-related variables that result in higher police, fire, and sanitation expenditure requirements. Others argue that greater nonwhite populations mean a lower level of governmental fiscal capacity and hence a lower level of expenditures, particularly for education. In all cases, the interpretation has been drawn from the demand side; that is, the emphasis has been on why larger concentrations of minority population might require more services. There has been little investigation of the cost issues—of the possibility that cities with large nonwhite populations have different patterns of public employment and compensation levels.

While comparisons of local government employment among central city areas may be misleading because of interstate variations in the assignment of functions as between state and local governments, data on overlapping central city governments show that local governments in minority cities provide an average of only five more common function municipal jobs per 10,000 of population than do those in white cities. They also, however, pay lower public-sector wages. For instance, in the common functions, in 1972, minority cities paid 6.7 percent less on average than did the white cities (see Table 4.6). However, since all income in the white cities was 9 percent higher, public-sector employees in minority cities received relatively high pay in relation to income of all families in their cities. This higher pay characteristic indicates that more employees could have been hired in these cities with the same amount of overall expenditures if their pay levels had been at the average level of that for all employees in the cities. If, as has been suggested, a 1 percent high wage results in a 0.7 percent lower level of employment, then the opportunity cost of this higher common-function wage in minority cities is 1.61 percent fewer common-function employees in return for the higher wage.

Finally, and still with respect to the public employment issue, it is useful to compare the components of change in common-function expenditures. The 1962-1972 change in labor costs is partitioned into a wage rate, an employment, and an interaction effect, as shown in Table 4.7.* Those results show little

---

*The "wage rate" effect is simply the increase in expenditures that would have occurred had employment remained constant, but the actual increment in per employee compensation had taken place. The "employment effect" is the increase in expenditures

# TABLE 4.6

Composition of Labor Cost Increase: Cities with Relatively Large and Relatively Small Nonwhite Populations

| | Common Functions | | | | | | | |
|---|---|---|---|---|---|---|---|---|
| | Average Salary | | | | Employment/10,000 Population | | | |
| | 1962 | 1972 | Increase | Percent Increase | 1962 | 1972 | Increase | Percent Increase |
| **Cities with Large Proportions of Nonwhite Population** | | | | | | | | |
| Washington, D.C. | 500.77 | 886.87 | 386.10 | 77.10 | 169.59 | 216.54 | 46.95 | 27.68 |
| Baltimore | 392.29 | 646.50 | 254.21 | 64.80 | 137.88 | 159.91 | 22.03 | 15.98 |
| Newark | 476.19 | 881.68 | 405.49 | 85.15 | 123.41 | 134.35 | 10.94 | 8.86 |
| Detroit | 506.07 | 1032.33 | 526.26 | 103.99 | 110.47 | 114.77 | 4.30 | 3.89 |
| St. Louis | 440.79 | 800.72 | 359.93 | 81.66 | 114.61 | 125.90 | 11.29 | 9.85 |
| Cleveland | 477.09 | 898.48 | 421.39 | 88.32 | 103.39 | 114.65 | 11.26 | 10.89 |
| Atlanta | 352.80 | 731.77 | 378.97 | 107.42 | 108.67 | 135.92 | 27.25 | 25.08 |
| New Orleans | 334.46 | 590.93 | 256.46 | 76.68 | 127.32 | 132.68 | 5.36 | 4.21 |
| **Cities without Large Proportions of Nonwhite Population** | | | | | | | | |
| Providence | 379.10 | 724.65 | 345.55 | 91.15 | 132.66 | 115.59 | −17.07a | −12.87 |
| Minneapolis | 529.05 | 949.74 | 420.69 | 79.52 | 97.14 | 109.01 | 11.87 | 12.22 |
| Milwaukee | 520.23 | 1012.07 | 491.84 | 94.54 | 120.76 | 103.81 | −16.95b | −14.04 |
| San Antonio | 350.20 | 706.31 | 356.11 | 101.69 | 63.97 | 67.34 | 3.37 | 5.27 |
| San Bernardino | 524.44 | 885.79 | 361.34 | 68.90 | 98.90 | 115.00 | 16.10 | 16.28 |
| San Diego | 552.02 | 948.91 | 396.89 | 71.90 | 73.98 | 76.38 | 2.41 | 3.25 |
| Denver | 480.56 | 744.12 | 263.53 | 54.83 | 105.56 | 122.91 | 17.35 | 16.44 |
| Portland | 504.17 | 896.87 | 392.70 | 77.89 | 96.72 | 106.01 | 9.28 | 9.60 |
| Seattle | 514.88 | 931.25 | 416.37 | 80.87 | 85.04 | 103.36 | 18.31 | 21.53 |
| **Averages** | | | | | | | | |
| Eight minority cities | 435.06 | 808.66 | 373.60 | 85.64 | 124.42 | 141.84 | 17.42 | 13.30 |
| Nine white cities | 483.85 | 866.63 | 382.78 | 80.14 | 97.19 | 102.16 | 4.96 | 6.41 |

aDecrease in Providence is due to decrease in sanitation employment.

bDecrease in Milwaukee is due to decrease in sewerage, parks and recreation, and water supply employment.

Source: U.S. Bureau of the Census, Local Government Employment in Selected Metropolitan Areas and Large Counties, 1970, Series GE 70, no. 3 (Washington, D.C.: U.S. Government Printing Office, 1971).

## TABLE 4.7

### The Components of Increase in Common-Function
### Labor Costs, 1962-72

|  | Percent of Total Increment Due to: | | |
|---|---|---|---|
| City | Wage Rate Effect | Employment Effect | Interaction Effect |
| Washington | 62.0 | 21.5 | 16.5 |
| Baltimore | 77.8 | 14.1 | 9.1 |
| Newark | 94.5 | 3.0 | 2.5 |
| Detroit | 113.3 | - 6.5 | - 6.8 |
| St. Louis | 124.7 | -13.6 | -11.1 |
| Cleveland | 111.8 | - 6.2 | - 5.5 |
| Atlanta | 65.2 | 16.8 | 18.0 |
| New Orleans | 103.4 | - 1.9 | - 1.5 |
| Providence | 207.0 | -56.0 | -51.0 |
| Minneapolis | 97.7 | 1.3 | 1.0 |
| Milwaukee | 152.9 | -27.2 | -25.7 |
| San Antonio | 74.5 | 12.7 | 12.9 |
| San Bernardino | 55.4 | 26.4 | 18.2 |
| San Diego | 62.0 | 22.1 | 15.9 |
| Denver | 62.1 | 24.5 | 13.4 |
| Portland | 77.3 | 12.7 | 9.9 |
| Seattle | 74.1 | 14.3 | 11.5 |
| Averages | | | |
| Eight minority cities | 94.1 | 3.4 | 2.5 |
| Nine white cities | 95.9 | 3.4 | .7 |

*Source*: Data compiled by author.

difference between the two city groups, but do show that wage rate effects on expenditures have dominated employment effects in all cities.

## DIFFERENTIAL FISCAL PERFORMANCE

With respect to the differential fiscal performance of minority cities, their expenditures indicate that they spend more than the white cities, in total and for

that would have occurred had average compensation remained constant, but the actual increment in employment had taken place. The difference between these two effects and the total increment in labor expenditures is a residual which we refer to as the interaction effect, since it describes the expenditure increment resulting from payment of a higher wage rate to an increased number of employees.

education. They also spend more, on average, relative to their suburbs than do the white central cities. Partial explanation for these differences include greater federal and state government aid and greater tax effort relative to their income for minority cities.

There are, as well, marked differences between minority and white cities in the structure of expenditures. Wage rates tend to be lower, and local government employment higher, in the black cities.

Though the evidence of relatively higher wages in minority cities presented here is far from conclusive, the policy implications of such a finding are important.

If minority cities choose to pay higher compensation to public employees, financed from property taxes that bear more heavily on the poor, the level of services to the community will, in turn, be lower than the level that would have resulted had the same expenditure been used to employ more workers, even at lower wages. By paying lower wages, these cities would be able to offer more services than they otherwise could.

The tradeoff between employment and wages is only one dimension of the possible decline in service levels to core city residents. A more severe financial constraint results if state and federal assistance does not increase. If tax limits prevent tax increases and local tax bases decline or remain constrained, these cities will simply be unable to finance an adequate level of services. One might conclude that previous increases in local employment in the minority cities have been possible mostly because of large increments in state and federal aid and greater local tax effort. Without such increments, but with tax rates so high as to push middle-income residents out of the cities, and with inflation pressures promoting higher pay rates, it is likely that public expenditure increases in all large cities may mean higher wages but reduced employment. Since the findings in this analysis suggest that minority cities are more likely to trade off more employees for higher pay, the resulting decline in services provided may be most pronounced in these cities.

## NOTES

1. The Advisory Commission on Intergovernmental Relations, *City Financial Emergencies: The Intergovernmental Dimension*, prepared by Seymour Sacks and John Callahan (Washington, D.C.: Government Printing Office, 1967).

2. Roy W. Bahl, *Metropolitan City Expenditures: A Comparative Analysis* (Lexington, Kentucky: University of Kentucky Press, 1969); Theodore Bergstrom and Robert Goodman, "Private Demands for Public Goods," *American Economic Review* 63 (June 1973): 280-96; Thomas E. Borcherding and Robert T. Deacon, "The Demand for the Services of Non-Federal Governments," *American Economic Review* 62 (December 1972): 891-901; John C. Weicher, "Determinants of Central City Expenditures: Some Overlooked Factors and Problems," *National Tax Journal* 23 (December 1970): 379-96.

3. The major works on this subject are Sacks and Callahan, op. cit., and Alan K. Campbell and Seymour Sacks, *Metropolitan America: Fiscal Patterns and Governmental Systems* (London: Collier-Macmillan Limited, 1967).

4. Weicher, op. cit.

# 5

## THE CITY AS
## THE CENTER
## OF EMPLOYMENT
Seymour Sacks

As far back as 1944, Hansen and Perloff noted:[1] "With each of the large industrial areas the dominance of the major city has tended to lessen significantly since the turn of the century. . . . The relative growth of the peripheral areas compared with central cities has been striking." The economic future of the central city continues to be an important issue. Some authors, such as Kain,[2] see a declining labor market, while others, such as Fremont[3] and Harrison,[4] find hope.

Information on the city as a place of work is fragmentary and inconsistent. The large central city is not an economic entity; it is part of a broader area, the Standard Metropolitan Statistical Area or SMSA. While these areas have many interactions with the rest of the nation, they achieve their main meaning as labor markets. The large cities and their surrounding areas cannot be viewed independently of one another.

For the 76 major metropolitan areas covered by this study, the employment increase from 1960 to 1970 was 18.9 percent, compared to 19.5 percent for the nation as a whole. The 76 areas represent all areas with central cities in excess of 150,000, except for the recently consolidated cities of Indianapolis, Jacksonville, and Nashville-Davison, the triple-city areas of Springfield-Chicopee-Holyoke, and Gary-Hammond-East Chicago, and the twin-city area of Norfolk-Portsmouth.

During the period 1960 to 1970, aggregate employment in the large cities in these 76 metropolitan areas covered by this study increased by 5.5 percent as compared to 43.0 percent in their outside areas. Thus, employment opportunities increased rather than declined—in central cities but the growth lagged way behind that of the suburbs.

It is possible that some of the growth is associated with annexation rather than real economic expansion. As shown in Table 5.1, the average central city

# TABLE 5.1

## Standard Metropolitan Statistical Areas, Percent Change in Employment and Area, 1960-70

| Name | City | Outside Central City | Metropolitan Area | Central City Area |
|------|------|------|------|------|
| Tulsa, Okla. | 35.4 | -9.8 | 23.0 | 263.8 |
| Honolulu, Hawaii | 21.7 | 58.8 | 32.8 | .0 |
| El Paso, Texas | 10.7 | 11.7 | 10.8 | 3.5 |
| San Bernardino, Calif. | 16.6 | 32.7 | 26.6 | 115.6 |
| Birmingham, Ala. | 5.7 | 23.9 | 12.1 | 6.7 |
| Rochester, N.Y. | .5 | 105.7 | 27.5 | .0 |
| Paterson, N.J.* | -2.0 | 36.5 | 24.2 | .0 |
| Wichita, Kansas | 21.2 | -15.1 | 7.4 | 68.6 |
| Akron, Ohio | -6.4 | 44.3 | 10.8 | .0 |
| Tucson, Ariz. | 57.9 | -27.0 | 30.2 | 14.2 |
| Jersey City, N.J. | -12.6 | -4.1 | -7.5 | .0 |
| Sacramento, Calif. | 55.1 | -1.2 | 25.3 | 106.6 |
| Austin, Texas | 53.9 | 69.7 | 55.5 | 46.9 |
| Richmond, Va. | 16.1 | 64.4 | 26.5 | 62.1 |
| Albuquerque, N.M. | 25.8 | 5.5 | 22.1 | 46.4 |
| Dayton, Ohio | 14.0 | 30.5 | 21.2 | 15.1 |
| Charlotte, N.C. | 41.8 | 54.2 | 44.4 | 18.7 |
| Corpus Christi, Texas | 18.4 | 18.3 | 18.4 | 170.2 |
| Des Moines, Iowa | 18.0 | 34.1 | 20.4 | 4.8 |
| Grand Rapids, Mich. | 10.9 | 40.6 | 24.4 | 83.3 |
| Syracuse, N.Y. | -7.6 | 42.5 | 13.8 | .0 |
| Flint, Mich. | 10.5 | 45.5 | 20.9 | 10.3 |
| Mobile, Ala. | -3.8 | 5.5 | -1.1 | -23.6 |
| Shreveport, La. | .2 | 7.9 | 2.4 | 55.5 |
| Fort Wayne, Ind. | 44.2 | 95.3 | 54.0 | 41.6 |
| Worcester, Mass. | 2.3 | 23.2 | 7.6 | .0 |
| Salt Lake City, Utah | 16.5 | 70.9 | 34.3 | 5.3 |
| Knoxville, Tenn. | 41.0 | -8.0 | 18.8 | 208.0 |
| Madison, Wis. | 49.2 | 38.4 | 46.6 | 37.1 |
| Spokane, Wash. | 9.1 | -.7 | 5.9 | 16.2 |
| Fresno, Calif. | 17.9 | 2.4 | 10.5 | 46.4 |
| Baton Rouge, La. | 34.4 | -1.9 | 25.6 | 29.0 |
| Hartford, Conn. | .0 | 45.9 | 22.9 | .0 |
| Bridgeport, Conn. | 1.6 | 44.0 | 17.7 | .0 |
| Tacoma, Wash. | -2.1 | 78.6 | 29.3 | .0 |
| Jackson, Miss. | 36.4 | 20.0 | 32.6 | 8.6 |

| Name | City | Outside Central City | Metropolitan Area | Central City Area |
|------|------|------|------|------|
| New York, N.Y. | -1.9 | 31.1 | 3.9 | .0 |
| Chicago, Ill. | -12.1 | 62.2 | 10.5 | .4 |
| Los Angeles, Calif. | 5.4 | 35.3 | 18.3 | 2.1 |
| Philadelphia, Pa. | -4.1 | 22.5 | 7.1 | .0 |
| Detroit, Mich. | -18.8 | 58.4 | 14.4 | .0 |
| Houston, Texas | 51.4 | 58.1 | 53.0 | 23.6 |
| San Francisco, Calif. | 5.6 | 38.0 | 19.1 | 1.0 |
| Baltimore, Md. | -4.6 | 56.9 | 18.2 | .0 |
| Dallas, Texas | 41.2 | 71.5 | 49.0 | 4.7 |
| Washington, D.C. | 8.2 | 96.2 | 41.0 | .0 |
| Cleveland, Ohio | -12.9 | 62.6 | 10.2 | .0 |
| Minneapolis, Minn. | 1.9 | 118.9 | 29.7 | .0 |
| Milwaukee, Wisc. | -10.2 | 76.5 | 13.9 | 5.5 |
| San Diego, Calif. | 17.0 | 62.0 | 31.1 | 9.2 |
| San Antonio, Texas | 49.4 | -25.1 | 26.0 | 24.3 |
| Boston, Mass. | -4.0 | 24.0 | 11.5 | .0 |
| Memphis, Tenn. | 22.4 | 18.5 | 21.7 | 37.9 |
| St. Louis, Mo. | -14.2 | 49.9 | 13.3 | .0 |
| New Orleans, La. | .0 | 78.6 | 16.6 | .0 |
| Phoenix, Ariz. | 51.1 | 61.9 | 54.5 | 32.6 |
| Columbus, Ohio | 20.5 | 45.8 | 27.1 | 55.1 |
| Seattle, Wash. | 15.5 | 65.8 | 29.3 | 2.4 |
| Pittsburgh, Pa. | 6.1 | -3.8 | -.1 | .0 |
| Denver, Colo. | 19.6 | 80.7 | 37.9 | 31.9 |
| Kansas City, Mo. | 11.1 | 37.4 | 21.1 | 143.0 |
| Atlanta, Ga. | 19.5 | 126.0 | 51.3 | 2.3 |
| Tampa, Fla. | 21.2 | 70.1 | 35.9 | 14.7 |
| Buffalo, N.Y. | -15.8 | 29.2 | 4.0 | .0 |
| Cincinnati, Ohio | -3.8 | 36.5 | 12.0 | 1.2 |
| Annaheim, Calif. | 113.9 | 128.7 | 122.5 | 25.8 |
| San Jose, Calif. | 48.9 | 85.7 | 70.7 | 151.8 |
| Fort Worth, Texas | 9.5 | 126.9 | 38.6 | 46.4 |
| Toledo, Ohio | 16.7 | 10.4 | 14.4 | 68.7 |
| Portland, Ore. | 11.6 | 60.0 | 28.0 | 32.8 |
| Newark, N.J. | -12.5 | 21.7 | 9.9 | .0 |
| Oklahoma City, Okla. | 38.5 | 21.1 | 34.7 | 97.8 |
| Louisville, Ky. | 15.1 | 57.6 | 28.4 | 5.2 |
| Omaha, Neb. | 15.8 | 33.2 | 20.2 | 49.0 |
| Providence, R.I. | 4.3 | 20.7 | 11.5 | .0 |
| Miami, Fla. | 7.4 | 80.7 | 40.4 | .0 |
| Average | 15.6 | 41.1 | 25.0 | 30.7 |
| Standard Deviation | 22.6 | 35.4 | 18.8 | 51.4 |

*Multiple central cities.

*Source*: U.S. Department of Commerce, Social and Economic Statistics Administration, Bureau of the Census, *1960-1970 Census of Population: Journey to Work.*

showed an increase of 15.6 percent in employment; but the most rapid growth occurred in the Anaheim-Santa Ana-Garden Grove (Disneyland) area where the suburban nature of the area, plus the annexation, made the cities indistinguishable from their outside area. In general, cities with above-average growth had annexed some adjacent area. In fact, only Honolulu, of all the cities with growth rates over 9.5 percent, had no annexation.

While not exclusively associated with large cities, the major declines in employment occurred in most large cities outside the South and West. The cities that lost in excess of 10 percent of their jobs between 1960 and 1970 were Milwaukee, Chicago, Newark, Jersey City, Cleveland, St. Louis, and Buffalo, with Detroit recording an 18.8 percent decline.

Table 5.2 also shows the pattern of growth in the outside or surrounding areas. Again with the exception of Anaheim, in which the entire area may be viewed as suburban, there is a clear indication of a major shift of employment from central cities to their outlying areas. This seems to be the usual case. The central city growth in employment is either modest or negative, but there is a substantial increase in employment outside.

## COMMUTING

What has happened to the city as a place of work? As shown in Table 5.2, in 1960 cities retained 85.5 percent of their employed resident labor force while the others worked outside of the city; by 1970 this had fallen to 78.3 percent in spite of annexations that should have made retention easier. Even in the most annexing cities, the retention rate fell. At the same time, the attractive power of the cities (the employment of nonresidents) fell slightly from 39.1 percent to 37.8 percent. It should be noted, however, that this decline was accompanied by a vast increase in the labor force residing outside the central cities and hence represented an absolute increase in the number of persons living outside of central cities but working in them.

## THE CHANGING PATTERN OF EMPLOYMENT IN LARGE SMSAs

Let us look at a broad picture of what is happening to the industrial structure of employment in large central cities and their surrounding areas. Two forces are involved: first, the growth of the central cities, and second, their changing importance relative to their surrounding areas. It appears from aggregate place of work data that in 1960 large central cities had 65.0 percent of employment in metropolitan areas with over 100,000 persons. This figure is almost identical with the 64.3 percent figure for the large SMSAs considered in this study. In spite of major annexation during the 1960s, the figure dropped to

TABLE 5.2

Central City Employment Characteristics, 1960 and 1970
(percent)

| | Residing in City Working in City | | | Residing in OCC Working in City | | | Residing in City Working in OCC | | | City Area Annexed |
|---|---|---|---|---|---|---|---|---|---|---|
| | 1960 (A) | 1970 (B) | B/A | 1960 (C) | 1970 (D) | D/C | 1960 (E) | 1970 (F) | F/E | |
| Tulsa, Okla. | 88.8 | 80.7 | 102.1 | 35.9 | 42.8 | 119.2 | 9.2 | 7.1 | 77.1 | 263.8 |
| Honolulu, Hawaii | 90.1 | 84.9 | 94.2 | 60.5 | 35.3 | 58.3 | 9.3 | 13.9 | 149.4 | .0 |
| El Paso, Texas | 90.8 | 86.6 | 95.3 | 14.7 | 25.8 | 175.5 | 5.3 | 9.0 | 169.8 | 3.5 |
| San Bernardino, Calif. | 67.2 | 62.5 | 93.0 | 26.8 | 17.7 | 66.0 | 25.4 | 27.4 | 107.8 | 115.6 |
| Birmingham, Ala. | 88.0 | 78.0 | 88.6 | 43.5 | 44.7 | 102.7 | 10.0 | 20.3 | 203.0 | 6.7 |
| Rochester, N.Y. | 94.7 | 80.6 | 35.1 | 76.7 | 45.5 | 59.3 | 4.5 | 18.5 | 411.1 | .0 |
| Paterson, N.J.* | 64.0 | 56.6 | 88.4 | 10.2 | 8.0 | 78.4 | 22.6 | 27.5 | 121.6 | .0 |
| Wichita, Kansas | 75.6 | 80.5 | 106.4 | 38.0 | 37.3 | 98.1 | 22.4 | 17.5 | 78.1 | 68.6 |
| Akron, Ohio | 86.0 | 70.4 | 81.8 | 47.0 | 28.0 | 59.5 | 9.0 | 19.9 | 221.1 | .0 |
| Tucson, Ariz. | 78.2 | 84.7 | 108.3 | 38.4 | 62.8 | 163.5 | 18.8 | 12.3 | 65.4 | 14.2 |
| Jersey City, N.J. | 56.4 | 50.0 | 88.6 | 10.8 | 8.4 | 77.7 | 16.6 | 18.2 | 109.6 | .0 |
| Sacramento, Calif. | 80.5 | 80.0 | 99.3 | 35.5 | 44.3 | 124.7 | 16.2 | 17.5 | 108.0 | 106.6 |
| Austin, Texas | 93.0 | 90.5 | 97.3 | 49.0 | 64.4 | 131.4 | 4.0 | 6.3 | 157.5 | 46.9 |
| Richmond, Va. | 87.2 | 81.4 | 93.3 | 60.7 | 58.2 | 95.8 | 6.0 | 15.5 | 258.3 | 62.1 |
| Albuquerque, N.M. | 86.0 | 83.9 | 97.5 | 56.0 | 70.6 | 126.0 | 11.0 | 13.2 | 120.0 | 46.4 |
| Dayton, Ohio | 85.9 | 73.1 | 85.0 | 38.9 | 40.2 | 103.3 | 13.1 | 21.6 | 164.8 | 15.1 |
| Charlotte, N.C. | 88.8 | 88.8 | 100.0 | 61.5 | 53.3 | 86.6 | 5.3 | 7.8 | 147.1 | 18.7 |
| Corpus Christi, Texas | 83.5 | 81.8 | 97.9 | 20.5 | 24.0 | 117.0 | 11.5 | 16.0 | 139.1 | 170.2 |
| Des Moines, Iowa | 91.5 | 87.9 | 96.0 | 47.2 | 62.8 | 133.0 | 5.8 | 9.1 | 156.8 | 4.8 |
| Grand Rapids, Mich. | 84.3 | 71.6 | 84.9 | 40.9 | 32.8 | 80.1 | 13.2 | 26.6 | 201.5 | 83.3 |
| Syracuse, N.Y. | 83.4 | 72.3 | 86.6 | 35.5 | 30.2 | 85.0 | 15.1 | 26.2 | 173.5 | .0 |

TABLE 5.2 (Cont.)

| | Residing in City Working in City | | | Residing in OCC Working in City | | | Residing in City Working in OCC | | | City Area Annexed |
|---|---|---|---|---|---|---|---|---|---|---|
| | 1960 (A) | 1970 (B) | B/A | 1960 (C) | 1970 (D) | D/C | 1960 (E) | 1970 (F) | F/E | |
| Flint, Mich. | 85.9 | 77.2 | 89.8 | 58.3 | 49.1 | 84.2 | 12.5 | 19.8 | 158.4 | 10.3 |
| Mobile, Ala. | 93.0 | 85.7 | 92.1 | 42.8 | 40.4 | 94.3 | 5.2 | 9.7 | 186.5 | -23.6 |
| Shreveport, La. | 89.0 | 81.9 | 92.0 | 37.2 | 39.6 | 106.4 | 8.4 | 14.3 | 170.2 | 55.5 |
| Fort Wayne, Ind. | 88.4 | 81.1 | 91.7 | 54.6 | 60.6 | 110.9 | 9.2 | 16.5 | 179.3 | 41.6 |
| Worcester, Mass. | 89.1 | 84.5 | 94.8 | 41.9 | 39.7 | 94.7 | 5.4 | 8.3 | 153.7 | .0 |
| Salt Lake City, Utah | 88.3 | 80.1 | 90.7 | 51.4 | 45.7 | 88.9 | 7.1 | 16.8 | 236.6 | 5.3 |
| Knoxville, Tenn. | 85.7 | 88.2 | 100.9 | 35.8 | 41.3 | 115.3 | 11.3 | 8.5 | 75.2 | 208.0 |
| Madison, Wisc. | 92.4 | 89.7 | 97.0 | 43.3 | 50.8 | 117.3 | 5.1 | 7.9 | 154.9 | 37.1 |
| Spokane, Wash. | 81.5 | 83.1 | 101.9 | 40.3 | 43.6 | 108.1 | 15.2 | 14.5 | 95.3 | 16.2 |
| Fresno, Calif. | 79.7 | 75.4 | 94.6 | 31.7 | 36.4 | 114.8 | 16.9 | 20.8 | 123.0 | 46.4 |
| Baton Rouge, La. | 88.0 | 77.8 | 88.4 | 50.0 | 62.3 | 124.6 | 7.0 | 11.6 | 165.7 | 29.0 |
| Hartford, Conn. | 77.0 | 64.0 | 83.1 | 33.1 | 27.6 | 83.3 | 18.4 | 28.3 | 153.8 | .0 |
| Bridgeport, Conn. | 77.4 | 68.2 | 87.5 | 36.5 | 31.0 | 84.9 | 14.0 | 20.5 | 146.4 | .0 |
| Tacoma, Wash. | 77.9 | 70.7 | 90.7 | 45.2 | 25.0 | 55.3 | 15.9 | 19.7 | 123.8 | .0 |
| Jackson, Miss. | 90.7 | 89.1 | 98.2 | 38.5 | 51.1 | 132.7 | 4.5 | 7.7 | 171.1 | 8.6 |
| New York, N.Y. | 95.2 | 94.3 | 99.0 | 30.7 | 27.4 | 89.2 | 2.7 | 3.6 | 133.3 | .0 |
| Chicago, Ill. | 92.6 | 81.7 | 88.2 | 33.8 | 25.8 | 76.3 | 6.6 | 17.0 | 257.5 | .4 |
| Los Angeles, Calif. | 78.8 | 72.4 | 91.8 | 30.8 | 30.4 | 98.7 | 20.2 | 25.4 | 125.7 | 2.1 |
| Philadelphia, Pa. | 91.7 | 85.3 | 93.0 | 23.7 | 20.6 | 86.9 | 7.1 | 12.3 | 173.2 | .0 |
| Detroit, Mich. | 81.7 | 65.4 | 80.0 | 33.8 | 23.2 | 68.6 | 17.2 | 33.2 | 193.0 | .0 |
| Houston, Texas | 94.0 | 90.0 | 95.7 | 45.1 | 45.6 | 101.1 | 4.5 | 8.9 | 197.7 | 23.6 |
| San Francisco, Calif. | 89.0 | 84.2 | 94.6 | 26.8 | 28.1 | 104.8 | 9.9 | 13.9 | 140.4 | 1.0 |
| Baltimore, Md. | 92.6 | 74.9 | 80.8 | 37.0 | 30.6 | 82.7 | 11.9 | 23.5 | 197.4 | .0 |
| Dallas, Texas | 94.3 | 86.7 | 91.9 | 35.6 | 47.0 | 132.0 | 3.8 | 10.9 | 286.8 | 4.7 |
| Washington, D.C. | 86.8 | 79.1 | 91.1 | 45.7 | 32.1 | 70.2 | 11.9 | 19.1 | 160.5 | .0 |
| Cleveland, Ohio | 95.1 | 74.5 | 78.3 | 51.3 | 41.4 | 80.7 | 7.6 | 24.3 | 319.7 | .0 |
| Minneapolis, Minn. | 92.4 | 79.5 | 86.0 | 51.3 | 42.6 | 83.0 | 6.3 | 19.5 | 309.5 | .0 |
| Milwaukee, Wisc. | 89.8 | 75.5 | 84.0 | 46.9 | 35.0 | 74.6 | 8.8 | 23.4 | 265.9 | 5.5 |

| City | | | | | | | | | | |
|---|---|---|---|---|---|---|---|---|---|---|
| San Diego, Calif. | 91.3 | 83.4 | 81.3 | 44.2 | 34.0 | 76.9 | 7.4 | 15.1 | 204.0 | 9.2 |
| San Antonio, Calif. | 82.7 | 87.9 | 106.2 | 29.2 | 61.6 | 210.9 | 15.6 | 10.7 | 68.5 | 24.3 |
| Boston, Mass. | 81.2 | 76.3 | 93.9 | 28.2 | 24.6 | 87.8 | 16.5 | 21.6 | 130.9 | .0 |
| Memphis, Tenn. | 94.2 | 90.7 | 96.2 | 60.5 | 38.0 | 62.8 | 4.0 | 7.0 | 175.0 | 37.9 |
| St. Louis, Mo. | 91.2 | 78.5 | 86.0 | 36.2 | 29.5 | 81.4 | 8.3 | 21.0 | 253.0 | .0 |
| New Orleans, La. | 94.2 | 85.9 | 91.1 | 42.7 | 40.4 | 94.6 | 9.2 | 12.5 | 135.8 | .0 |
| Phoenix, Ariz. | 86.4 | 84.2 | 97.4 | 28.2 | 33.1 | 117.3 | 12.2 | 13.8 | 113.1 | 32.6 |
| Columbus, Ohio | 90.5 | 79.2 | 87.5 | 46.2 | 52.4 | 113.4 | 7.6 | 18.7 | 246.0 | 55.1 |
| Seattle, Wash. | 88.1 | 85.7 | 97.2 | 39.8 | 44.7 | 112.3 | 7.2 | 12.5 | 173.6 | 2.4 |
| Pittsburgh, Pa. | 87.7 | 78.8 | 89.8 | 16.1 | 23.4 | 145.3 | 11.1 | 20.1 | 181.0 | .0 |
| Denver, Colo. | 89.3 | 83.2 | 93.1 | 42.0 | 40.9 | 97.3 | 9.1 | 15.3 | 168.1 | 31.9 |
| Kansas City, Mo. | 86.0 | 78.0 | 90.6 | 42.0 | 39.9 | 95.0 | 12.0 | 19.9 | 165.8 | 143.0 |
| Atlanta, Ga. | 90.6 | 76.5 | 84.4 | 47.0 | 41.4 | 88.0 | 7.6 | 20.7 | 272.3 | 2.3 |
| Tampa, Fla. | 89.8 | 80.4 | 89.5 | 33.5 | 37.8 | 112.8 | 8.2 | 17.6 | 214.6 | 14.7 |
| Buffalo, N.Y. | 82.3 | 72.5 | 88.0 | 36.7 | 29.8 | 81.1 | 17.0 | 26.6 | 156.4 | .0 |
| Cincinnati, Ohio | 87.1 | 72.8 | 83.5 | 43.5 | 36.4 | 83.6 | 10.9 | 24.6 | 225.6 | 1.2 |
| Annaheim, Calif. | 52.0 | 48.8 | 93.8 | 16.6 | 19.8 | 119.2 | 25.0 | 30.4 | 121.6 | 25.8 |
| San Jose, Calif. | 66.8 | 52.5 | 78.5 | 24.5 | 18.1 | 73.8 | 26.4 | 38.4 | 145.4 | 151.8 |
| Fort Worth, Texas | 89.4 | 75.0 | 83.8 | 36.0 | 29.5 | 81.9 | 7.4 | 20.2 | 272.9 | 46.4 |
| Toledo, Ohio | 86.2 | 85.2 | 98.8 | 53.9 | 35.4 | 65.6 | 8.6 | 12.6 | 146.5 | 68.7 |
| Portland, Ore. | 89.9 | 78.9 | 87.7 | 40.5 | 40.7 | 100.4 | 8.4 | 18.9 | 225.0 | 32.8 |
| Newark, N.J. | 64.9 | 56.1 | 86.4 | 16.2 | 12.4 | 76.5 | 22.2 | 28.0 | 126.1 | .0 |
| Oklahoma City, Okla. | 92.1 | 89.3 | 96.9 | 47.7 | 55.2 | 115.7 | 5.7 | 8.8 | 154.3 | 97.8 |
| Louisville, Ky. | 89.2 | 76.0 | 85.2 | 39.6 | 46.9 | 118.4 | 8.9 | 22.1 | 248.3 | 5.2 |
| Omaha, Neb. | 91.5 | 86.0 | 93.9 | 36.4 | 41.1 | 112.9 | 6.7 | 11.9 | 177.6 | 49.0 |
| Providence, R. I. | 81.0 | 73.4 | 90.6 | 30.0 | 28.7 | 95.6 | 14.4 | 19.6 | 136.1 | .0 |
| Miami, Fla. | 77.7 | 56.6 | 72.8 | 40.0 | 30.7 | 76.7 | 20.6 | 40.8 | 198.0 | .0 |
| Average | 85.5 | 73.3 | 91.5 | 39.2 | 51.8 | 98.8 | 11.1 | 17.6 | 174.1 | 30.7 |
| Standard Deviation | 8.6 | 9.9 | 6.8 | 12.4 | 13.2 | 27.2 | 5.7 | 7.4 | 62.5 | 51.4 |

*Multiple central cities.

*Source:* U.S. Department of Commerce, Social and Economic Statistics Administration, Bureau of the Census, *1960-1970 Census of Population: Journey to Work.*

56.0 percent for all areas over 250,000 and to 57.0 percent in the areas covered in this study. The changes were, however, different among industries. At the other extreme, several areas outside of central cities recorded employment losses, but, with the exception of the areas around Pittsburgh and Jersey City, they reflected the loss of territory through annexation by others.

The overall pattern of employment growth of large cities may be summarized geographically: the greatest losers were the Great Lakes cities—such as Detroit, Buffalo, and Clevelend, and the older cities such as Jersey City, Newark, New York, New Orleans, and Hartford.

## ANNEXATION AND EMPLOYMENT GROWTH

To what extent does annexation help the rate of employment growth of cities? Does population growth, which often accompanies annexation, increase faster than employment and thus place increased pressures on the central city or suburban labor market? Does population decline—a phenomenon of central cities—mean a more than proportionate loss of jobs? To answer these questions, I have used regression analysis to separate out the effects of annexation from the effects of population growth in determining employment growth. What are the separate effects of population and annexation change on employment?

The findings show that above-average growth in city employment between 1960 and 1970 was clearly associated with annexation. Both weighted and unweighted models were used to statistically "explain" the patterns of change. Since all the variables are percentages, they can be interpreted as elasticities. Specifically:

$P$ = percent change in population between 1960 and 1970

$A$ = percent change in central city area between 1960 and 1970

$E$ = percent change in employment between 1960 and 1970

Cities:

$$E_c = \overline{.8486P_c} - 0.0327A_c - 0.0023E_{occ} \qquad R^2 = .5327$$
$$\phantom{E_c =} (.1183) \quad (.0481) \qquad (.0557)$$

Outside Cities:

$$E_{occ} = \overline{1.3215P_{occ}} + .1469A_c - 0.7745E_c \qquad R^2 = .5389$$
$$\phantom{E_{occ} =} (.1564) \qquad (.0733) \quad (.1812)$$

Where:

cities = the subscript c

outside cities = the subscript occ

values in parentheses are the standard errors

The analysis, while it follows the traditional approach, poses a dilemma because small central and outside central areas may have a major effect, whereas important large city or outside city areas tend not to be recognized. In order to deal with this problem, a weighted regression analysis was undertaken.

Cities (weighted by 1970 employment in central city areas):

$$E_c = \overline{.9115P_c} = 0.0059A_c = 0.0213E_{occ} \quad R^2 = .5617$$
$$\phantom{E_c = }(.1202) \quad\;\; (.0544) \quad\;\; (.0568)$$

Outside cities (weighted by 1970 employment in outside areas):

$$E_{occ} = \overline{1.5966P_{occ}} + 0.1332A_c - .7639E_c \quad R^2 = .7330$$
$$\phantom{E_{occ} = }(.1232) \quad\quad (.0642) \quad\;\; (.1369)$$

The results imply that for cities with declining populations–which is the case of cities with a high proportion of minorities–employment will fall, but not as rapidly as population. This is the phenomenon of whites moving out of the city but keeping their jobs there. On the other hand, in the rapidly growing surrounding areas, employment grows, but more rapidly than population. This stimulates employment opportunities for inner-city residents able and willing to commute. The analysis further shows that annexation is more important in increasing employment in central cities than it is for the suburbs.

During the period 1960 to 1970 there were substantial declines in construction, manufacturing, and personal service employment in cities, as shown in Table 5.3. At the same time there were minor declines in transportation, communication, and public utilities, and in wholesaling and retailing. There were increases in finance, insurance, and real estate, business and repair services, and public administration, with the most substantial increase in professional services (which includes educational and health services). Most of those categories in which increases occurred are not usually filled by blacks. While there was a suburban gain in manufacturing, it was not large enough to offset the losses of cities of these kinds of jobs.

All of these changes altered the economic base of the cities and their outside areas. As shown, in Table 5.4, manufacturing has fallen in relative importance in the city but also in suburban areas. In 1960, 28.7 percent of all

## TABLE 5.3

### Change in Employment by Place of Work, Large SMSAs, 1960-70
(percent)

| Category of Employment | City | Outside City | City as Percent of Total 1960 | 1970 |
|---|---|---|---|---|
| Construction | - 8.9 | +26.6 | 58.9 | 50.9 |
| Manufacturing | -27.9 | 18.5 | 61.9 | 51.8 |
| Transportation, communication, utilities | - 1.1 | 51.6 | 74.8 | 66.0 |
| Wholesaling and retailing | - 3.5 | 70.7 | 69.1 | 55.8 |
| Finance, insurance, real estate | +17.4 | 81.0 | 79.5 | 71.5 |
| Business and repair service | +22.4 | 92.7 | 71.2 | 61.1 |
| Personal services | -32.3 | 6.3 | 67.2 | 56.6 |
| Professional services | +39.9 | 89.9 | 65.2 | 57.8 |
| Public administration | +10.9 | 34.7 | 68.7 | 64.4 |
| Total | - 2.1 | 45.3 | 66.7 | 57.5 |

*Source*: Adjusted place of work data, 1960 and 1970 census.

## TABLE 5.4

### Distribution of Employment by Place of Work, Large SMSAs, 1960-70
(percent)

| Category of Employment | City 1960 | 1970 | Outside City 1960 | 1970 |
|---|---|---|---|---|
| Construction | 5.2 | 4.9 | 7.3 | 6.3 |
| Manufacturing | 28.7 | 22.4 | 35.4 | 28.8 |
| Transportation, communication, utilities | 9.1 | 9.2 | 6.1 | 6.4 |
| Wholesaling and retailing | 21.4 | 21.0 | 19.2 | 22.5 |
| Finance, insurance, real estate | 6.6 | 7.9 | 3.4 | 4.2 |
| Business and repair services | 3.3 | 4.1 | 2.6 | 3.5 |
| Personal services | 6.5 | 4.6 | 6.4 | 4.7 |
| Professional services | 13.0 | 18.5 | 13.9 | 18.2 |
| Public administration | 6.2 | 7.0 | 5.6 | 5.2 |

*Source*: Adjusted place of work data, 1960 and 1970 census.

employment in cities was in manufacturing; ten years later this had fallen to 22.4 percent. The decline in manufacturing was offset by a major increase from 13.0 to 18.5 percent in what the census calls professional services, a category that includes education and health services. At the same time, manufacturing employment in the suburbs also fell sharply, but in the case of these areas there was not only a substantial increase in professional services, but also increases in wholesaling and retailing and other functions that were formerly associated with central cities.

## NOTES

1. Alvin H. Hansen and Harvey S. Perloff, *State and Local Finance in the National Economy* (New York: W. W. Norton Company, 1944).

2. John F. Kain, "The Distribution and Movement of Jobs and Industry," in *The Metropolitan Enigma*, ed. James G. Wilson, rev. ed. (Cambridge, Mass.: Harvard University Press, 1968), pp. 1-31.

3. Charlotte Fremont, *Central City and Suburban Employment Growth, 1965-67* (Washington, D.C.: The Urban Institute, 1970).

4. Bennett Harrison, *Urban Economic Development* (Washington, D.C.: The Urban Institute, 1974).

# 6

## MANAGING
## A BUDGET
## IN CRISIS
Kenneth A. Gibson

Newark has suffered the traditional problems facing most of our large cities. The flight of whites from the city created a 70 percent black and Hispanic population of mostly poor and unskilled persons. As a result, approximately 20 percent of the work force is unemployed.

The city finds itself at the mercy of the state in its efforts to retain industry. Since property taxes are utilized to finance public education, Newark finds itself with a tax rate of $9.94 per $100 of assessed valuation, an exorbitant rate. Industry is finding the suburbs more and more attractive.

The Newark city government has established the Newark Economic Development Corporation (NEDC) to develop methods of attracting and retaining industry. NEDC helps businesses get economic development grants, train workers, and locate property, and has been moderately successful in its search for new industry for the city.

Newark's assets are at times difficult to observe. Nevertheless, Newark is located in New Jersey's meadowlands, where all facets of transportation (air, sea, rail, and highway) and proximity to New York City create a valuable potential location for industry.

Many large corporations—including the largest insurance company in the world, the state's utility companies, and the state's leading financial institutions—

---

Mayor, Newark, New Jersey. The most recent budget data (1976) have been substituted for the 1974 data used in the paper delivered by Mayor Gibson at the conference.

have remained in Newark throughout its most difficult years. Rutgers University Law School, Newark School of Engineering, the New Jersey College of Medicine and Dentistry, and local community colleges serve as centers of higher education for its inhabitants. In addition, new housing construction begun in 1975 totaled nearly $100 million.

In spite of this picture of progress, many problems remain. The city needs a comprehensive program to train its unskilled population. The cost of such a program will pay for itself in the long run through the returns made by productive workers. Newark needs a more equitable tax structure so that the burden of supporting city programs will be shared by a greater portion of the population. It needs a program of housing construction and/or rehabilitation, and even greater effort must be made to attract industry into the city to provide jobs and revenue.

At this point, Newark must look to the federal and state governments as well as its own resources for help. Any change in the tax structure must be made at the state level. The economy of Newark is tied to the economy of the nation, and a commitment to improve both must be mustered at the federal level of government. My 1976 budget message gives the cold realities of the fiscal pressures on large cities with high percentages of minority populations.

## THE BUDGET MESSAGE

Today our city faces its most serious economic challenge since I took office. Without question this has been the most difficult budget I have had to prepare. The fundamental problem with which I and my staff have had to grapple is to strike a reasonable balance between providing basic services to residents and holding the property tax as low as possible. What follow are my budget proposals to provide services to Newark citizens and to raise the necessary revenues for this fiscal year. State law (New Jersey State Statutes Annotated 40A:4-3) requires the budget to be prepared on a cash basis. What this means is that during any fiscal year a city must collect sufficient cash to provide its services and meet its outstanding debts. In short, the state of New Jersey does not permit deficit financing.

In preparing this budget, we were once again confronted with the realities of a shrinking revenue base, an archaic state tax structure, an increase in operational expenses, and an unprecedented level of uncertainty about the budgetary implications of pending action by other levels of government. During periods of economic growth, these realities are burdensome. Faced as we are with inflation, high unemployment, and recession, they are devastating. Yet, notwithstanding these many constraints, I have developed a budget that best meets the needs of Newark's citizens.

# A LOOK AT 1975

The beginning of fiscal year 1975 saw the city of Newark confronted with a $35 million budget gap. That is, Newark had $35 million less than it needed to finance its budget and maintain the tax rate of the preceding year. To restrain the rate of escalating taxes, I implemented austere measures. These measures included the layoff of approximately 430 employees, a reduction in the city's contribution to the Board of Education, a reduction in overtime appropriations, and a reduction in positions due to attrition. We eliminated the remainder of the budget gap by increasing the tax rate from $8.60/100 assessed valuation to $9.94/100 assessed valuation.

Even with the austere measures and the increased tax rate, we had to continue to live within our means. However, we were confronted with large cutbacks in state aid. These cutbacks resulted in a loss to the city of Newark of $2,276,843. The state had promised us this aid during the development of our 1975 budget and we had anticipated it. In addition, the state withheld from the city excess aid of $3.5 million. Hence, in total, the state confiscated $5,776,843 from the city of Newark.

## FINANCIAL OUTLOOK

### Decline in Revenues

Because the state plans to confiscate the same aid in 1976, we are not permitted to include it in the balancing of our budget. If one calculates the loss to the city in state aid for 1975 and 1976, the result would be approximately $11,553,686. All of this loss has to be absorbed by the taxpayer in 1976. As a result of this cash deficit and other losses in miscellaneous revenues, the city had to use its 1975 surplus to offset the loss.

An additional problem that confronts us each year is the decline in the percentage of property taxes collected. Over the past five years our percentage of property tax collection has fallen from 88.21 percent to 85 percent. What this means is that 85 percent of the assessed properties are paying taxes while 15 percent are not, and additional appropriation (reserve for uncollected taxes) has to be made to offset this loss in revenues. The financing for the additional appropriation is borne by the 85 percent that are paying properties. As the collection rate decreases, the appropriation for "reserve for uncollected taxes" increases. I If the collection rate of the present year falls beyond the collection rate of the previous year, the city will encounter a deficit.

The city has also faced a shortfall in the receipt of delinquent property tax revenues. The loss—$1.8 million.

The net reduction in revenues (other than property taxes) from 1975 is as follows:

| 1. Surplus | $1,800,000.00 |
| 2. Miscellaneous revenues | 1,729,401.80 |
| 3. Delinquent property taxes | 1,836,600.00 |
| Total reduction | $5,366,001.80 |

## Increase in Appropriations

The large increases in 1976 appropriations are due mainly to the payment of interest and principal on municipal and school bonds and notes, and the cash deficit of 1975. A summary of the increases in municipal appropriations is as follows:

| 1. Operations | $ 771,123.53 |
| 2. Municipal debt service | 3,628,738.00 |
| 3. Judgments | 25,000.00 |
| 4. Cash deficit of preceding year | 4,301,047.95 |
| 5. School debt service | 5,429,179.00 |
| 6. Reserve for uncollected taxes | 4,093,646.05 |
| Total increase | $19,248,734.53 |

## Budget Preparation Trail

Budget preparation began in June 1975, with departments developing their plans and the dollar costs attached. Based on information available in September 1975, Newark was confronted with a $33,373,000 budget gap for fiscal year 1976. Realizing that the taxpayers could not bear a large increase in property taxes, I immediately began to define other options that would considerably reduce the gap.

Each department director was told to review his budget and to identify areas where cutbacks would least jeopardize the most essential operations. This process was followed three times and resulted in the termination of 480 municipal employees. The bulk of these employees came from the police, public works, and recreation and parks departments; and 14 from the office of the mayor. The savings generated from the layoff is $4,135,000.00. With the layoffs, other reductions, and updates of other budget data, the budget gap was reduced to $17,834,204, or a savings of $15,538,796 from the original gap of $33,373,000. We obtained permission from the state legislature to enact several taxes in Newark—a 1 percent payroll tax and a parking lots receipts tax, which the municipal council approved. We have also asked the city council to enact a liquor tax and to authorize an increase in water rates. Action on this request has not been forthcoming. The latter tax would allow us to further reduce our deficit by an additional $1 million.

As was the case last year, we are seriously limited in our ability to provide a definitive budget because of the incredible number of uncertainties associated with other levels of government. The uncertain variables projected in the budget include:

1. the city's tax obligation to Essex County

2. the date and fiscal impact of the State Supreme Court's decision regarding the funding of a "thorough and efficient" educational system for school districts

3. passage of legislation to return to the municipalities $25 million taken from the business personal property replacement tax surplus

4. final adjudication of court suits initiated by several New Jersey municipalities to restore $25 million taken by the state from sales tax receipts

5. final adjudication of a court suit initiated by the city of Newark to increase in in-lieu tax payment to Newark by the Passaic Valley Sewerage Commission

6. passage of legislation to increase the 1976 urban aid appropriation by $2 million

7. return of bus receipts replacement tax revenues to the municipalities

If the above uncertainties are resolved in Newark's favor (although this is highly unlikely), it would mean approximately $5.2 million of additional revenue. There are also several uncertainties related to the posture of the municipal council once this budget is received:

1. the municipal council's action taken in changing the proposed budget, including

   a. projection on anticipated revenues

   b. projection of the city's tax collection rate

2. municipal council action on the proposed water rate increase

3. municipal council and Board of School Estimate action in appropriating funds for the board of education

Clearly this year's budget realities are a double-edged sword. We can either hold down the tax rate increase and drastically reduce services by eliminating departments and laying off more than 20 percent of our work force, or provide our citizens with the basic services they rightly deserve and expect and permit the tax rate to skyrocket above what they can and should pay. Because neither alternative is plausible, I have sought to ensure that basic services will be maintained while not letting the tax rate escalate prohibitively. While some may question the wisdom of this course of action, it is the one I felt most rational.

I am well aware that the balance we have sought—between reduced municipal services and an increase in the tax rate—is tenuous indeed.

Although my recommendations do not project more and better programs or provide the financial relief that Newark residents and business people deserve,

I do believe they will permit the city and the citizens to survive the economic crisis that almost all American cities now face. They represent this administration's best judgment regarding the allocation of the city's resources for the coming year; but I am not closed to exploring additional options.

As you know, 1976 is the nation's bicentennial. It is indeed tragic that one of this country's oldest cities is beset by economic woes that would not be insurmountable were there sufficient concern at the state and federal government levels.

There are several measures that the federal government can undertake to relieve the fiscal pressure on our cities. Among these are the extension of revenue sharing, a full employment policy, and a countercyclical measure that would trigger further aid to cities during periods of high unemployment. It must be recognized that a significant part of the economic crises of cities small and large is national in origin.

# 7

## MANAGING THE
## SMALL CITY
Howard Lee

Small cities are beginning to experience an overwhelming increase in population that is causing a complete change in the approach to problem solving, new demands for citizen involvement in decision making, a different set of priorities, increased pressures, and new styles of administration. Unfortunately, small cities are no more prepared for this new role than are large cities.

In the next three decades this nation's population will grow by 60 to 80 million and smaller cities and towns will experience the greatest percentage of population increase.

To this point, many small cities have not had the problems of mass exodus, dying inner cities, or creeping suburbs. They are still small enough that suburbs and city continue to support each other economically. The downtown businessman still feels a sense of responsibility to the total city. Blacks and whites, the rich and the poor, have frequent contact with each other, the level of sensitivity and responsibility can be fairly easily stimulated, and citizen participation is usually vigorous. Strong leadership can produce a sense of hope, and the chief executive can identify problems early and become a catalyst for working out solutions.

Nevertheless, the pressures and the demands of growth have strained our administrative and fiscal resources. The problems of running a small city today do not differ significantly from those of running a larger city, except that part-time elected officials are expected to do it. Yet national policy gives the greatest portion of federal resources to larger urban areas. Therefore, the problems of small cities that could be solved today continue to grow and may become unsolvable tomorrow.

---

Mayor, Chapel Hill, North Carolina.

The biggest problem that such cities face is the mounting cost. Mayor John Lindsay once said that it would take more than 50 billion dollars to cure the ills of New York City, while another estimate states that more than 3.5 trillion dollars would be required to build the urban facilities to accommodate the population increase. Chapel Hill and most cities of similar size could meet present needs and be able to accommodate to the needs of population expansion and overall growth for the foreseeable future with a bare fraction of this amount of money.

It seems to me that the real hope for solving the problems of both small and large cities will be in changing the national policy that denies them adequate support. Most of the problems in Chapel Hill during the past six years could have been solved with slightly more than 15 million dollars. This amount would not only have met practically every need within the city, but would have averted many problems experienced by big cities today. More importantly, all blight could have been removed, all slums cleared up, facilities could have been built, adequate service delivery systems implanted, and an environment created to insure humanistic living for decades to come.

There is still hope for solving most of these problems; but the small city hall must be committed to responding creatively and adopting a different mode of operating. First, cities must be run like good businesses and subjected to a greater sense of accountability. Second, the mayors must provide strong leadership and give undivided attention to the office. Currently most small cities have only part-time ceremonial mayors. Until adequate salaries are provided, small cities will not have the necessary leadership. Third, nearby small and moderate size cities must develop cooperative relationships. While this increases the burdens, pressures, and time demands, it offers possibilities for resources that might otherwise be unavailable. Fourth, small cities must highlight their problems and call national attention to their value in solving urban problems.

In Chapel Hill and most small cities, we fall victim to the federal definition of an urban area: "One with a population of 50,000 inhabitants or more as reflected in the 1970 census report." This definition is made without regard to the priorities, urgent needs, or uniqueness of the particular city. It is assumed that any city with a population under 50,000 does not have the same cross-sectional needs as a city above 50,000. Therefore, while it does not qualify for certain federal funds and support, it still grapples with tremendous problems. It must rely on local resources while getting only crumbs from the federal government.

Today a majority of small cities are forced to write proposals, design programs in advance, develop plans for future development, and compete with one another for funding. None of these cities can justify hiring competent specialists for this purpose. Local funds must be spent for consultants, or already limited staff time is stretched further. These facts tend to discourage many small cities from seeking federal funds. The most constructive answer is for small cities to develop plans for hiring joint personnel to fill this specialized need.

The real hope, however, will be to support and sponsor intergovernmental programs, either on a regional basis or with other smaller cities or nearby larger cities.

In the Chapel Hill area, the seed of one such intergovernmental effort was the creation of the Research Triangle Planning Commission, a group of local officials and community leaders in the Raleigh-Durham-Chapel Hill area. Its organization in 1950 was a logical extension of the establishment and promotion of Research Triangle Park, a park where industry and research projects are concentrated and can draw on the resources of the three surrounding universities—North Carolina State University, Duke University, and the University of North Carolina at Chapel Hill.

This Research Triangle Planning Commission later served as the nucleus for the Triangle Council of Governments (COG), organized in 1972 and designated as the lead regional organization for a larger governor-designated six county area.

For Chapel Hill, there have been advantages to functioning as part of a regional group that looks on us and treats us just like everyone else. Chapel Hill citizens have a disproportionately large influence on the organization and on-going COG programs. Chapel Hill, though, is not a unique municipality; it has the same needs for sewers and water, housing, crime control, refuse disposal, job training, public transit, and recreation as the other COG municipalities.

In 1974, Chapel Hill had a tremendous need for manpower training, could identify vast manpower development potential, and had prepared acceptable plans; but it was still "too small" to be considered for federal funding under the comprehensive employment and training act. The city was eligible to compete for state discretionary funds, but instead established a consortium relationship with the city of Durham and two counties to seek federal funds. There is no question that Chapel Hill's gains have been greater than if it had sought the funds from the state.

Because most small cities have difficulty in acquiring housing grants, there is the danger of pricing the poor completely out of the community. Therefore, the leadership must develop other methods for ensuring a fairly balanced housing mix. In Chapel Hill today, the moderate and low-income housing pace has been inadequate. In order to at least partially rectify this situation, it was necessary to create local mechanisms. First, the city acquired additional public housing through the direct aid of former assistant Department of Housing and Urban Development (HUD) secretary Samuel Jackson. His attention provided a few units to accommodate the most urgent needs of the poor.

Second, Chapel Hill encouraged local nonprofit groups to construct and sponsor moderate-income housing projects. A 100-unit project so built is now occupied. Third, a $1 million housing loan trust fund was established with an initial investment of $350,000 from federal revenue sharing funds. It guarantees mortgage loans by local banks to high risk low-income citizens, provides for a 3 percent interest rate to the borrower, and subsidizes the difference charged by the lender. Fourth, the city acquired federal funds, added local funds, and completely renovated a seven-square-mile blight-filled section of the city for less than $2 million.

The cities of Raleigh and Durham have also taken advantage of federal funding for neighborhood redevelopment. However, the cities alone cannot begin to attack the housing needs of the Triangle area. They are small and do not have vast suburban areas. Expansion of the universities, and the even greater expansion of the health complexes at the University of North Carolina and Duke, has brought job seekers, young medical students, graduate students—many with families—in great numbers to seek low and moderate cost housing that does not exist. The too-little-regulated mobile home, alone or in parks, has sprung up in rural areas, while the too-high-priced and inadequately built apartment complexes spread out on the edges of the cities.

The nonprofit Research Triangle Housing Development Corporation was incorporated in September 1973 and is at work on projects for a six-county area. The first ground-breaking was held in March 1975 and other projects including rehabilitation have been funded and are on the drawing boards. For Chapel Hill and other small North Carolina cities, this intergovernmental approach seems to be our only real hope.

Another very special problem for Chapel Hill was the grave need for public transportation. Recognizing mobility as a major factor for raising the economic standard of the state's poor, the city successfully lobbied in Washington for $800,000 in capital funds for buses and other equipment for our councils on aging.

Few of us, however, understand the cost complexities for setting such public transportation service in motion. While the citizens of Chapel Hill passed a referendum and levied a $.10 tax on each household to finance the operations of its municipal system and authorized the sale of $350,000 of municipal bonds for construction of other facilities, under current Urban Mass Transit Administration (UMTA) legislation the city does not qualify for federal operating subsidy. While the system is the second largest in the state in terms of daily riders, Chapel Hill must provide an operating subsidy from local tax revenues because its under-50,000 population does not qualify it as an urban area. Both Durham and Raleigh, meanwhile, do qualify to receive federal operating subsidies for expensive, privately owned, nonresponsive systems. This may be considered one of the greatest discriminatory acts against small cities. Plans are on the boards to rectify this situation by instituting an intergovernmental system along with Durham and Raleigh—the most reasonable and efficient direction to take.

Another big problem facing small cities is their inability to attract competent employees, especially administrators. The only apparent solution is to employ competent personnel on a joint and cooperative basis.

While the crime problems of small cities are far from the magnitude of big city problems, the small city crime rate has soared over the past few years; but what little federal aid small cities get has not been productive. Under the impact program created the Law Enforcement Assistance Administration (LEAA) in 1972 to experiment in criminal justice planning for five specific crimes (murder, rape, aggravated assault, robbery, and burglary), for instance, grants of $20 million were given to eight medium-sized cities. Little basic planning was done, however, and problems already have begun to surface:

1. Only one of the eight cities appears to have been able to spend its entire $20 million within the arbitrary time frames of the program, and even that city will be hard put to show that the infusion of this money did, in fact, reduce crime.

2. The arbitrary goal of reducing crime by 5 percent in two years and 25 percent in five years was not realistic, given the limited funds allocated.

3. Several cities encountered tremendous problems in getting community participation. Other cities experienced serious problems in dealing with the effects of increased arrests on courts and jail facilities.

4. All cities suffered through an evaluation crisis—which is still going on— because evaluation methods and goals were often changed.

Meanwhile, Chapel Hill has been forced to funds its own police social work unit, which has been tremendously effective in reducing criminal repeaters and providing crisis intervention services, but no LEAA funds were available to support our efforts.

I believe that small cities would greatly benefit from greater criminal justice funds made available directly to the city without the mountains of paper work and bureaucratic red tape. Formation of a small cities' LEAA advisory task force also would be helpful. It could serve as an informational and programmatical clearing house exclusively for small cities, provide outside expertise to evaluate programs, and help write proposals.

Similarly, consideration should be given to ways of changing the distribution of national resources, perhaps by adopting a 50-smallest-cities concept as a way of keeping more people in their home areas. If this were adopted, small towns and cities would be greatly aided in planning community growth, developing mechanisms to deliver services quickly and efficiently, and equipping themselves to prevent the deteriorating effects of pessimism and hopelessness.

Unfortunately, the current national policy provides insufficient funds to the small city, destroying its hope for viability and the ability to anticipate and to stay on top of problems. And so the headaches of running cities such as Chapel Hill increase with time and with the explosion of population.

In the meantime, small cities' banding together, cooperating with counties and nearby big cities—in short, improved intergovernmental relations—appears the best hope of at least making progress on the daily operational problems of local government.

# III

## THE SHIFT OF POWER FROM CITY HALL

# 8

## THE RISE OF
## REGIONAL, COUNTY,
## AND STATE GOVERNMENTS
David Walker

Cities are major participants, yet frequently pawns, in current intergovernmental relations. As the most multifunctional of all units of local government, cities stand as the prime revenue raisers and service providers at the local level.

Despite the legal constraints of operating within unitary systems and generally under the ramifications of Dillon's Rule, most cities in earlier periods possessed—as a practical matter—some independence. Now, in the face of mounting intergovernmental pressures, the question is: Can or should cities preserve independence?

## INTERGOVERNMENTAL INITIATIVES AND IMPACTS

Being most immediately and most heavily on the local servicing firing line, cities are in an especially vulnerable position vis-a-vis the intergovernmental initiatives of others. The formal powers, fiscal authority, and functional capacity of cities have always been subject to state-municipal and sometimes county-municipal controversy. However, the battle over formal municipal powers is now subsiding. At least half of the states have granted greater home rule powers to their localities over the past five years.

### Servicing Shifts

Nevertheless, on the service front, subtle but significant shifts have been occurring:

1. State functions have expanded significantly. Traditional state activities have grown and new ones—as in the environmental, land use, and transportation

fields—have emerged. Since the late 1950s, 20 states have assumed predominant (85 percent or more) or exclusive fiscal responsibilities for welfare, corrections, health, hospitals, and airports.*

2. County modernization in some states is putting these jurisdictions into a more significant servicing role. Approximately one-fourth of all urban county expenditures went for municipal-type services in 1972. Moreover, home rule counties—and their number is growing (over 60)—generally are more energetic in providing regional and urban services.

3. The growing servicing role of special districts and authorities also has special meaning for municipalities. There are over 24,000 such districts. They provide a wide range of services and have independent budgets.

4. Still another dimension of the servicing scene is the increase in inter-local contracts and agreements. Recent Advisory Commission on Intergovernmental Relations, and International City Management Association (ACIR-ICMA) survey data indicate that the typical city has entered into about nine formal or informal servicing agreements. Most dealt with physical developmental and auxiliary support activities. Housing, zoning, basic police services, and other controversial services were usually not covered. Central and independent cities tended to be less involved with interlocal contracting than suburban units.

Now, most of the state-local servicing shifts have involved other than municipal jurisdictions. Only in those cases where cities that are treated simultaneously as counties (Baltimore, San Francisco, New York, and others), where interlocal contracting is involved or where certain special district efforts have emerged, have cities been affected significantly by these developments.

When certain federal categorical and block grant programs are considered, an expansionist view of current municipal services emerges. Early social (or human-related) assistance programs, while impacting on city residents, rarely were administered by cities. Instead, a state-county pattern of implementation prevailed.

With the Housing Act of 1949 and the beginning of federal support for urban renewal, cities began to focus on problems of physical decay and poverty. Sometimes this local role was assumed by independent or dependent special districts; but, in time, city halls exerted a dominant influence over the activities of many of these units. Moreover, by the end of the Great Society, the earlier small package of grants available directly to cities had grown to over 70. While some of these were place-related programs, many were human-related, a fact that put some cities, especially central cities, into a new and expanded servicing role. The impetus for this, it should be noted, was federal, not state.

---

*This is measured in terms of state-local fiscal outlays, and excludes federal contributions.

The new manpower and community development block grants seem to have furthered this trend. Under the Comprehensive Employment and Training Act of 1973 (CETA), over 400 local governments—cities and counties of over 100,000 population—are eligible to serve as "prime sponsors," individually or through local consortia. The Housing and Community Development Act of 1974 (HCDA) provides entitlement grants to all cities of over 50,000 population and "urban counties," as well as to a large number of smaller jurisdictions on a "hold harmless" basis.

These provisions certainly increase the responsibilities of urban counties as well as cities. HCDA funds will go to about 76 counties. More than 200 counties are participating in CETA. Similar changes are occurring in some cities, especially in the smaller eligible cities. For example, in Illinois, 35 communities—8 more than the 27 that previously participated in one or more of the Department of Housing and Urban Development's (HUD's) categoricals—will receive community development allocations. Overall, perhaps 20 percent of the metropolitan entitlement cities have had little to no experience with HUD's earlier community development programs. Although comparable figures have yet to be compiled in the manpower area, it seems clear even now that a number of communities are being drawn into new community development and manpower roles. Overall, then, the net effect of shifting these programs over from a project (categorical) to a block grant (with entitlements) basis is to extend the jurisdictional coverage of these mostly human-related program efforts to more cities as well as counties.

## Municipal Monies

The foregoing, recent developments as well as others, clearly underscore the growing intergovernmental impact on city finances. For instance, the local property tax, still the dominant tax revenue source for cities, has been heavily affected by state actions on both the reform and relief fronts.*

While property taxes represent 65 percent of city tax revenues from their own sources, they represented only 31.5 percent of total municipal general revenues in 1972, compared to more than 43 percent a decade earlier. The dramatic shift in the role of intergovernmental revenues is the reason. Between 1963 and 1972, city revenues from intergovernmental sources soared from less than $3 billion to over $11 billion and grew to account for one-third of all cities'

---

*During 1970-74, two-thirds of the states enacted major state-financed property tax relief programs for the elderly (25 of these were of the circuit-breaker type). An ACIR survey of 21 states revealed that their circuit-breaker programs provided a total of $467 million in relief to over 3 million claimants in fiscal year 1974.

In addition to this recent relief effort, a gradual trend towards local property tax reform by the states emerged during the past decade. Over one-third of the states reorganized or strengthened their property tax supervisory units. Four states joined Hawaii in centralizing assessment; 15 established or revamped assessor-training programs; 14 launched or beefed up their assessment ratio studies; and at least a dozen adopted a full disclosure policy regarding the average level of assessment in the community.

general revenues. While this increase clearly was significant and part of a general trend toward intergovernmentalizing city finances, it was not so great as that experienced by counties or school districts. Intergovernmental revenue in 1972 accounted for more than 40 percent of their total revenues.

About one-fifth of the intergovernmental revenues of cities came directly from the federal government (a higher proportion than that of any other local government unit except for special districts). Another three-quarters of the total came from state aid. Though no accurate figures as yet exist on the extent of state pass-through of federal aid funds (one "guesstimate" put it at one fifth), we do know that nearly nine out of every ten state-aid dollars are chiefly conditional. In 1972, all but 4.9 percent of these conditional dollars went for education (64.1 percent), highways (7.8 percent), public welfare (21.1 percent), and health and hospitals (2.1 percent)—functions in which school districts or counties are heavily involved. In other words, except where a city is also a county or where it runs its own dependent school system, the extent of state pass-through of federal grant funds to most municipalities is probably minimal. Most state assistance systems simply are not geared to city-type programs.

Of growing significance to cities is the increase of state general support payments and federal revenue sharing or "no strings aid."* With the former, cities, as well as counties and sometimes all local taxing units, nearly always are included as eligible recipients. At the same time, the city share of the overall state general support payments (in 1972) came to nearly 55 percent of the total ($2.1 billion) and the proportion of federal general revenue sharing funds amounted to approximately the same proportion (56) of the total local share.†

## The New Metropolitan Mosaic

Another dimension of the growing intergovernmental impact on municipal activities is the mushrooming of mechanisms, procedures, and institutions at the metropolitan (and nonmetropolitan multicounty) level. Nearly all of these have an impact on cities—fiscally, functionally, and/or administratively—and practically none of them existed a dozen years ago.

Developments in four broad areas must be noted:

1. Over 1,800 federally encouraged districts (charged with areawide planning) have been established at the substate regional level in 19 different categorical and block grant programs (comprehensive health planning, law enforcement, transportation, air pollution, and so forth).

---

*These include programs involving the sharing of specific state taxes on an "origins" basis and of general state revenue on a "needs" basis.

†Based on the first two payments.

2. Independent special districts and authorities (such as school, transportation, and water supply) surpassed the 24,000 mark in 1972, making them the fastest-growing unit of local government.

3. Over 600 regional councils of government, largely controlled by city and county representatives, have come into being in approximately 250 metropolitan and 350 nonmetropolitan areas, thanks largely to federal funds or requirements. In addition, some 470 A-95 clearinghouses with review and comment powers have been designated, most of them having a council-of-governments structure.

4. Partially in response to federally encouraged districting efforts, 44 states now have at least designated substate districting systems.

## The Rare Reorganizational Alternatives

In contrast to the growing fragmentation that characterizes the overwhelming majority of our metropolitan areas, a handful have opted to restructure.

Eleven city-county consolidations (out of some 40 attempts) between 1962 and 1974 have resulted in more federal grant funds, more professional managerial capacities, and improved public services for the areas involved. However, these consolidations have led to higher costs for local government and have not caused fundamental shifts in the collection and distribution of local tax revenue.

Another view of the one-tier approach emerges when cities such as Oklahoma City and Tulsa annex large portions of adjacent unincorporated territory to preclude "defensive incorporations" and to extend their boundaries to match actual urban development.

A semifederated approach is illustrated by Miami-Dade County, where a state-authorized new county charter established an essentially two-tier government. Existing municipalities are authorized to enact regulations not enacted by the expanded county government. The latter performs all municipal services and is the prime provider for the county's unincorporated areas. Municipalities can transfer functions to the county when such services have assumed countywide significance. Governmental costs have risen along with the level of services and professionalism.

Multipurpose metropolitan servicing authorities (or districts) is another approach. The municipality of metropolitan Seattle is the prime example.

The most innovative three-tier approach of the last decade is the Metropolitan Regional Council in Minnesota's Twin Cities area. This state-supported multipurpose unit has responsibility for developing area-wide plans, authoritatively coordinating the major area-wide functional agencies operating in its region, and guiding metropolitan development. It also prepares "policy plans" for regional functions. These plans guide special districts (commissions), counties, and other bodies in drafting "development programs" that they will run. Atlanta has a similar unit.

These variations on a reorganizational theme have involved only about 6 percent of metropolitan areas. All of them, however, have a body (council of governments—COG) to handle areawide problems.

## SOME THEMES FOR TROUBLED TIMES

A "go-it-alone" approach toward the municipal future seems inappropriate; yet the assessment that the cities have already been overwhelmed by intergovernmental forces generating greater interdependence is decidedly premature. Cities can retain some of their traditional independence in an era of growing interdependence, but some shifts in city attitudes and strategy are essential.

1. There is a basic need to develop a healthier sense of what is feasible. Ideally, this would emerge in the broader context of a systemic state-local process geared to sorting out and reassigning servicing roles.[1] The present pattern of functional assignments in most states is largely an uncoordinated patchwork. The time has come to formulate general servicing criteria such as economic efficiency, fiscal equity, manageability, and political accountability in determining which level of government should be responsible for each function. Labor-intensive, strong accountability-oriented, and various human-related—as well as place-related—services should be functions of cities.

2. There is a need to recognize fully the jurisdictional jungle that characterizes the local government. The fiscal, functional, and administrative styles and needs of cities vary widely and higher levels of government must detect and cope with these disparities. Further, cities must be tolerant of their own comparative advantages and be willing to aid one another through interlocal agreements and other multijurisdictional arrangements.

3. There must be an end to municipal ambivalence over regional governance. Some cities would like to opt out of the whole metropolitan mosaic. Some have fought all regional developments, while still others have tried to co-opt the process by strengthening the "umbrella" role of regional councils and the cities' position in them. Still, a few cities are in a position to call for and benefit from wholesale regional reorganization. The "go it alone" approach seems untenable. Isolationism is as foolish for cities in urban areas as it is for nations. The real question then, is: What kind of "foreign policy" should a city pursue: combative, co-optive, collaborative, and/or reconstructionalist?

4. There is a desperate need to recognize the growing role of the states. Despite variations and some unevenness, the overall performance record of states is to be commended. Their traditional legal powers over cities and their newer financial assistance, regulatory, and servicing roles are of critical significance in defining the future role of cities.

5. The cities need to face the implication of the changing intergovernmental fiscal system. This, at the outset, means confronting the growing "intergovernmental component" in their own budgets. It means carefully sorting out the federal aid (direct and channeled) from state aid. It means focusing on the equalization provisions in all of the aid sectors. It means facing the fact that cities are the least aided of all categories of local governments, save for townships. It means a balanced assessment of the extent to which states have picked up servicing responsibilities; of the pattern of state aid (to what jurisdictions and by what means); and of the degree to which the local property tax is still a prime provider of state-local services. Above all, it now means a vigorous representation to the federal government as to the relative rigidity of local revenue sources and the mounting social and dollar demands being made on cities in this period of recession-depression and inflation. In short, cities must insist that states and, especially, the federal government consider the intergovernmental fallout of their budgetary and program actions and inactions. This, of course, means a different appeal to Washington than heretofore has been the case. National (even international) economic policy; finance and budget committees; the Treasury, the Council of Economic Advisors, and U.S. Office of Management and Budget (OMB)—these must be the new areas of municipal attention, and not just the legislative committees and departments dealing with urban-oriented programs.*

Finally, cities, more perhaps than any other jurisdictional group, should cut through the conceptual confusion of recent years and see clearly the myths that have mesmerized others (and occasionally some of their own members). Some, in effect, already have been noted. Others are the following:

1. There is a misconception or fear that general revenue sharing and block grants will replace categorical grants altogether. American federalism needs all three of these forms of intergovernmental fiscal transfers, not just one.

2. Many view a block grant as merely a big categorical program. In some respects this is true, especially when large formula-based categoricals are used as the sole basis of comparison; yet a block grant is different. It arises when categoricals are merged (as in the case of the Partnership in Health and of manpower and community development programs), or when a broad program area that could be categorized is treated as a whole from the outset (as with the Safe Streets legislation). Rigorously defined eligibility provisions usually are stipulated. Both matching and apportionment formulas generally are applied, but significant discretion in terms of specific program emphasis usually is left to

---

*Recent National League of Cities and U.S. Conference of Mayors presentations before the Joint Economic Committee and Senate Budget Committee and their *The Federal Budget and the Cities: A Review of the President's FY 1972 Budget in Light of Urban Needs and National Priorities* (National League of Cities/U.S. Conference of Mayors, Washington, D.C., 1971–annual) begin to reflect the new trend.

recipients. Nevertheless, the higher-level government retains the power of substantive review prior to expenditures, and audits comprise a basic means of providing long-term accountability.

3. Many confuse decentralization and devolution. Decentralization involves the breaking up of concentrated authority at the center of a government and distributing it more widely among its administrative units. Devolution, on the other hand, is the delegating of power or authority by a central government to lower-level governing units.

4. Many supposedly general-purpose jurisdictions are really limited-purpose units halfway between single-purpose districts and full-fledged multi-purpose governments. A jurisdiction's ability to raise revenue from its own sources, its pattern of expenditures, its degree of reliance on interlocal contracts, and the presence of a large number of overlying independent special districts—all these provide clues as to whether it is actually a general or essentially a limited-purpose unit.

5. The belief that a fragmented local government system will guard against overcentralization needs clarification. With the increased dependence on intergovernmental fiscal transfers, and with the many spillovers in urban areas, higher-level intervention is resulting.

## NOTE

1. See Advisory Commission on Intergovernmental Relations, Substate Regionalism and the Federal System, Vol. 4, *Governmental Functions and Processes: Local and Area-wide* (Washington, D.C.: Government Printing Office, February 1974).

# 9

## REGIONAL GOVERNMENT
## AND THE MINORITY MAYOR
Lee Calhoun

There are serious doubts as to whether the types of changes advocated in the metropolitan reform movement will make a significant difference in coping with the critical problems of urban areas. These essentially incremental approaches to problem solving often overlook the essential problem of a capitalistic system that generates income inequalities among the citizenry, creating social classes with contradictory economic and political interests. Such approaches tend to perpetuate the status quo, with cosmetic changes thrown in when necessary.[1] There are benefits to participating in the American political system that outweigh the costs and make participation almost mandatory for blacks, even though radical or complete change will not occur. More specifically, this paper seeks to offer some insight into black participation in regional councils and the problems and prospects of that participation, and to make some observations about the future of the regional council movement.

It may be said that new regional political forms were an inevitable response to the rapid deterioration of the central cities and the subsequent growth of suburban areas. Second, there are costs to nonparticipation in regional councils that must be evaluated before participation is dismissed. Third, contrary to the views of Piven and Cloward that the potential for control of the cities by blacks consistent with their majority status will not be achieved due to the growth of metropoliswide planning and coordinating agencies,[2] it is argued that such new political forms may be the survival mechanisms for many of the majority black central cities.

## HISTORICAL OVERVIEW

Regional councils, as defined in this study, include councils of governments (COGs), regional planning commissions (RPCs), economic development districts (EDDs), and certain other voluntary, multijurisdictional and multi-functional organizations representing local elected officials.[3] Perhaps the best known, and of primary interest in this study, are the councils of governments, which are invariably defined as multifunctional regional associations of elected local officials (or of local governments represented by these elected officials) who come together on a voluntary basis at regular intervals to discuss common problems, exchange information, and develop consensus on policy questions of mutual interest.[4] Roscoe C. Martin, in his much-cited work on regional councils, says that "COG's basically embody a confederal approach to area-wide coordination."[5] This is true because a COG has no governmental powers or operating responsibilities. Indeed, because it has no authority to compel either participation, attendance, or acquiescence in policy decisions, its existence rests solely on the good will of the member local governments. It functions primarily as a planning and problem solving body.

The use of the regional council approach originated in 1954 with the establishment of the Supervisors Inter-County Committee in the Detroit area. After this inauspicious beginning, it was not until the 1960s that regionalism became a generally accepted approach to planning and problem solving in the metropolitan and nonmetropolitan areas of the United States. The National Association of Regional Councils states that there were over 600 regional councils in 1972 compared with 142 in 1969. This rapid growth rate has been attributed to federal and state government regulations that made participation in regional councils almost mandatory for local governments if they wished to become eligible for many types of federal aid. COGs grew by leaps and bounds during this period also because of the expansion of the 701 comprehensive planning assistance program in 1965 to include COGs as eligible recipients of funds. Section 204 of the Demonstration Cities and Metropolitan Development Act of 1966 stated, "Applications for loans and grants in a variety of functional areas shall be submitted for review to any area-wide agency which is designated to perform Metropolitan or regional planning for the area within which the assistance is to be used."[6] Another piece of legislation that aided the expansion of the regional council movement was title 4 of the Intergovernmental Cooperation Act of 1968, which called for the "establishment of rules and regulations governing the formulation, evaluation and review of federal programs and projects having a significant impact on area and community development."[7] On July 24, 1969 Circular A-95 was issued by the executive branch. In it, administrative regulations were set forth that encompassed both of the above pieces of legislation. The circular, revised in 1971, implements those sections of the legislation requiring that applications for federal assistance to a large number of public facilities-type programs in metropolitan areas be accompanied by the comments of an areawide comprehensive planning agency or clearinghouse. An early-warning Project Notification and Review System (PNRS) was also a part of the circular; it requires potential applicants to file a summary statement of the project with the regional clearinghouse for review before the formal proposal is submitted.[8]

Although COGs receive certain authority from the A-95 Circular, they are influenced more by the 701 planning program funds they receive from the Department of Housing and Urban Development (HUD)—the bulk of COG operating funds. In addition, HUD's guidelines require that a significant percentage of the metropolitan area governments be on the COG policy board. HUD has also begun to move towards increasing citizen participation on policy boards of COGs, and towards directing their attention to social as opposed to strictly physical problems.

Along with this prodding by the federal government through various pieces of legislation, executive orders, administrative guidelines, and the like, the movement towards regionalism has been aided by the various reform movements that have been in existence at the local level for decades. Much of the push for metropolitan consolidation came about during the 1950s as a drastic (more far-reaching than COGs) attempt to achieve governmental efficiency, reduce governmental fragmentation, and/or head off black control of the cities. This type of response, however, never reached the numbers that one might have expected.

Even though city-county consolidation and other forms of metropolitan government have not achieved the numbers expected, they have served as a spur towards milder forms of regionalism such as COGs. This has happened because both black and white elected officials have recognized the need for some form of regional cooperation; and it has happened even though the masses of white and black citizens are unaware of the existence of COGs and of their role and purpose in local government affairs.[9]

## OPERATION OF COGs

In examination of the operation of councils of governments, certain issues such as method of representation and voting, types of policy questions to be discussed, and sources of leadership are common threads running through the studies of COGs. Whereas these were problems that transcended race, they took on a heightened sense of urgency where the central city had a black majority.

Victor O. Jones suggests that "ideological warfare over the representational base of the governing body"[10] is perhaps the greatest danger to the existence of COGs. In a major survey of mayors and county chief executives conducted by the ACIR and ICMA,[11] one of the most common reasons cited for not participating in a COG was the fear of a loss of autonomy or domination by the largest member jurisdiction.

The most frequently used methods of voting in COGs are a weighted system based on population and a unit of government system whereby each government receives the same number of votes. The arguments for the latter scheme suggest that to move to a weighted system moves farther away from the original idea of a "council" of equals and towards dominance of the confederation by the local government with the largest population, usually the central city. The ACIR-ICMA study conducted in 1972 noted that 38 percent of the cities and 36 percent of the counties reporting cited use of the one-unit, one-vote scheme of representation, while 33 percent of the cities and 34 percent of the counties noted use of a population-based voting scheme. Some regional councils employed a combination of procedures in their voting schemes. The study noted that central city areas appear to be somewhat less satisfied with the method of representation than suburban areas. Mogulof suggests that if the large central city is the most obvious victim of unit-of-government voting schemes, in most cases it appears to be a willing vicim. He posits that central city leaders know that COGs are unwilling to risk taking action that might hurt the central city, and therefore voting becomes a formality not worth arguing over; that the COG simply is not important enough to justify a struggle over voting strength; and that the COG might evolve into a new level of government if a population-based voting scheme were enacted.[12] This was not, however, the case in Cleveland when Carl Stokes was mayor, nor is it the case in Washington, D.C.

Cleveland, Ohio filed suit in March of 1970 in the U.S. District Court to increase its representation on the regional planning authority. It was only after HUD intervention by decertifying the regional agency that Cleveland's representation of the board was increased. In Washington, on the other hand, the district's representation on the COG general assembly was increased by resolution of the board after negotiation.

## MINORITY CONFIDENCE IN COGs

Harris found in his survey of locally elected officials that there was little difference between blacks and whites in their support for or confidence in the potential of COGs for dealing with urban problems. Those blacks who were officially connected with COG were more favorable towards it, while those not connected opposed participation primarily on the political elective aspects of the regional movement, and did not consider the broader pros and cons of the urban problem complex and the resolution of these problems in the long term. He further suggests that participation in COGs might lead to a greater understanding of the potential of such bodies, and that because of the voluntary nature of COGs it was imperative to have strong political leadership within the organization if they are to succeed.[13]

While Harris was not so eager to write regional councils off, even though he viewed them as an "extention of the establishment,"[14] others such as Zimmerman[15] and Norton Long[16] appear to have given up on regional councils as incapable of meeting metropolitan needs. Royce Hanson suggests that this lack of enthusiasm for regional councils is due to the feeling on the part of many re-formers that the regional council approach is only half a loaf and that it may impede movement towards true metropolitan government.[17]

ACIR has noted the lack of knowledge about minority perceptions of re-gional council strengths and weaknesses and called for further research in this area. They do, however, raise two major points about minority participation in COGs that are worthy of discussion. The two points are:

(1)  If minority groups do not comprise a majority of the population in a Metropolitan area, they may improve their political status under an area-wide form of government because this body may be subject to various federal requirements which would over-come the racially restrictive policies of smaller individual units of local government.
(2)  In areas where minority groups are in control of the central city or comprise a significant political majority, they could lose po-litical power in an area-wide body because it may be responsive to a majority coalition of suburban and central city whites.[18]

Mogulof, in his 1971 study, noted that certain new arrangements of govern-mental forms could serve to maximize blacks' capacity for gaining benefits from resources available in the region and yet maintain their political power.[19] While these observations suggest that benefits can accrue to blacks through participa-tion in regional councils or some extension of that concept, to date not enough analysis has been carried out of the effect of regional forms on blacks. Instead, what we have had to rely on have been premonitions of doom, educated guesses, and isolated fragments of evidence that have only recently begun to flow in.

In the following pages an attempt will be made on an elementary basis to analyze the impact of black participation in regional councils by a case study of the Metropolitan Washington Council of Governments (WASH COG). Although there are several difficulties in trying to generalize from the Washington experi-ence—the lack of governmental proliferation in the area, its relationship to the nation's capital, greater federal involvement in the Washington area, and the recent advent of home rule for the District of Columbia—there are several other factors that make it attractive for comparison and generalization. The demo-graphic characteristics of the Washington metropolitan area are common to most other large central-city-dominated regions; it is an interstate area, as are 32 other regions; even though there are fewer general governmental jurisdictions, there are a host of specialized planning jurisdictions and programs that make the regional planning process a complex task; and many of the same fears concerning regional councils expressed in the ACIR-ICMA study and the Harris Survey are also found in the Washington metropolitan area.

## WASHINGTON, D.C.—A CASE STUDY

The metropolitan Washington experience with regional councils dates back to 1957 with the creation of the Metropolitan Washington Council of Governments, a pioneer in the regional council movement.[20] Established as a meeting place for the governing officials of the various local governments to come together and become acquainted, Washington COG has also served as the mechanism for cooperative agreements. A focus of WASH COG in recent years has been on the District of Columbia's proposal to institute a commuter tax on those who work in the district but reside in surrounding areas. It has been successfully defeated by the surrounding jurisdictions' representatives in Congress, which has final approval of such proposed legislation emanating from the district.

Governmental structures in the Washington metropolitan area are relatively simple in terms of the number of governmental units operating. As of 1971, there were 61 municipalities, 6 counties, 25 independent local authorities, and 17 regional and subregional agencies.[21] In the suburban areas of metropolitan Washington, a strong county government apparatus exists that limits the number of governmental units operating within WASH COG. Fifteen local governments belong to the COG, along with area members of Maryland and Virginia legislatures and of the U.S. Senate and House of Representatives. The complexity of regional cooperation within the Washington metropolitan area is to be found in its interstate character as alluded to earlier. Since the city is a child (or creature) of the state, regional cooperation is doubly difficult because there are two states (Maryland and Virginia) that comprise the metropolitan area along with the District of Columbia. In addition, because Washington, D.C. is a unique entity, being a child (or creature) of the federal government, regional cooperation must be not only between states, but must include the parent federal government as well. This is further complicated when one considers that representatives to Congress from the states of Maryland and Virginia sit on the House and Senate District Committees and in effect act as overlords of the district, while at the same time representing their suburban Washington constituencies that may be hostile towards the district. Another level of complexity is added when one considers that the federal government acts not only as the parent of the district, but also acts towards the district in many respects as if it were another state or city. Finally, because the District of Columbia is the seat of the federal government, the region's proximity to the various branches of government adds to the complexity of regional cooperation.

WASH COG is a nonprofit corporation. Membership is voluntary, and COG lacks coercive authority. Because of its interstate character, it would appear that COG will never move beyond this type of arrangement, as is possible for regional councils found within the boundaries of a single state. An increasing reliance on the creation of special districts as the only legal form of independent subregional interstate government is noted not only in the Washington area but in other interstate areas as well.

WASH COG receives approximately 71 percent of its financing from the federal government in the form of grants-in-aid, 22 percent from the participating cities and counties in the form of dues (prorated by population), and approximately 7 percent from the states and other sources.[22] The District of Columbia is the largest local government contributor to COG on the basis of its population. With the overwhelming percentage of its operating funds coming from the federal government and much of the impetus for its existence from the same source, there is little wonder that many of COG's detractors view it less as a means of interlocal cooperation and more as another tool of federal intervention in local affairs.

The District of Columbia, which is approximately 77 percent black, comprises close to 28 percent of the region's population. With home rule, the district recently elected its first city administration in over 100 years, the overwhelming majority of whom are black. Mindful of the adage, "There's power in numbers," blacks in the district are wary of any regional movements that may dissipate any of its newly acquired powers. In looking at the staff of COG at the professional and managerial levels, it was found that blacks hold only 9 out of 81 positions. Because the District of Columbia is the largest single local government in the COG, its leadership (or lack of it) will go a long way in determining the future directions of the organization. The mayor of Washington appears to lack interest in the activities of COG, and COG staff, as well as the policy board, appears to be affected by this seeming lack of interest. His failure to appear at policy board meetings and to send his top assistants is, however, somewhat offset by the active participation of several members of the city council, one of whom serves as chairman of the board of COG. Although membership on the COG board is viewed as a prestigious position by many, city council members who were recently elected to the board seem to understand the value of a strong district posture within the region and the possibility that tangible benefits may accrue to the district from its participation.

COG has begun to move in the direction of more socially oriented programs in response to the concerns of the black representatives. Through the workings of its various policy advisory boards, COG has developed such programs as Consumer Alert, which advises the consumer of his rights, and Minorities in Management, which, in conjunction with several universities, trains minority group members to become effective city and regional administrators. Another COG effort that has received considerable attention has been its successful project to meet federal goals for joint city-suburban planning in housing. The fair share program, a federally financed leasing program under HUD control, seeks to distribute housing in the region on the basis of the suburban jurisdiction acceptance of larger shares of housing for low-to-moderate-income families.[23] The efforts of Sterling Tucker, the D.C. city council chairman who is also the chairman of the council of governments, were cited by the Washington *Post* for not only meeting the federal goals but also successfully pleading for increased funding for the region (which would also ensure a much higher level of funding for the District's housing program).[24]

COG staff members interviewed pointed out that the transformation of WASH COG from what Cox calls a "Metropolitan marching and chowder society"[25] to a full-fledged regional planning organization has taken place in large part because of efforts by black representatives from the district that have helped to decrease central city-suburban tensions. This regional perspective that has been adopted by some black leaders must be viewed as a very pragmatic assessment of federal financing trends and as a realization that regional cooperation does not necessarily have to lead to regional government, especially in an interstate region.

With the adoption of a weighted voting scheme based upon the "one man, one vote" principle, the District of Columbia has an adequate representational base from which to operate within the COG general assembly. This further encourages black participation in COG, even though the district's mayor has chosen, in recent years, to send as his representatives white members of the city administration.

While there are few dissenting votes within COG, as Cox suggests, it does appear that the organization is growing increasingly stronger and more capable of dissention that will not destroy the progress already made towards regional cooperation. Even though the idea of a commuter tax is anathema to suburban representatives, it is being made increasingly clear by district officials that the suburban areas must play a greater financial role in solving problems that relate to the district.

It is true that

> WASH COG is illustrative of the "conference approach" to procedural adaptation to changing urban problems. Metropolitan Conferences of Governments are the weakest kind of alliance conceivable, one which has no sanctional authority with regard to its members, one from which a participant may withdraw without citing cause. It is not a body politic, nor could it by any reasonable definition of the term be called a government. COG's should "... not be written off as a futile exercise," since they have "... demonstrated a capacity to achieve some alleviation of those Metropolitan problems which lie within the purview of existing governments and there are many such.[26]

COGs can, however, be looked at as another mechanism for raising the political sophistication of black elected officials. If American politics is based on compromise, the COGs are a wonderful mechanism for black officials to practice the art of negotiation in a setting that will provide them with a great deal of contact with suburban and federal officials through the grant review process and the development of regional programs. With an attitude of "cautious pragmatism," blacks should participate in regional councils to achieve economic and political gains.

The failures of the 1960s should serve to caution black central city leaders against the false belief that the federal presence will necessarily bring about the positive changes they envision, and that they can simply ignore the areas surrounding the central city. Black officials must be aware that if urban problems cannot be solved by utilizing existing structures, then new structures and institutions must be built.

## NOTES

1. David M. Gorden (ed.), *Problems in Political Economy: An Urban Perspective* (Lexington, Mass.: Heath, 1971).

2. Frances Fox Piven and Richard A. Cloward, "Black Control of Cities II: How the Negro Will Lose," *New Republic*, October 7, 1967, pp. 15-19.

3. Advisory Commission on Intergovernmental Relations (ACIR), *Regional Decision Making: New Strategies for Substate Districts*, Vol. 1 (Washington, D.C.: ACIR, May 1973), p. 114.

4. See American Society of Planning Officials, *Voluntary Metropolitan Governmental Councils* (Chicago, August 1962), p. 2; National Service to Regional Councils, *Regionalism: A New Dimension in Local Government and Intergovernmental Relations* (Washington, D.C., 1971), p. 6.

5. Roscoe C. Martin, *Metropolis in Transition: Local Government Adaptation to Changing Urban Needs* (Washington, D.C.: Housing and Home Finance Agency, September 1963), p. 6.

6. Melvin B. Mogulof, *Governing Metropolitan Areas: A Critical Review of Councils of Governments and the Federal Role* (Washington, D.C.: The Urban Institute, 1971), p. 5.

7. Mogulof, Ibid., p. 5.

8. See Executive Office of the President, Office of Management and Budget, *Circular No. A-95 Revised* (Washington, D.C.: February 9, 1971).

9. Charles W. Harris, *Regional Council of Governments and the Central City* (Detroit, Mich.: The Metropolitan Fund, Inc., March 1970), pp. 19-20.

10. Victor O. Jones, "Metropolitan Detente: Is It Politically and Constitutionally Possible?" *George Washington Law Review* 37, no. 4 (May 1968): 742.

11. ACIR, op. cit., vol. 1, p. 115.

12. Mogulof, op. cit., p. 81.

13. Harris, op. cit., pp. 19-21.

14. Harris, Ibid., p. 26.

15. Joseph H. Zimmerman, "A Proposal for Substate Regional Governments" quoted in Tobe Johnson, *Metropolitan Government: A Black Analytical Perspective* (Washington, D.C.: Joint Center for Political Studies, 1972), p. 10.

16. Norton E. Long, "Regions Within States" quoted in Tobe Johnson, op. cit., p. 10.

17. Royce Hanson, *Metropolitan Councils of Governments* (Washington, D.C.: ACIR, August 1966), p. 34.

18. ACIR, op. cit., vol. 1, p. 129.

19. Mogulof, op. cit., p. 82.

20. For more detailed examination of the early history of COGs and the Metropolitan Washington Council of Governments, see James L. Cox, "Federal Urban Development Policy and the Metropolitan Washington Council of Government: A Reassessment," *Urban Affairs Quarterly* 3, no. 7 (September 1967): Royce Hanson, op. cit., and Roscoe C. Martin, op. cit.

21. American Institute of Planners, *The ABC's of a Metropolitan OPD: The WASH COG Experience,* Technical Report no. 1 (Washington, D.C.: The Institute, 1972), p. 20.

22. Ibid., p. 22.

23. Washington *Post*, editorial, Sunday, March 30, 1975.

24. Ibid.

25. Cox, op. cit., p. 77.

26. Quoted in ACIR, op. cit., Vol. 1, p. 63.

# 10

## NEIGHBORHOOD
## GOVERNMENTS
Milton Kotler

Neighborhood governments represent an institution that could help resolve some urban problems for minority as well as other citizens; yet one of the most persistent criticisms of neighborhood government in our cities is that the autonomy of small territorial units would increase the fragmentation of government. This would in turn decrease efficiency, isolate neighborhoods, and increase hostility among them.

These are serious charges. In my book *Neighborhood Government* I did not carry the argument for local democracy far,[1] nor did I discuss the potential for intercommunal cooperation and thus raise neighborhood governmnent as a plausible general principle of municipal government. I wish to do so now, and to show that the administration of public services and welfare can proceed efficiently on a neighborhood and intercommunal basis and that political cooperations between neighborhoods can result.

I propose that neighborhood government become the basic unit of urban life and that the interrelation of these governments compose the metropolitan community. This goes farther than proposing a means of securing more citizen participation in city government; neighborhood government is an alternative, not just a corrective to our present system. Autonomous neighborhood governments should replace city government.

The fundamental justification for this new system of urban governance must be inherent in citizenship—in liberty and democracy—rather than in efficient management or civil order.

Today many poliitical scientists view the city as Charles Levermore did nearly a century ago—as an economic rather than a political unit, and as a business corporation created for business purposes.[2] Many oppose neighborhood governments by claiming that the neigborhood is too small a unit to administer public services efficiently. They further argue that the autonomy of neighborhoods would lead to competition, hostility, and violence among them.

Such criticism implies, first, that the city, in contrast to the neighborhood, is indeed an efficient, closed system of administration. It also implies that, unlike the fragmented horizon of neighborhood government, the unified city exhibits less hostility and violence. Let us examine these implications.

The supposition of the self-sufficient city is one of the major myths of local government. Dr. Joseph F. Zimmerman, in studies of intergovernmental service agreements and transfer of local functions,[3] has found that three-fifths of nearly 6,000 incorporated municipalities surveyed receive services from other units—including jails and detention houses, police training, street lighting, refuse collection, libraries, solid waste disposal, water supply, and crime laboratory services. Moreover, he found that, in general, "the larger the unit, the more agreements it enters into."[4] Furthermore, council-manager governments are more inclined to enter into service agreements than council-mayor governments. Thus, in reality, the modern, large, professionally managed city is not a self-contained system but rather an open system of interlocal and intergovernmental relations.

As if to epitomize the reality of interlocal cooperation, the California Local Government Reform Task Force Report of 1974 recommends the partitioning of existing cities and counties as a means of increasing functional efficiency.[5] Optimal population units would be able to relate for each given function without the impediments of unitary jurisdiction, and neighborhoods would be able to separate easily from large cities when smaller units could provide better services, by themselves or through contract, than the city could.

"Contracting for services will be important to neighborhood governments, many of which will be relatively small and may not desire to produce all of their own services," one report says. "They could contract for neighborhood services with the larger city, the country, a private firm or adjacent community, wherever they could get the most efficient package of the public goods and services they desire."[6] As new studies in public administration (works by Vincent and Elinor Ostrom, Robert Bish, and William Niskanen) demonstrate the inefficiency of the large-scale centralized administration of public goods and services, the political forces behind consolidation and centralization will shift their case from efficiency to the political arguments of equal justice, the redistribution of wealth, and the preservation of urban peace. Let us turn to the problem of economic justice and then to the peaceful potential of intercommunalism.

There is a range of rich and poor communities within our present centralized cities. Certainly neighborhood government cannot be faulted for creating that disparity; nor do the historic trends of income distribution in the United States show any reduction of inequality between communities as a result of the urban centralization of the past 40 years.

In 1969, a preliminary inquiry was made into the redistributive function of the centralized city.[7] Shaw-Cardoza is a poverty area in Washington, D.C.

with a population of 80,000 people. Our 1969 study showed a net outflow of the dollar value of goods and services ($35 million).

Studies done by Richard Schaffer showed a similar net outflow in the working-class community of Borough Park in Brooklyn.[8] In his comparative case, Schaffer showed that Bedford-Stuyvesant received more than it paid out in taxes. Yet, upon careful scrutiny, it appeared that this net inflow did not result in any increase in capital value of the community. It is likely, he concluded, that the net balance "passed through" the Bedford-Stuyvesant community, in the form of payments to government employees who worked in the community but resided elsewhere.

If the Shaw-Cardoza area were able to spend its own $45 million in taxation annually for its own services and capital development, rather than relying on the city of Washington, that community would be more prosperous today. Neighborhood government thus may be a more sound basis, both for the increase of wealth and for its distribution among communities.

As for the fear that independent neighborhood communities will war against one another, let us remember that we already have many adjacent neighborhood-size municipalities in our metropolitan areas, each with its own small police force that performs local duties and shares numerous cooperative agreements with surrounding muncipalities. Statistics show conclusively that the incidence of crime in these small communities is less than in large cities. Furthermore, citizen dissatisfaction with many police services increases with the size of municipalities.[9]

Let us imagine the new intercommunal city that integrates the values of liberty, democracy, efficiency, and peace.

We shall use the city of Washington, D.C., which would be composed of 40-50 neighborhood government municipalities. These would include the familiar areas of Adams-Morgan, Georgetown, LeDroit Park, Trinidad, Chevy Chase, Cleveland Park, Petsworth, Brookland, and numerous other municipalities. The neighborhood populations would vary from 5,000 to 30,000 and their boundaries would be determined by negotiations among citizens of the areas.

The neighborhood governments would have full municipal powers to tax, zone, license, legislate, and draw up criminal codes. They would have authority for the health, education, and safety of their citizens and would administer police, recreation, libraries, housing, health, schools, refuse collection, and other functions. They could contract for the performance of these services, or even transfer these functions to other municipal, state, federal, and private units.

The neighborhood governments would vary in constitution. Legislative powers could be invested in the general meeting of citizens, devolved into sub-neighborhood units like block organizations, or vested in representative town meetings.

Executive power could be held by elected officers, or granted to an executive officer chosen by lot to rotate responsibility, or even vested in committees of the assembly to avoid a division of legislative and executive powers.

The organization of judicial power would also vary. In some cases the general assembly, or a committee of the assembly, might sit as a jury. Jurors could serve directly or be selected by lot. Judges could be elected or appointed.

The most characteristic feature of the system is that most public goods and services would be shared among neighborhood governments. High school education, sewerage disposal, and crime laboratories might be arranged jointly by a number of neighborhood governments, for example.

Because of the diverse needs of the neighborhoods, there would be a greater variety of public goods and services than presently exists—different health programs, corrections programs, educational alternatives, and housing programs. There would be numerous interneighborhood organizations for different functions, and the legislative bodies of each neighborhood would regularly evaluate the performance of interneighborhood service agreements, functions, transfers, and joint ventures.

Public service would be responsive to citizen decision, and more service functions would be voluntarily performed by citizens as their civic responsibility. Professionals, however, would continue to perform expert tasks wherever necessary.

Increasingly, the intercommunal agreements of Washington would spread to relations with neighborhood governments in Maryland and Virginia, so that intercommunalism would assume the form of metropolitan government.

Neighborhood assemblies and councils would maintain steady legislative relations with one another so that laws could be deliberated within the context of intercommunal relations. Legislative uniformities could be achieved as desired, but, far more important, variation in laws would exist with mutual understanding and notice. Confederative councils would harmonize the independence of law making.

There would be a comparable system of metropolitan interrelations for judicial organization and powers. While there would be a strong tendency for uniformity of criminal and civil codes, the neighborhood governments would impose their own requirements of civil law and procedure.

This model of the intercommunal city stresses the autonomy of neighborhood government and the right of neighborhoods to confederate into common councils for various purposes. In a real sense we turn the current two-tier[10] and three-tier[11] metropolitan schemes on their heads.

The Committee for Economic Development (CED) offers decentralization through community districts with appropriate legislative representation, while intensifying the executive power of the centralized metropolitan government. Its main purpose is to establish centralized regional government, and it recognizes the need to trade off citizen participation in order to gain this end.

Our own aim is the opposite—to gain power and autonomy for the community—and we recognize that a regional confederative capacity is required for this end. The CED stresses managerial centralism, leavened by citizen participation; we stress citizen responsibility with an interlocal management capability.

There is no "central government" for our metropolitan model. Instead there are many governments, in many constellations of relationship. Four neighborhood governments will have a junior high school; five neighborhood governments will jointly contract for fire protection; one neighborhood government will publicly own and operate a food collective; eighty neighborhood governments will operate the electric utilities, and so on.

Our model of intercommunalism is not revolutionary. It has its roots in American municipality 100 years ago. At that time, in Massachusetts, there were many service agreements and joint ventures between Boston and other nearby communities over water supply, bridges, highways, police, and fire protection. Boston was certainly the dominant municipality, but other neighborhood governments had independence of decision. This is more than they would have today with centralized downtown control.

Today's technology and economy require a more complex interrelation than the Boston region exhibited 100 years ago, but the general description of our model resembles the administration of local government in Massachusetts in 1830, when Alexis de Toqueville wrote, "what we find there is a presence of a power which, if it is somewhat wild, is at least robust, and an existence checkered with accident indeed, but full of animation and effort."[12]

Indeed, our model of intercommunalism is not that remote from the present autonomy and interrelationships of present suburban neighborhood governments. However, the most unsatisfactory aspect of present small municipalities is that they are not constituted democratically. Instead of practicing direct democracy, our thousands of neighborhood-sized municipalities are run by small elective cliques that retard rather than cultivate citizenship.

We are not drawn to neighborhood government for the sake of local liberty if that liberty is to be exercised by a few. We are drawn to local liberty for its democratic potential of human freedom. By saying that a groundwork already exists for our intercommunal city, we also mean that present neighborhood size suburban governments must open their doors to the deliberative responsibility of citizens.

## NOTES

1. Milton Kotler, *Neighborhood Government: Local Foundation of Political Life* (New York: The Bobbs-Merrill Co., 1969).

2. Charles H. Levermore, *The Republic of New Haven* (Baltimore: Johns Hopkins University, 1886), p. 196.

3. Joseph F. Zimmerman, *Intergovernmental Service Agreements and Transfer of Functions*, in ACIR, *Substate Regionalism and the Federal Systems*, Vol. 3 (Washington, D.C.: U.S. Government Printing Office, 1974).

4. Ibid., p. 51.

5. State of California, Governor's Office, Office of Planning and Research, *Local Government Reform Task Force Report* (Sacramento, Calif.: 1974).

6. Robert Bish and Vincent Ostrom, *Understanding Urban Government* (Washington, D.C.: American Enterprise Institute for Public Policy Research, 1973), p. 99.

7. Earl F. Mellor, *Public Goods and Services: Costs and Benefits, A Study of the Shaw-Cardoza Area of Washington, D.C.* (Washington, D.C.: Institute for Policy Studies, October, 1969).

8. Richard L. Schaffer, *Toward an Economic and Social Accounting System for Bedford-Stuyvesant*, Ph.D. dissertation, Department of Economics, NYU, April 1973.

9. Elinor Ostrom et al., *Community Organization and the Provision of Police Services*, ed. H. George Frederickson, Series No.:03-001, Vol. 1 (Beverly Hills, Calif.: Sage Publishers, 1973).

10. Committee of Economic Development, *Reshaping Government in Metropolitan Areas* (Washington, D.C.: Government Printing Office, February 1970).

11. Joseph Zimmerman, *The Federated City* (New York: St. Martin's Press, 1973).

12. Alexis de Toqueville, *Democracy in America*, Vol. 1 (New York: Random House, 1945), pp. 95-96.

# 11

## NEIGHBORHOOD DECLINE
Marcus Alexis

For minority residents of the central city, the issue of neighborhood preservation is linked to neighborhood governments. Neighborhood forces may be needed to obtain and implement policies of preservation. But how does the central city housing stock decline? How are neighborhoods destroyed?

One of the most comprehensive studies of housing decline in any city is that of the New York City Rand Institute. This study, commissioned by the city of New York, took a detailed look at the housing situation in that city. In appraising what it calls the "current crisis" in New York City rental housing, seven variables are identified: (1) shortage of rental housing; (2) deterioration of the housing stock; (3) abandonment; (4) service cost-price squeeze; (5) disinvestment; (6) increasing friction between tenants and landlords; and (7) family income and rent expenditures.[1]

Since 1965, 7,000 units per year have been removed from the New York housing stock and between 1960 and 1967, the inventory of sound housing increased by only 2.4 percent. In the same period, the "dilapidated" inventory increased 44 percent, and the "deteriorating" inventory grew 37 percent. In addition, roughly 15,000 units were abandoned annually during the 1960 period. From 1960 to 1967 the abandonment rate rose 38,000 units per year.

Since 1945 the cost of supplying well-maintained rental housing in New York City increased at an annual average rate of 6 percent.[2] In the uncontrolled rental sector, these cost increases have resulted in frequent rent increases. In the controlled sector, rent ceilings have risen at an annual rate of 2 percent—much less than the cost of a constant level of maintenance. This service cost-price squeeze has contributed to the deterioration of the available housing stock and has accelerated both disinvestment and abandonment of residential structures.

In neighborhoods troubled by other social problems, rental property has ceased to be attractive to investors and mortgage lenders. Owners unable to sell on economically acceptable terms "disinvest" by not maintaining and ultimately by abandoning their properties.

The New York crisis has increased the friction between tenants and land-lords. In the controlled sector, there has been increasingly militant action by tenant organizations, often resulting in rent strikes and other challenges to the traditional prerogatives of property owners. In the uncontrolled sector, there have been frequent, unexpected, and large rent increases demanded for lease renewals.

The crisis is only partially attributable to inadequacy of tenants' incomes. In the past 15 years both real income and consumption of housing have grown substantially. Real family income increased substantially between 1950 and 1960. Much of that increase went to low-income families. However, the rapid inflation since 1967 has in all likelihood eroded the growth in New York City real incomes. When one looks at per capita housing expenditures between 1950 and 1960, one discovers that per capita space consumption increased 18 percent for nonwelfare families and that the rent-to-income ratio was the same in 1968 as it was in 1950—19 percent. When welfare families are included, the increase was from 19 to 21 percent of family incomes.

## RACIAL DISCRIMINATION

An element in the current crisis not explicitly discussed in the New York City Rand Institute study, but one that surely contributes to the crisis of housing and neighborhood deterioration, is racial discrimination.

One expression of this discrimination is that municipal school districts underspend in declining neighborhoods, so that overcrowding of schools, deteriorating facilities, and less experienced teachers are common in these neigh-borhoods. In addition, municipal services such as sanitation removal, fire and police protection, and parks and recreational facilities are more in demand, and noise and foul air pollution, are more prevalent. Job opportunities are also more limited in highly segregated communities and are becoming increasingly so as jobs shift from central cities to outlying suburbs. Increased transportation cost and reduced information about jobs in those outlying regions hamper blacks in getting those jobs. These factors exacerbate neighborhood deterioration.

As neighborhoods deteriorate, a discriminatory housing market makes it impossible for blacks to move to other areas. To understand the housing environ-ment in which most blacks operate, we must first comprehend the structure of inner-city housing markets. One important fact about such markets is that immigrants, whatever their race, tend to pay more than established residents for housing of comparable quality. There are two reasons for this: (1) immigrants are less familiar with the market; and (2) they compete with one another for a limited supply of housing.

Another characteristic of inner-city housing markets is that there are observable black-white rent differentials. Some have argued that existing differentials might reflect (1) larger family sizes for blacks—meaning more intensive use of premises and therefore greater maintenance costs; and (2) greater uncertainty of rental payments due to the generally low incomes of blacks. But there is considerable evidence that blacks pay higher housing premiums than these two factors can explain.

A study conducted in St. Louis in 1967 found that as the non-white population in census tracts increased from 0 to 100 percent, the median value of owner-occupied homes increased by $2,600; this reflects a discriminatory markup of 20 percent. Note here that this finding is for owner-occupied and not rental property, and therefore the two points mentioned earlier, namely, larger family size and uncertainty about rental payments, could not be operative. In another study of the Chicago housing market there was a discriminatory markup of 30 percent. A third study in Syracuse, New York also found large discriminatory markups paid by blacks. The most complete study to date is one completed in 1971 in New Haven, Connecticut.

## THE NEW HAVEN STUDY

The New Haven study produced the following results:

1. Blacks pay 11 percent rental premium.

2. Female-headed households pay a premium of 5.7 percent.

3. Newcomers, those in the city less than two years, pay a 7.4 percent premium.

4. In all-black neighborhoods, blacks pay 19 percent more than whites in all-white neighborhoods.

5. Households headed by black males pay 7.2 percent more than white households headed by males.

6. Households headed by black females pay 17 percent more.

7. Welfare families pay an additional 6.2 percent more.

8. There is no evidence that black families residing in the white boundary or in the white interior pay more than white households in all-white neighborhoods, but they do pay more than white families in the white boundary.

9. Increases in the educational attainment of black male-headed families have no effect on the rents they pay, whereas for black female-headed households, increases in educational obtainment are associated with significant decreases in rents.[3]

If one adds up the premiums paid by a black female-headed household on welfare, the total premium is 23 percent. If that family is also a newcomer to the city, the premium rises to more than 30 percent. These results are for rental properties; however, they are remarkably consistent wiith the results found for owner-occupied housing and thus cast some doubt on the notions that housing premiums paid by black renters reflect the larger family size or greater uncertainty about rental payments.

## ABANDONMENT

Housing abandonment has increased substantially since the middle 1960s. Neighborhoods with high proportions of blacks have some of the highest rates of abandonment. Some have argued that this is due to rent control. However, St. Louis, which has no rent control, has a higher abandonment rate than New York. This indicates that the abandonment is more complex than it appears on the surface. A study by the Center for Community Change and the National Urban League identifies six steps in the abandonment process. They are:

1. decline in neighborhood socioeconomics status (as middle class whites leave)
2. racial or ethnic change as newcomers find expansion space
3. property speculation followed by exploitation
4. weakened market conditions—emergence of "crisis ghetto" conditions
5. disinvestment
6. abandonment[4]

Another element in the abandonment process not explicitly listed in the six steps above is the cost-price squeeze. This cost-price squeeze is itself a multi-dimensional phenomenon. It includes rising maintenance cost, intensified code enforcement, and rising real estate taxes, and finally results in disinvestment and then abandonment.

A typical scenario might go as follows. Real estate investors purchase property in the inner city because of attractive rates of return. The attractiveness of this property is partially due to the ability of owners to purchase for cash and thereby earn capital premium in areas in which traditional financing (partly because of red-lining) is not available. Sometimes speculators with large cash resources purchase property and then resell, refinancing themselves at very high rates. Another device is for owners to purchase property with the intent of "mining" the property. Such investors have no intention of providing maintenance or upkeep. The gains provided by rent and depreciation are all pocketed. These investors count on lax code enforcement to permit the process to continue for years. In some cases, these investors also neglect to pay real estate taxes, permitting the property to go into default, and, of course, realizing a gain on the taxes not paid. Agitation by tenant groups increases the intensity of code enforcement, but by that time, properties have become so deteriorated that restoring them to code levels is economically infeasible. In areas with static or declining land values, the properties cannot be sold to other investors who might be interested in the land alone. The speculative owners thus abandon the property, finding this cheaper to do than to attempt to either sell or restore to code levels.[5] The Urban League study shows this process to have taken place in St. Louis, the Hough area in Cleveland, the east New York section of Brooklyn, and Chicago's Lawndale.[6] As this process proceeds and touches other neighborhoods, a central question for blacks becomes, "Neighborhood control over what?"

# NOTES

1. Ira S. Lowry (ed.), *Rental Housing in New York City*, Vol. 1, *Confronting the Crisis* (New York: The New York Rand Institute, 1970), p. 37.

2. Ibid.

3. Thomas King and Peter Mieszkowski, "An Estimate of Racial Discrimination in Public Housing," *Cowles Foundation Discussion Paper* no. 307 (New Haven, Conn.: Cowles Foundation for Research in Economics, 1971), mimeo., p. 44; also see their paper, "Racial Discrimination, Segregation and the Price of Housing," *The Journal of Political Economy* 81 (May-June 1973): 590-606.

4. Center for Community Change and the National Urban League, *The National Survey of Housing Abandonment*, 3d ed. (Washington, D.C.: Center for Community Change and the National Urban League, 1972), p. 118.

5. F. E. Case, "Code Enforcement in Urban Renewal," *Urban Studies* 5, no. 1 (November 1968): 277-89.

6. Center for Community Change and the National Urban League, op. cit.

# 12

## URBAN GROWTH AND
## URBAN GOVERNMENT

Harvey Garn
Nancy Tevis

In 1970 Congress enacted the Housing and Urban Development Act calling for the development of a national urban growth policy. The act specifies that a biennial report on urban growth be prepared for the Congress, and in response, the Domestic Council of the President submitted the *Report on National Growth 1972* and the *Report on National Growth and Development 1974.*

The 1972 report was widely criticized for lacking positive policy formulation, and, by default, supporting past approaches to urban growth problems—a position that would promote continued uneven growth patterns and further aggravation of urban problems. To many, this implicit policy failed to fulfill the congressional intent that the federal government assume responsibility for the development of a national urban growth policy designed to promote balanced and orderly growth.

The second biennial report emphasizes the same principles as the 1972 report, again with no explicit urban growth policy statement. The implicit policy of the report is summarized by the project director, James F. Selvaggi: "Although our social, economic and governmental systems are not conducive to the establishment of a single national policy on growth, we can manage . . . by achieving greater coordination of our various public sector activities."[1]

Both of these reports have fallen far short of their legislative purpose. More seriously, they have obscured the major issues at the heart of deciding whether a change in growth trends is a sensible policy objective. This chapter seeks to clarify these issues by focusing on two basic questions: (1) Do differences in levels and change in economic conditions (and, therefore, benefits and costs to residents) across and within metropolitan regions call for an explicit public policy on urban growth? (2) If so, what should the major components of such a policy be?

The first question is usually avoided because it entertains the possibility of positive governmental intervention in private decision making. Not surprisingly, avoiding this issue means that attention is seldom focused on whether or not an active public role is valid in influencing spatial patterns of growth and development. Thus, the potential components of a coherent national urban growth policy have not been articulated because consideration of the prerequisites has been precluded.

We conclude that an explicit national policy on urban growth is necessary, and that such a policy should have both programmatic "channeling" components and institutional "structural" components. ("Channeling" programs are designed as incentives to affect the behavior of individuals and groups, and "structural" components deal with governmental and other institutional changes.)[2] These conclusions are based on evidence suggesting that inter- and intrametropolitan differentials in economic conditions will persist over time and that these differentials do not reflect either equilibrium outcomes or those that are equitable. The evidence further suggests that improvement will have to be sought through a combination of private actions (including the movement of persons, capital, and jobs) and public policies. The appropriate public policies will have to recognize key interactions between private choices and governmental structures, powers, and relations.

## FUNDAMENTAL ISSUES

Before further supporting this view, we will outline three fundamental issues involved in establishing a viable urban growth policy. First, such a policy should recognize that it is hard to distinguish public from private incentives. The consequences of many private decisions are partially attributable to public policy decisions. An obvious example is the effect of federal highway construction on an individual or firm choosing a location; another concerns benefits to builders from water and sewer facilities supplied by the government. This implies the legitimacy of a public interest in the channeling of individual choices. (To say that such public efforts are legitimate does not, however, imply that any given set of public actions is "best" or effective.)

The second issue is that a viable urban growth policy will require innovation in the structural organization of our governmental institutions. Governmental structures are, paradoxically, both too small or lacking in power to meet the needs of metropolitan society, and too large or unreceptive to respond to the needs of subgroups of citizens. Neither the federal experiments in the 1960s nor the "new federalism" of the 1970s has effectively dealt with these problems. Institutional innovation, therefore, is central in an urban growth policy.

The third issue to be incorporated in the development of a viable urban growth policy concerns processes. The current state of affairs in metropolitan

America is the result of extensive historical processes. A policy to change the effects of this process cannot sensibly be devised that does not itself incorporate the idea that urban growth policy is a process. Many of those who talk and write about urban growth policy seem to presume that it consists primarily of the identification of optimal future arrangements.

"Urban growth policy" development requires at least as much attention to processes as to desired directions for change.* Unfortunately, relatively little of the debate about urban growth policy to date has faced this. Arguments abound about channeling options without reference to governmental structures and their implications; and, conversely, most of those who concern themselves with structure seem to assume implicitly that there is some structure that is so persuasive that the outcomes are bound to be satisfactory. Our argument, however, is that urban growth policy requires the formulation of channeling programs as well as structural innovations as part of an ongoing process of adjustment and adaptation to achieve collective ends.

## Implications of Differentials

It is not necessary to belabor the fact that significant differentials exist in economic and social conditions across and within metropolitan areas. The critical point is how these differentials are interpreted. Many persons view these differentials as "natural" or as representing the working out of equilibrium or optimal arrangements in our national system. To the contrary, we believe that in part these disparities represent market failures, the absence of corrective or compensatory mechanisms, and inadequate arrangements between private activities and government.

There is considerable support for this point of view. We shall cite only a few examples. Many persons, especially economists, believe that market forces respond optimally to real disparities, or move toward an equilibrium, or that government action will rectify market failures.

With respect to intermetropolitan differentials, however, Lee Donne Olvey reached a different conclusion when he tested the hypothesis that factor mobility in a market economy produces equilibrating results. He found "reason to expect persistent problems of stagnation in certain regions of a growing economy. Paradoxically, the analysis further suggests that such problems are exacerbated rather than reduced by factor mobility."[3] He sums up his point by saying:

---

*Here we include individuals, families, firms, and so forth.

The obvious difficulty with migration as the solution to the unemployment problem is the implication that investment rates will continue to be low, with consequent adverse effects on the quality of the capital stock, and that the quality of the region's labor force may decline as well. Insofar as the more energetic, better educated, and potentially more productive members of the labor force tend to be more mobile, a net loss of labor force members through migration will further reduce the productivity of the labor force and the attractiveness of the area to investment. The problem here is that a region which is losing employment growth because of high wages, and hence losing labor as well can go on and on in this posture, since there is no corrective mechanism. Clearly this kind of continuing erosion of a metropolitan area's competitive position can mean a serious and long term problem.[4]

Olvey concludes that the issue is unlikely to be resolved without public intervention, although he thinks the most likely public policies are politically infeasible. Note, however, that his analytic result obtains in the fact of factor mobility, which is supposed to be the equilibrating force.

Not only intermetropolitan differences, however, have this characteristic. Intrametropolitan affairs are affected by interdependencies and externalities that raise important questions about the corrective ability of market forces. Bennett Harrison says it this way:

Cities abound in "market failures." Indeed, it has been argued that the present "urban crisis" is largely the result of the inability of private profit-oriented market systems to deal with such post-industrial phenomena as high-density development (with its attendant indivisibilities), joint production of valued goods with unwanted residuals which pollute an environment whose absorptive capacity is steadily declining, and the growing sensitivity of the profitability of any urban investment to the nature of adjacent land uses, with the result that small-scale investments are increasingly more difficult to finance, as banks and other lenders give preference to projects large enough to "internalize" adjacent activities and turf. It is such market failures which have led to a remarkable kind of paradox which mathematicians call a "prisoner's dilemma": to the extent that high risk and low profitability within the city induce private lenders and investors to "red line" whole areas of the core and take the "action" to the suburbs, conditions in the core deteriorate further, which only increases the risk, reduces the private profitability of investing in the center, and reinforces the "suburbanization" of capital. To any individual investor, looking around for the most profitable opportunities, it is clearly in his own private, self interest *not* to invest in the core. Yet the pursuit of his self-interest creates a social situation in which the condition of the core must get even

worse (thereby reinforcing his original decision). Unlike the promises
of the standard economic theory textbooks, the private pursuit of
profit does *not* lead to an unambiguous improvement in social welfare. Indeed, in the present example, it most certainly leads in the
opposite direction!

As societies become more complex—and there is no social
institution created by men which is more complex than the modern
city—these market failures become more common, necessitating public intervention in the private market. It does *not* follow that
unwieldy, inefficient Federal government bureaucracies are necessary in order to overcome these market failures. It *does* seem to follow that *some* sort of collective action is necessary. I suspect we
shall need to combine public subsidization of private producers, the
selective expansion of federal, state and local government programs,
and ultimately the creation of wholly new political-economic institutions (such as neighborhood development corporations and multi-
level regional governments.)[5]

A summary is appropriate at this point. Everyone agrees that there are
great inter- and intrametropolitan variations in economic and social conditions;
but Table 12.1 shows how graphic these differences can be for poverty areas; the
central city as compared with the remainder of the metropolitan area. Some
view these variations as naturally resulting from a system seeking equilibrium or
optimal conditions. We argue that this is not true. Government actions may
exacerbate problems as well as fail to relieve them. Governments have their own
imperatives, which do not necessarily correlate with the economists' ideas of an
institution that will regulate and correct for market failure or compensate for
interdependencies and externalities. Problems cited here require adjustments of
private and public activities and roles. Persistent evidence of adverse effects and
market failures resulting from current activities and choices calls for significant
changes in our ways of thinking about problems and in our institutional arrangements for dealing with them.

## Recommendations for Change in Local Government

In 1972 hearings on the first national urban growth report, Richard
Burton and one of the authors of this chapter argued for nonincremental
changes in the federal system as it operates in metropolitan America.[6] The direct
federalism of the 1960s, built on direct links between program recipients and the
federal government, undermined state and local governments and failed to facilitate restructuring of local government. The new federalism of the Nixon
administration, while built on considerable rhetoric about returning power to
state and local government, turned out to be only revenue sharing without any

TABLE 12.1

Intrametropolitan Differentials

| City | Unemployment Rates | | | Median Income (dollars) | | | Percent of All Families Earning $15,000 or more | | | Percent of All Families with Income Below Poverty Level | | |
|---|---|---|---|---|---|---|---|---|---|---|---|---|
| | SMSA* | Central City | Poverty Area | SMSA* | Central City | Poverty Area | SMSA* | Central City | Poverty Area | SMSA* | Central City | Poverty Area |
| Atlanta | 3.0 | 4.0 | 8.2 | 10,693 | 8,398 | 5,709 | 26.1 | 18.8 | 4.0 | 9.1 | 15.9 | 27.2 |
| Boston | 3.5 | 4.3 | 8.5 | 11,448 | 9,133 | 7,968 | 30.1 | 18.1 | 14.0 | 6.1 | 11.7 | 16.9 |
| Chicago | 3.5 | 4.4 | 10.6 | 11,928 | 10,239 | 6,432 | 31.9 | 23.2 | 7.0 | 6.8 | 10.6 | 29.1 |
| Cleveland | 3.5 | 5.2 | 8.9 | 11,399 | 9,098 | 7,038 | 28.1 | 15.3 | 9.0 | 6.9 | 13.5 | 24.3 |
| Detroit | 5.7 | 7.2 | 14.0 | 12,112 | 10,038 | 7,506 | 33.0 | 22.6 | 11.0 | 6.5 | 11.3 | 24.1 |
| Kansas City | 3.3 | 3.8 | 10.0 | 10,564 | 9,904 | 6,839 | 23.0 | 20.1 | 7.0 | 6.9 | 8.9 | 19.7 |
| Los Angeles | 6.2 | 7.0 | 12.5 | 10,968 | 10,530 | 6,785 | 28.4 | 28.1 | 8.0 | 8.2 | 9.9 | 21.1 |
| New York | 3.8 | 4.2 | 8.1 | 10,862 | 9,673 | 6,282 | 29.2 | 23.5 | 7.0 | 9.3 | 11.5 | 21.9 |
| Philadelphia | 3.7 | 4.6 | 8.7 | 10,780 | 9,361 | 7,372 | 25.3 | 18.2 | 9.0 | 7.3 | 11.2 | 19.3 |
| Portland | 6.1 | 6.6 | 11.9 | 10,458 | 9,789 | 6,581 | 22.1 | 20.4 | 7.0 | 6.9 | 8.1 | 19.9 |
| St. Louis | 4.9 | 6.4 | 10.5 | 10,495 | 8,173 | 5,851 | 22.8 | 12.9 | 5.0 | 8.1 | 14.4 | 28.6 |

*Standard Metropolitan Statistical Area.

Sources: U.S. Department of Commerce, Bureau of the Census, County and City Data Book 1972 (A Statistical Abstract Supplement) (Washington, D.C.: U.S. Government Printing Office, 1973), for SMSA and central city data; and U.S. Department of Commerce, Bureau of the Census, Census of Population: 1970, Employment Profiles of Selected Low-Income Areas, final Report PHC(3)-16, Chicago, Ill., summary (Washington, D.C.: U.S. Government Printing Office, 1972), for data on poverty areas.

impetus for state and local change. Further, the latter has drawn repeated charges from local officials of a substantial net reduction in available funds and a withdrawal of federal commitments to alleviating urban problems.

The appropriate governmental units for large metropolitan regions appear to be metropolitan states, rather than COGs (councils of government), two-tier governments, or the current proliferation of special districts to achieve economies of scale for activities requiring large capital outlays. The organization of metropolitan states would politically decentralize state government to align with our largest metropolitan areas.

We argued that such an institutional realignment would:

(1) preserve intact the current polycentric structure of local government in the metropolitan area;

(2) provide metropolitan-wide areas with a fiscally and constitutionally viable form of government;

(3) redress the city/suburban imbalance of political power;

(4) provide functionally meaningful state boundaries within which "comprehensive planning" would stand a far better chance of becoming comprehensive;

(5) preserve the local political gains of blacks and other minority groups;

(6) respond to the governmental problems created by fragmentation of the metropolitan area along inter-state lines;

(7) force state responsiveness to problems of the urban crisis and obviate the need for "direct federalism;" and would, therefore,

(8) check the tendency toward centralism in a pluralistic society.[7]

The creation of metropolitan states, however, needs to be supplemented by some means of enhancing the representation of neighborhoods and, especially, minority interests. Unfortunately, much of the political strength for regional government in metropolitan areas has been organized to prevent minority groups from capitalizing on growing political strength in urban neighborhoods. We noted, therefore, the need for creation of neighborhood governments within current central cities or alternative mechanisms to allow political "voice" within neighborhoods.[8]

Neighborhood governments, to be most effective, need to be placed in a metropolitan state context. Milton Kotler has argued persuasively for neighborhood government, but would leave the present city as a unit to deal with the intercommunity needs. We argued, on the contrary, that

> While Mr. Kotler has accurately pointed to the failure of the city boundaries to accommodate the needs of individual communities (neighborhoods), he somehow assumes that the territorial limits of the city are appropriate to their inter-community (collective) needs.

Such an assumption clearly disregards the spatial structure of modern metropolitan society and its major socioeconomic characteristic: community interdependence. Obviously, the inner-metropolitan, low-income communities (neighborhoods) have important stakes in public functions that extend well beyond artificial city boundaries into the outer (suburban) reaches of the metropolitan area, functions that include transportation, jobs, housing, recreation, etc. These vital non-local interests must be accounted for in an appropriate area-wide institution just as their local interests are to be recorded in neighborhood government. We would therefore amend Mr. Kotler's plan for governmental reorganization to the extent that cities would be replaced by our proposal for Metropolitan States as the most logical object of federation.[9]

In low-income neighborhoods particularly, community development corporations (CDCs) are a potentially useful institutional device. Even with the creation of neighborhood governments, a CDC's ability to internalize a mix of private market activities and quasipublic activities could be an asset. Essentially, CDCs attempt to identify deficiencies in the operation of private markets and in the delivery of public goods and services. At the same time, they try to reduce the constraints on private market operation and delivery of public goods and services; or to more effectively deliver appropriate public and private goods and services.

A CDC has the potential to achieve these improvements. It can assist a community with a smaller private market or fewer public goods and services than the community is capable of producing. This low production level can be attributed to:

1. a lack of information about opportunities or profitable markets among private market decision makers

2. the existence of "neighborhood effects" that prevent investment or expansion by private investors, or cause relocation of community activities

3. a failure of market units (firms, retail outlets, housing owners) to be large enough or well enough organized to reap economies of scale or positive externalities

4. an absence of complementary public goods or infrastructure

5. a lack of public or private programs to address unique community problems.

The management of a CDC, with both knowledge of the community and sympathy with it, can be expected to have more relevant information than others, and either to discount adverse neighborhood effects or to eliminate some of them—at least with respect to its own activities. A CDC management with experience might be expected to be skillful in overcoming problems of size or organization of market units, and better able to perceive and take advantage of positive externalities.

The historical constraint on scale has resulted from deteriorating assets in the community, lack of investible resources, and lack of sufficient local purchasing power. A CDC may arrest the deterioration of community assets in housing stock and commercial property. It also generates investment funds from external sources and from its own revenues. A CDC can do little to extensively expand local purchasing power, even though its expenditures have some multiplier effects. However, it can focus the existing demand by engaging in activities responsive to community needs.

Moreover, a CDC (partly because it is eligible for public service grants as a nonprofit organization, and partly because it represents at least potential local political interests) is likely to have more influence than other individual private firms or investors in providing complementary goods and services or in inducing government to provide them.* The CDC experience to date shows mixed results, but CDCs remain one of the most interesting innovations for community or neighborhood improvement.

The need remains, however, for political decentralization. Efforts to achieve economic and racial integration of the suburbs have resulted in attacks on the right of local jurisdictions to control land use, particularly through zoning. Such attacks may well prove shortsighted if political decentralization could be achieved. In many urban areas, the major question is not whether central city areas will be redeveloped but when and under whose control such redevelopment will occur. If neighborhoods are to be sustained, better planning authority is needed in central city neighborhoods than appeals to central city governments. For these purposes, CDCs are weaker than political jurisdictions.

## CONCLUSIONS

We believe that urban problems are unlikely to be solved without a considerable overhaul of our governmental structure, at least as it operates in metropolitan areas. Rather than undermine the federal system, as did the direct federalism of the 1960s, or abandon national purposes concerning urban areas, as does the current new federalism, we must take broader approaches. Two specific activities are crucial: gathering information on channeling options within this structural framework and developing strategies for moving toward the new arrangement.[10] Innovation in social technologies is essential for providing services as well as for determining the degree of concern for public good in

---

*This view of community development corporations is based on a recent evaluation of CDCs conducted by the Urban Institute for the Ford Foundation. The authors of this chapter, as well as Herrington Bryce and Carl Snead, participated in the evaluation.

private choices, to better meet the needs of all citizens and to address the social implications of their actions and choices for a national growth policy. No less innovation is required to develop governmental structures that are more consistent with the needs of our metropolitan society than are present arrangements, and that take into account the elaborate interactions between public choices and private decisions.

## NOTES

1. James F. Selvaggi, "National Growth Policy-Making: Illusion or Illumination?" in *Management and Control of Growth* (Washington, D.C.: The Urban Land Institute, 1975), p. 436.

2. For a more detailed discussion of these components, see Harvey A. Garn and Michael Springer, "Formulating Urban Growth Policies: Dynamic Interactions Among People, Places, and Clubs," *Problems of Policy Choice in Intergovernmental Relations, Publius* 5, no. 4 (special issue, fall 1975): 25-49.

3. Lee Donne Olvey, "Regional Growth and Inter-Regional Migration—Their Pattern of Inter-Action," thesis presented at Harvard University, April 1970, p. 110.

4. Ibid., p. 129.

5. Bennett Harrison, *Issues in National Urban Growth Policy: Summaries of Eight Congressional Seminars* (Washington, D.C.: National Planning Association, February-May 1973), pp. 50-51.

6. Richard P. Burton and Harvey A. Garn, "The President's 'Report on National Growth 1972': A Critique and an Alternative Formulation," *National Growth Policy*, part 2, selected papers submitted to the Subcommittee on Housing, of the Committee on Banking and Currency, House of Representatives, 92d Cong., 2d sess. (Washington, D.C.: Government Printing Office, pp. 647-703.

7. Ibid., p. 30.

8. "A Theory of Neighborhood Problem Solving: Political Action vs. Residential Mobility," John M. Orbell and Toru Uno, *American Political Science Review* 66 (1972): 471-89.

9. Ibid., pp. 80-81. (See Kotler's Chapter 10 in this volume.)

10. For discussion of these issues, see Harvey A. Garn, "Public Services on the Assembly Line," *Evaluation* 1, no. 2 (1973): 36, 41, 42; Harvey A. Garn and Michael Springer, "Formulating Urban Growth Policies: Dynamic Interactions Among People, Places, and Clubs," *Problems of Policy Choice in Intergovernmental Relations, Publius* 5, no. 4 (Fall 1975): 25-49.

## PARTICIPATION OF
## MINORITY CITIZENS
## IN POLICY DECISIONS
## AND THEIR IMPLEMENTATION

# 13

## CITIZEN PARTICIPATION
## AND MODEL CITIES
Ricardo A. Millett

Viewed in the context of resident participation, the Model Cities experience resulted in a series of compromises and frustrated expectations among minorities. Among its most noticeable impacts was the development of the concept of citizen participation. A negative impact was the creation of a middle bureaucracy of upwardly mobile people who, it seems, channeled the demands of the deprived through the bureaucracy.

Some students of the participation issue view the provisions for resident participation in the Model Cities program as a conscious attempt to decrease the emphasis on this factor—particularly where "resident" is interpreted to mean ethnic minorities.[1] Elsewhere this de-emphasis has been identified with the ghetto rebellions of the 1960s and the increased political awareness of ethnic minorities during this period.

The historical frustrations of ethnic minorities with the inability and/or unwillingness of institutions to respond to their needs led them to believe that it was necessary to control some part of any program allegedly designed to help them. Hence, from the perspective of the powerless of the American slums, the program could have become responsive and meaningful only to the extent that they could seize the opportunities Model Cities offered and make it serve the needs of the community.

Although the Department of Housing and Urban Development (HUD) was unambiguous in respect to the role the municipal chiefs were to play in the program, the specific form of "widespread citizen participation" was left largely open. The performance standards for widespread citizen participation are suggestive rather than prescriptive, permissive rather than assertive. In large measure, as H. Ralph Taylor stated, the outcome of the Model Cities program (and thus inherently the form of resident participation) would be determined by the "will and competence of the communities to meet the problems of the slums."[2]

The Model Cities planning effort, insofar as it attempted to integrate wide-spread citizen participation in its operational process, was a recognition of the need to provide participatory mechanisms for target communities. How, then, did such participation unfold in the ghettos of urban areas? How did the decision-making processes that evolved in the Model Cities program relate to the ethnic minorities' demands for increased influence? Specifically, were minority groups able to use the participation mechanisms in the Model Cities program to resolve their sense of powerlessness, and if so, under what conditions? This chapter attempts to find empirical answers to these questions.

## STUDY METHODOLOGY

The major data source for the study is a series of chronological case histories compiled and written by Marshall Kaplan, Gans, and Khan (MKGK). These chronologies provide a reliable, continuous history of both the Model Cities program in each city and the range of interaction among municipal staff, HUD regional personnel, local service institutions, and local residents. Although focused primarily on recounting the activities of the City Demonstration agencies, the chronologies also recorded other activities in the city (such as elections or riots) that had, or should have had, an impact upon the Model Cities program. In addition, specific attention was paid to developing an accurate picture of the political cohesiveness of Model Neighborhood residents.

The selection of cities for study was conducted jointly with the staff of HUD's Model Cities Administration and was based on a conscientious effort to choose cities with characteristics considered both representative of most American cities and essential to an understanding of the impact of federal intervention programs on local communities.*

The first step in the study was to read each chronology in its entirety to screen out the observable variations in the degree of influence Model Neighborhood Area (MNA) residents were able to exercise in the program's operation. The literature on citizen participation and interviews conducted with key Model Cities administrators influenced the choice of variables. Three sets of variables are identified:

1. Intervening variables used are of two types. The first, labeled Environmental 1, includes the population size of the city, kind of municipal government,

---

*The cities selected were Atlanta, Georgia; Dayton, Ohio; Denver, Colorado; Detroit, Michigan; Cambridge, Massachusetts; Gary, Indiana; Reading, Pennsylvania; Rochester, New York; Richmond, California; San Antonio, Texas; Pittsburgh, Pennsylvania.

racial composition of the city and that of the MNA. The second, labeled Environmental 2, includes indices of racial conflict in the city occurring either during the two years prior to Model Cities or during the two-year period studied by MKGK. This subset also includes a measure of the political cohesiveness of the MNA residence vis-a-vis the Model Cities program. These variables are not exhaustive, but they do adequately describe the model neighborhood. Environmental 1 identifies the city from a broad population and political organization perspective, Environmental 2 identifies the degree of overt racial hostility that might have occurred in that city and the cohesiveness of the minority population.

2. Independent variables measure those program activities taken either by residents or City Demonstration Agency (CDA) staff resultant from the award and operation of a Model Cities grant. These variables constitute actual measures of resident participation, and the preconditions necessary for effective participation.

The independent variables measure:

a. resident involvement in the application phase for a Model Cities grant

b. resident activity for an increased role in the Model Cities process

c. resident participation in the selection of the CDA director

d. representativeness of the resident structure of neighborhood constituency

e. CDA director's sympathy to community control

f. role of the resident in designing the prerogatives of the resident participation structure

g. structure of the resident participation body

h. role of the resident in designing the structure and prerogatives of the CDA structure

i. percent of ethnic minorities in the citizen participation structure

j. information flow from the CDA to the resident structure

k. extent and nature of "professional cooperation" with residents

3. The dependent variables are measures of resident control as manifested in the degree and extent of influence residents were able to exercise in the hiring and firing of Model Cities personnel, allocation of Model Cities budget, and operation and initiation of Model Cities projects.

These variables are criteria by which the degrees of resident influence in the decision-making process in the Model Cities could be measured, since the above four decision areas are the key to control in most federal intervention programs that require resident participation. In particular, the demands of ghetto residents for community control of various municipal institutions and intervention programs have clearly focused on these four variables.

All the variables are summarized in Figure 13.1.

FIGURE 13.1

Variables in Model Cities Analysis

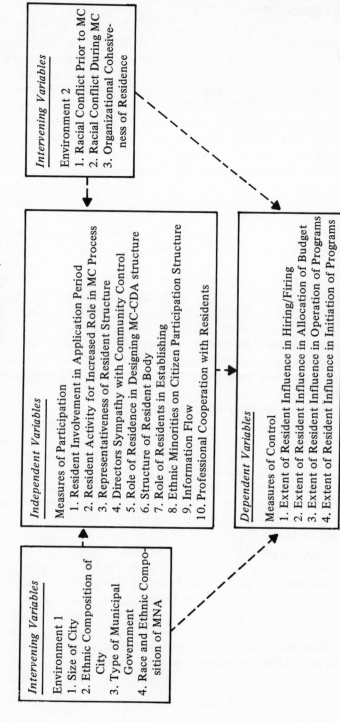

*Source:* Compiled by author.

## SUMMARY OF FINDINGS

Rank-order correlations were found between the intervening and independent variables and a summed index of all four dependent variables. The rank-order correlations are shown in Table 13.1.

Clearly, many of these variables are closely interrelated, but Table 13.1 shows some interesting correlations. The index of community control was not closely related to the percentage of minority representatives on the resident participation boards, an indication that participation was frequently without power on these boards where there were high numbers of minorities. A similar finding was observed in those model neighborhoods in which there was a high percentage of minorities.

Participation, however, tended to be positively correlated with the eventuality of a racial disturbance in cities while the Model Cities program was functioning. This suggests, among other things, that participation was a method of appeasement.

Further, control was inversely correlated to city size. Large cities were less likely than smaller ones to yield to community control over decisions. Another fact closely related to size is that cities with city managers (weak mayors) were more favorably disposed to community involvement. Since city managers are not elected, this suggests that strong mayors viewed community control as a high political risk.

Finally, as may be expected, control was most likely in those cities in which a great number of the Model Cities neighborhoods residents were directly involved in the program.

These findings outline the various actors, institutions, and social factors that need to be brought into concerted action to ensure the attainment of a viable resident participation process.[3] Where these conditions were absent, resident participation seemed to lock the residents into a position of little or no influence on major decisions (as was the case in Atlanta, Georgia). In Dayton, Ohio, where most of these conditions held, residents exerted considerable influence on the program.

## CASE STUDIES

Perhaps the most obvious outcome of the Model Cities program is its failure to lead urban institutions to meet the needs of minorities and the poor. In part, this failure can be seen as an overestimation of what Taylor has called the will and competence of communities to meet the problems of the slums (a politically naive view). Or, in general, it could be the result of inaccurate assumptions and analyses that underlie participation policies. Or, even more seriously,

## TABLE 13.1

### Relationship of Each of the Independent and Intervening Variables to an Index of Control

| Variables | Rank-Order Correlation (GAMMA) |
|---|---|
| 1. Size of city | -.250 |
| 2. Type of municipal government | .492 |
| 3. Race and ethnic composition of city | .500 |
| 4. Race and ethnic composition of MNA | -.185 |
| 5. Indices of racial conflict prior to Model Cities | -.083 |
| 6. Indices of racial conflict during Model Cities | .500 |
| 7. Community cohesiveness generated by Model Cities activity | .852 |
| 8. Resident involvement in Model Cities application | .478 |
| 9. Indices of resident activity for increased role in MC process | .846 |
| 10. Resident participation in selection of MC director | 1.000* |
| 11. Representativeness of resident structure of MN | .923 |
| 12. Director's sympathy with community control | 1.000* |
| 13. Role of residents in establishing the prerogatives of the CDA structure | .775 |
| 14. Autonomy of citizen participation body | .667 |
| 15. Role of residents in establishing the prerogatives of the resident participation structure | .692 |
| 16. Percentage of ethnic minority on resident participation structure | .124 |
| 17. Information flow from CDA to resident participation | .446 |
| 18. Extent of professional cooperation with residents. | .583 |

*These ordinal coefficients suggest that there is perfect congruence between these variables and the criterion variable.

*Source*: Compiled by author.

this failure may be the result of an underestimation of the factors and conditions that make up the will of ethnic minorities to "control their own destiny."

Hence, the overall qualities for which a program director was selected had a minimal relationship to the qualities of leadership that ethnic minority communities seem to require. The criteria by which he was selected and the responsibilities delegated to him by the municipal chief often worked against the development of working relations with the more politically conscious segments of the minority community. In most communities where there was a large ethnic minority population in the Model Neighborhood area, the program director was challenged. More often than not, these community organizations were frustrated by the inability of the project director to respond adequately to community needs. Hence, in Pittsburgh, the United Black Front, whose members were outside the traditional leadership structure, presented a constant challenge to the Model Cities program.

In Atlanta, where the mayor directly appointed a program director who was "educated" enough to adhere to the well-ordered planning schedule of the Model Cities process, only a small segment of the ethnic minority community was involved in the program or even knew of its existence. Yet at the end of the first action year (two years of actual operation) the program was the "eyes and ears" of the community. Given the inability of the Atlanta program either to make an impact on the Model Neighborhood area or to enlist the support of its population, this statement heightened the alienation of many local organizations.

In Gary, the program director was also appointed directly by the recently elected black mayor, who was himself anxious that the program not create any additional waves in a political situation that already promised to be turbulent. Accordingly, the program director was charged with steering the Model Cities program clear of potentially political issues, and this meant playing down resident participation. The program director's administrative style limited resident involvement largely to the review of program materials, and relied heavily on the intensive efforts of a few professional city staff members. It appeared that most residents acknowledged that Model Cities was a "mayor's program" and relied on the mayor's sensitivity to black residents and their condition.

In San Antonio, the conflicting allegiance of the program director to the chief municipal executive and the residents was a model case. The director, appointed by the municipal chief, reflected, on the one hand, pressures in the community for Mexican-American representation in the decision-making process and, on the other hand, the desire of the city council for someone loyal to the Good Government League.* The Mexican-American community was convinced that the director saw his role as a representative of the city first and as a representative of the Mexican-American community second, if at all.

To some extent, the failure of the Model Cities program to reach the majority of the lower-class ethnic minorities might be correlated with this problem of leadership. Like most previous federal intervention efforts, Model Cities attracted a small segment of the minority community. Those who were attracted were already geared toward a middle-class value orientation. As a result, the program tended to attract a cadre of upwardly mobile types who alienated the majority of the lower-class ethnic population.

---

*The Good Government League is a strong political organization in San Antonio dedicated to the goals of eliminating corruption and providing sound municipal government. For the past 20 years, the majority of the city council have been members of this organization.

Any real effort to deal with the problem of poverty should recognize the factors which prevent resident participation. Thus, an appropriate approach to planning might be what Herbert Gans calls the problem-oriented method. The thrust here is to concentrate on people, and on the social, political, and economic forces that foster their deprivation, rather than on the neighborhood conditions that are themselves consequences of these factors.

Model Cities planning schemes concentrated on instituting mechanisms and processes to affect the economics of managing resources. Cities largely depended on their own professional planners, who themselves traditionally resisted joint planning with the lower-class residents. This tendency highlights the contradiction of placing a human-oriented program in the hands of city hall.

## IMPACT OF WIDESPREAD CITIZEN PARTICIPATION ON THE ETHNIC MINORITY COMMUNITIES

On the whole, residents were extremely distrustful of the sincerity of a program run by city hall. Their distrust became even more acute as the program director and the professional planners manifested an inability to respond to their needs, or to fully integrate their inputs into the final planning products. Moreover, it seems that significant resident input into the planning process occurred largely as a result of political pressure exerted through protest actions. This reflects the reality that racism is so entrenched and pervasive in this country that often the greatest power the exploited have is the power to disrupt.

Insofar as it has increased distrust or failed to coordinate the interest of the "have-nots" with the general interest of city hall, Model Cities has been negative. To the extent that residents might have been forced to confront city hall, the program increased distrust and vitiated its ability to relate to the needs of the community. Residents of the Philadelphia Model Cities program concluded at the end of their unsuccessful effort to increase their decision-making influence in that program:

> It might be beautiful if city hall and HUD were trustworthy. But our history testifies to the fact that we'd be fools to trust the politicians. We were cheated each time we let our legal guard down. We only succeeded when we insisted that the politicians live up to their promises, and when we demonstrated that we had some power.

> All four Model City directors used us to achieve their own ends. Each was willing to negotiate with us when he assumed the job and had some important HUD deadline to meet. Right after that goal had been achieved, each tried to range on the partnership agreement by creating an outrageous crisis around the renewal of our contract. Though some of the staff of the city and federal agencies were

clearly honest and helpful, most of them lied, equivocated, cheated and distorted.[4]

In terms of economic impact, Model Cities cannot claim great success. Bennett Harrison's research on the extent to which Model Cities increased employment of minorities concluded that the urban poor did not receive its share of Model Cities resources or jobs.[5] Briefly, he found the following:

1. Citizen Boards were active in most cities, yet relatively few of their members received actual salaries.
2. Model Neighborhood residents shared in the direct, salaried employment created by the program. Less than a quarter of all Model City professionals during the planning period were residents of the target area. About two-thirds of the paraprofessionals and 49 percent of the clerical workers were residents.
3. Even after removing the effects of age, sex, education, hours and occupation, it was still apparent that MN residents received $800-$1,300 less per year than outsiders.
4. CDAs appeared to recruit a disproportionate number of MN women relative to men and to place considerable weight on educational credentials for all jobs.*

These are among the reasons why many minorities see the Model Cities program as enhancing the conditions that foster a "paracolonial" relationship, rather than as an agent to promote autonomy or yield benefits to their communities. Ralph A. Metcalf, in an article entitled "Chicago Model Cities and Neocolonization" in the April 1970 issue of the *Black Scholar* magazine wrote:

> . . . the community itself received little if any benefit from these programs. Moreover, these liberal pacifiers took a devastating psychological toll on the masses of black people in this country by increasing their physical dependence on a system which has exploited and oppressed them for over 440 years. This pacification is a form of neocolonialism.

Sam Yette's national best seller, *The Choice*, is another account that supports the notion that national intervention efforts have had a "colonizing" impact on ethnic minority communities.

The Great Society pacification programs, then, must be judged as failures, both in the honesty of their designs and in their truer aims

---

*Harrison's study employs multivariate analyses to investigate the rates of employment of ghetto residents and the salaries of all Model Cities employees during the program's planning period. His sample consisted of "first round" cities, nine of which (Richmond, Denver, Gary, Cambridge, Detroit, Rochester, Dayton, San Antonio, Pittsburgh) were cities in the present study sample.

of placating people justly aroused. In view of their maximum goals, the funds and the personnel provided, and the authority to do the job, the OEO and civil rights program did not relinquish the original aims of white establishment exploitation. They left ultimate control and financial benefits with the colonialists—not with the colonized; nor even were control and profits shared equitably between them.6

Of course, "widespread citizen participation" has also had some positive impact; in particular, the exposure of communities to the complexities and subtleties of governmental activities and operations. Ethnic minorities are realizing that the present institutional order will not change itself, and they have accepted the onus of change.

## CONCLUSION

The official rationale for the present de-emphasis on resident participation claims that the government cannot subsidize "revolution"; that the poor do not know what is good for them; that the real needs are jobs, not organization into troublemaking groups; that citizen participation only stirs controversy and polarizes the differences between races and classes; that citizen participation bent on community control is inimical to governmental honesty, equity, and professionalism; and that it hinders local governments in their effort to act on decisions based on citywide rather than more parochial considerations. These claims basically serve to maintain the present societal order.

Of course, no government can be expected to organize against itself. In the end, what is expected is that the government of a democratic society should recognize how remote its large and most influential institutions are from their clients and support new institutional organizations that are more responsive.

## NOTES

1. Sherri Arnstein and Daniel Fox, "Technical Assistance Paper on Citizen Participation," Department of Housing and Urban Services (Washington, D.C.: Government Printing Office, July 8, 1968), p. 220.

2. Herbert Gans, "Social and Physical Plannings for the Elimination of Urban Poverty," in *Urban Planning and Social Policy*, eds. Bernard J. Frieden and Robert Morris (New York: Basic Books, Inc., 1960), p. 49.

3. Sherri Arnstein, "The Eight Rungs On The Ladder On Citizen Participation," *Journal Of American Institute of Planners* 25 (July 1969): 2; Hans Speigel, *Citizen Participation in Urban Development: Cases and Programs* (Washington, D.C.: NTL Institute for Applied Behavioral Science, 1969); James Sundquist, *Making Federalism Work* (Washington, D.C.: The Brookings Institution, 1969), p. 4; Marshall Kaplan, "HUD-M.C. Planning System" (paper).

4. "Maximum Feasible Manipulation in Philadelphia: What the Power Structure Did to Us," *City Magazine* 4, no. 3 (1970): 37.

5. Bennett Harrison, "The Participation of Ghetto Residents in the Model Cities Program," *American Institute of Planners Journal* 4 (January 1973).

6. Sam Yette, *The Choice; The Issue of Black Survival in America* (New York: G. P. Putnam and Sons, 1969).

# 14

## POLITICAL COSTS
## AND BENEFITS OF
## PARTICIPATION
Charles Hamilton

There is now sufficient evidence that no clear agreement existed among policy makers and others on the meaning and intent of "maximum feasible participation" as stated in section 202(a) of the Economic Opportunity Act of 1964.[1] Apparently, guaranteeing maximum feasible participation was motivated mainly by a desire to stop hostile Southern whites from excluding blacks' participation in the development and administration of community action programs.[2] Other motivations and interpretations of the language quickly developed, however, and these hampered the program from its inception.

This chapter focuses on what I perceive to be one major political consequence of the emphasis on "maximum feasible participation." My basic conclusion is that it created a brand of social action that, at best, institutionalized a politics of protest but did very little toward establishing the conditions for a politics of governance. The policy makers intended to write legislation that was service oriented rather than politically oriented; in actual practice, however, local community groups not only became politicized, but did so in a narrow and most circumscribed way—focusing on temporary funded programs and on protest as a means of political leverage. "Maximum feasible participation" thus became, ironically, dysfunctional for development of a politics of governance—that is, for gaining control of real institutional power.

## SOME OPTIMISTIC ASSESSMENTS

In an article entitled "Citizen Participation in Community Action and Model Cities Programs," John H. Strange recognized the successes and failures of the programs. Regarding the former, he concluded that certain minority group members had acquired political experience and skills as well as significant control over jobs and opportunities for disseminating information, recognition, and money.[3] He also noted that the requirement that the poor participate in jobs and in decision making may lead to compatible revisions in the civil service system, as it already has in other employment areas[4] and as it has influenced the operation of the Model Cities and community action programs.[5]

In 1974, when the Nixon administration was showing a clear intent to cut back many antipoverty program funds, another observer commented that previously powerless groups were beginning to wield power through community action programs' funds. He also noted that "the network of poor people" across the country was learning to manipulate the system to alleviate poverty.[6]

These and other assessments[7] have emphasized the value of the participatory experience in increasing political awareness and skills: that is, poor people have experienced the process of going to meetings, dealing with budgets, responding to bureaucracies, and vying for offices on local boards. Without underestimating these benefits, my point remains that participation did not lead to the capture of control over local institutional budgets.

## THE TRADITIONAL PATRON-CLIENT RELATIONSHIP

The 1960s witnessed a growing disenchantment with old-style party politics, bossism, and "the machine." Nevertheless, the old-style parties at least mobilized local citizens around goals, and got results.

A classic patron-client relationship was developed as local politicians courted the new ethnic immigrants. The parties provided important benefits and services—favors—and, in return, received support, loyalty, and votes.[8] Ostrogorski has observed:

Germans, Italians, or Slavs arrive without knowing the language, the manners and customs, and the institutions of the country. But thereupon they find a fellow-countryman already naturalized and at home in the New World, who puts himself fraternally at their disposal; he guides their early steps, he helps them to look for work, he appears on their behalf before the representatives of the public authority in the ward with whom they have to deal; later on, when the legal term has expired, or even earlier, he procures their naturalization. Day by day the ties which grow up between him and them are drawn closer, he becomes for them not only a friend, an adviser, but an oracle; and full of gratitude for his friendly services, and of admiration for his intelligence, they make over to him with perfect good faith the votes which have just been given them, and which as a rule they do not know what to do with. Here again is an "owner" of votes, who will find a good investment for his modest pile in the electoral market.[9]

These patrons and clients thus mobilized their resources to capture local political offices that controlled local budgets. These offices and budgets in turn provided them with control over citywide dispensation of services, over taxing and revenue powers, over schools, the police, the courts, over the administration of key services cities provide, and, of course, over a multitude of jobs. Surely their performance was mixed; but the fact remains that there were important stakes to be gained. The patron-client relationship laid a foundation for a politics of governance.

## THE PATRON-RECIPIENT RELATIONSHIP AND A POLITICS OF PARTICIPATORY PROTEST

Notwithstanding the aspirations of some persons who saw the community action programs as a means for developing a newly politicized cadre of activists in all instances, such programs were essentially service-oriented. They existed to provide services and only incidentally involved their constituencies in certain kinds of political action such as voter registration and protest.[10]

Most descriptions of political action related to the programs show that the action merely involved protest—for example, against a city agency, a landlord, or merchants. Describing the situation in Detroit, Greenstone and Peterson wrote:

> In another area of the city, CAA organizers intervened on behalf of tenants demanding enforcement of the city's building code, even though these activities were known to arouse the ire of health department personnel. In other instances the NSCs helped community organizations to demand improved government services, registered voters, developed low-cost housing projects, and improved their members' buying practices. And the CAA was also "instrumental in . . . recruiting area residents for citizens' review boards in most of the city's police precincts." In sum, representatives and organizations of the poor at neighborhood and city-wide levels used CAA resources to develop a base of power with which to influence a wide variety of city policies. The poverty program, and later the Model Cities program . . . would become institutional bases of power for an increasingly strong and militant black leadership.[11]

Institutional bases of power is a highly questionable expression. These programs were funded by government agencies (federal and local); that is, the local groups had to rely on periodic grants in order to stay in business. Moreover, whereas the old-style precinct captain would dispense favors in return for votes, the "patrons" under the Great Society programs only asked their residents to be available to be serviced. There was no quid pro quo. There were no local offices to capture, with the power to distribute benefits throughout the city, and with control over tax-supported budgets.

Thus, we saw the development of a patron-recipient relationship. The patron would be funded from outside and would (hopefully) provide services (Head Start, legal services, consumer education, child care, manpower training, tenant counseling, senior citizen lunches, drug rehabilitation) to target areas. Periodically, a mass protest action would be staged against a reluctant bureaucracy or landlord or whatever; and, also periodically, the patron would submit another proposal to the appropriate agency to be funded.

The basic politics that developed around this process centered on intra-community fights to control positions on the local board. But beyond the provision of services, the most that can be said for the creation of institutional bases of power is that in some places community groups became more adept at pressure politics.

## THE POLITICS OF GOVERNANCE: THE PENULTIMATE OF PARTICIPATION

Many local community activists emerging from this participatory protest process became aware of the intricacies of the bureaucracy and of the power of local political (electoral) structures; but they did not mobilize to control these elements. They did not put together structures to maximize voter turnout, for example. They might have developed protesters, but they failed to develop precinct captains.

As important as a politics of protest has been (and will continue to be), it is only a piece of the political process. It is best calculated to influence policy and programs, and can have only minimal impact on determining the occupancy of (and thus control over) positions of institutional power.

Earlier ethnic groups did not make this mistake. They used their resources in a concerted, organized way to influence who got elected. And yet, after ten years of "maximum feasible participation," many local black communities have not learned this lesson. In New York City, frequently cited as a better model of participation, the residents of Harlem still are unable to exert adequate political leverage on city hall.

Saul Alinsky understood that there was more involved than tending to the goal of a more equitable distribution of goods and services; namely, the achievement of a more equitable distribution of decision-making power. Moynihan was certainly correct when he concluded that "the problem of the poor is not only that they lack money, but that they lack power. This means they . . . [need] organization first; antipoverty programs second" if they plan on changing the status quo.[12]

The critical lesson to be learned from the "maximum feasible participation" experience is that organizations must precede programs; programs must not be the source of organizations. Too many activists believed they could flourish through funding, without recognizing that funding for programs could easily be stopped.

Ethnic groups did understand that political strength derived from the control of elective offices. Community-based political action should be geared to capturing and controlling positions of institutional power, not just getting money for programs.

## NOTES

1. John C. Donovan, *The Politics of Poverty* (New York: Pegasus, 1967), p. 40.

2. Ibid., pp. 41-42; Daniel P. Moynihan, *Maximum Feasible Misunderstanding* (New York: The Free Press, 1969), p. 87

3. John H. Strange, "Citizen Participation in Community Action and Model Cities Programs," *Public Administration Review* 32 (October 1972): 660.

4. Ibid.

5. Ibid., p. 661.

6. New York *Times*, June 4, 1974, p. 37.

7. See, for example, Sar A. Levitan, *The Great Society's Poor Law: A New Approach to Poverty* (Baltimore: Johns Hopkins Press, 1969); Melvin B. Mogulof, *Citizen Participation: A Review and Commentary on Federal Policies and Practices* (Washington, D.C.: The Urban Institute, January 1970); U.S. Senate, Committee on Labor and Public Welfare, *Examination of the War on Poverty* (Washington, D.C.: U.S. Government Printing Office, September 1967).

8. Raymond E. Wolfinger, "Some Consequences of Ethnic Politics," in *The Electoral Process*, eds. Harmon Zeigler and Kent Jennings (Englewood Cliffs, N.J.: Prentice-Hall, 1966), pp. 42-54.

9. M. Ostrogorski, *Democracy and the Organization of Political Parties*, vol. 2, *The United States* (New York: Anchor Books, Doubleday & Company, 1964), p. 181.

10. Frances Fox Piven and Richard A. Cloward, *Regulating the Poor* (New York: Pantheon Books, 1971), p. 294.

11. J. David Greenstone and Paul E. Peterson, *Race and Authority in Urban Politics* (New York: Russell Sage Foundation, 1973), pp. 37-38.

12. Daniel P. Moynihan, op. cit., p. 186.

# 15

## OTHER ETHNICS AND
## CITIZEN PARTICIPATION
Ira Katznelson

In the early 1960s, a whole genre of today's urban institutions was virtually unknown. In the 1970s, little city halls, offices of neighborhood government, community planning boards, decentralized school boards, and neighborhood service delivery cabinets are commonplace features of urban political landscapes. Why, in the middle and late 1960s, was there a proliferation of mayorally-initiated programs of this kind? How, in the past decade, have these new institutions altered the existing web of social and political relationships between public officials and neighborhood residents? In what ways do these experiences contribute to an assessment of strategies of localism for transforming the conditions of black and white working-class urban communities?

I have been exploring these questions as part of an ongoing community study of Washington Heights-Inwood, an area that includes all of Manhattan north of Harlem. Virtually all its residents are members of working-class families. The area is segmented racially, ethnically, and geographically. Its 200,000 Irish, black, Jewish, Dominican, Greek, and Cuban residents live "much as do people in a great hotel, meeting but not knowing one another."[1] The northern part of the territory, with extensive parkland and good public transportation, is the most livable working-class neighborhood in Manhattan. Its population is predominantly white. The part to the south and east is a developing slum. Here the majority of the population is Hispanic and black.

In 1965, party organizations, synagogues, and the Catholic church were the most important institutional links between the residents of the area and the urban polity. Most of the political actors were white.

By the mid-1970s the older organizational pattern had been superseded by a new set of local political structures: an elected school board, a land-use community planning board, and instruments of political and administrative decentralization (the neighborhood action program—NAP—and the office of neighborhood government, respectively). A growing minority of neighborhood political activists were black and Hispanic.

Northern Manhattan's new boards and agencies were results of a conscious strategy to resolve what Reinhardt Bendix has called a crisis of the civic incorporation of the lower classes.[2] In liberal democracies, social cohesion depends heavily on the manner in which "potential partisans"[3] are linked to the polity. This is precisely the case because order in capitalist societies must be maintained by the liberal state in spite of the wide gap between nominal legal equality (inherent in citizenship and right to vote) and the structural inequities produced by the routine operation of the economic system.

In the late nineteenth century, the mass migration of Catholic and Jewish workers from Europe and blacks from the South challenged the traditional hegemony of the protestant ruling class. The political behavior of the new proletariat was unpredictable. Significant outbreaks of labor unrest and organizational activity caused the elite concern. During this period, urban political machines helped keep things under control. The machines stressed ethnicity, community, and concrete rewards. Run by specialist politicians, they exercised social control over newcomers by organizing both the input and output sides of politics; they provided the only coherent direct access links to government and acted as the key distributor of political rewards. By organizing political life, the machines provided a buffer to soften the relationships between elites and the masses.

The machines, though part of a national apparatus, were local institutions exerting strong local influence. Thus, when unions sought to create local political instruments of their own, as in the New York mayoral election of 1886, they were successfully opposed by Democratic and Republican machines. As a result, working-class political life in the United States was segmented into two distinctive sets of collectivities and organizations: working-class and unions; community-class and local politics. This enduring feature of American politics contributed to elite responses to the crisis of political incorporation of blacks in the 1960s.


## ORIGIN OF CITIZEN PARTICIPATION PROGRAMS

The remarkable political ferment in the black communities in the 1960s was an amalgam of a wildcat strike against traditional leadership practice and of a rebellious communal and territorial anticolonial impulse. In its full complexity, this political thrust closely resembled the form of English and Continental urban unrest Eric Hobsbawm calls populist legitimism, where the politically unincorporated populace used proscribed forms of political action to demand justice according to the manifest logic of prevailing arrangements: ". . . the ruler . . .

represents justice. Though it is patent that the local lords, officials, clergymen and other exploiters suck the blood of the poor, this is probably because the monarch does not know that is being done in his name. . . . The populace therefore riots for justice under the banner of King or Tsar."[4]

It was precisely this set of working assumptions that undergirded campaigns of civil disobedience in the South and participant behavior during ghetto revolts in the North. Like the members of many nineteenth-century working-class movements, black activists defined their demands in terms of citizenship. Local democracy and the capitalist social order were not directly attacked (though implicitly they inevitably were); at issue instead were their boundaries of inclusion.

Because of its content, the call for civil or citizenship rights could be answered by an elite strategy of political incorporation or co-option. Thus, Alan Altshuler addressed himself to "fellow whites" with an urgent plea to achieve a legitimate "peace of reconciliation" and to "sustain the interest of blacks in peaceful compromise . . . with the white majority" through community control.[5] John Lindsay similarly justified "plans for a structured, formal link between the neighborhoods and the city" to end the "discontent and alienation" that "were at the breaking point" within "the ghetto."[6]

Though most big-city administrations, including New York's, identified the black revolt as the main item on the local political agenda, they also—for reasons partially racist and partially economic—came to identify rapid racial turnover with urban decay and heightened political demands. Moreover, many urban political coalitions depended on traditional bases of electoral support. As populations moved, so did certain votes. But urban political elites had little to offer white working-class populations. Jobs were moving to the suburbs; urban civil service employment did not require urban residence. The quality of urban life was generally insusceptible to municipal solutions. As in their responses to black unrest, urban elites sought to define their concern for racial stabilization in largely political-institutional terms.

These considerations explain why the new programs of created participation were established. They also explain why, in cases where city officials had some discretion over where they would be located,* neighborhoods like Washington Heights-Inwood were selected—frequently without manifest demand from within the areas themselves. Northern Manhattan had a large and growing minority population, and, in the words of the draft pilot program for neighborhood government, was "still relatively stable, but in serious danger of decay," with "enough positive attributes to offer good chance for success."

---

*A related issue, of course, was that of location within the local neighborhood. Who would have easy access to the new institutions' offices proved to be less a matter of intent than of the availability of free city office space.

Most of the new programs, of course, were implemented citywide. The imperatives of political universalism made it impossible to create local planning and school boards in one neighborhood and not another. Thus, as a result of both area-specific and city-inclusive programs, by 1970 Washington Heights-Inwood had an elected school board, an appointed community planning board, and the rudiments of a new multifunctional neighborhood level government, the Neighborhood Action Program. Each of these local political structures will now be considered in turn.

## SCHOOL BOARDS

Under the impact of major shifts in urban labor markets and populations, and the increased political coherence of black activists, the politics of education broke out from its traditional isolation. The thrust of black demands, as well as the counterthrust of municipal unionization, threatened to turn school fights into a much more general social conflict whose consequences were unpredictable. As Henry Wells has noted,

> the New York schools were no longer deemed fit to perform their traditional role in bolstering the social order, the policing of the offspring of the deprived populations of the city, and the instilling of a sufficient variety of marketable skills to insure the continued prosperity of the region. These failings struck directly at the corporate and financial concerns which lie at the heart of the local and national economy.[7]

The decentralized school board structure created by the School Decentralization Law of 1969 was a structure of uncertain powers. To the city educational establishment as a whole, the board's major function was not the decentralization of governance, but the disaggregation of conflict. From the perspective of neighborhood politics, however, the local boards loomed very large. In a reform-minded city, they shifted considerable patronage (hiring nonprofessional staff, influencing the selection of some teachers and all supervisory personnel) to distinctive and visible neighborhood units.

Broadly speaking, there have been two major consequences of school decentralization for urban cohesion. First, in northern Manhattan, the politics of education has emerged anew as a distinctive political field. Local party officials and leaders of voluntary organizations have withdrawn from school politics, due largely to the volatility of school issues (in the two-year period almost a third of the school board's monthly meetings ended prematurely because of fights in the audience), the racial character of electoral and patronage competition, and the city-level example of how urban political elites have been burned by interposing themselves in school affairs. As a result, the realm of school politics has been opened to black and Hispanic leadership.

The emergence of new ethnic leaders facilitated the transformation of education from a redistributive to a distributive issue. Indeed, as David Protess has argued, a machine city is "a local polity whose political actors expect almost all public policies which affect it to have a distributive impact; that is, to be convertible to patronage."[8] From this perspective, school conflicts are now functional.[9]

## COMMUNITY PLANNING BOARDS

In stark contrast to the deafening political noise of school board elections and meetings, the Washington Heights Community Board, as the organ of the traditional elite under demographic pressure, has developed a strong sense of unity and group solidarity.

Such advisory community planning boards have existed in Manhattan for over 25 years. They have provided borough presidents, who appoint board members, with a source of symbolic patronage, with intelligence about local reactions to major land use decisions, and with a forum for promoting favored programs. In 1969, the Lindsay administration sought to capture this political resource by attaching local boards more closely to the City Planning Commission it controlled, and by expanding the boards to all city neighborhoods. Legislation passed in that year gave the community boards the authority to hold public hearings on proposals and programs affecting their districts, and increased the boards' advisory powers with respect to capital construction projects.

The tradition of appointing the most visible voluntary group leadership and party club nominees to the board has continued in Washington Heights. Of its 46 members in 1973, 36 were white, 9 black, 1 Hispanic. Virtually all members were professionals.

In addition, the formal and relatively closed structure of board meetings makes it difficult for the relatively unorganized and politically inexperienced to be heard. At these meetings, the public can participate only in the first half hour and does so without the benefit of an advance agenda, with the result that this half hour has little relevance to the substantive board meeting that follows.

Although the practice of community board politics reinforces prevailing patterns of organization instead of providing an alternative vehicle of political and social expression for the relatively unorganized, the board plays an important role in maintaining the social cohesion of the area. The board has given confidence and resources to a declining white political and organizational leadership, and thus has been an important part of the city administration's policy of racial stabilization. Moreover, by being a conclave of the area's visible leadership, especially in the white communities, the board appears to the white public to be a representative neighborhood legislature. Most land use decisions continue to be reached behind closed doors; but they now are enveloped in the patina of representative democracy.

## THE NEIGHBORHOOD ACTION PROGRAM

The legislative appearance and functions of the community planning board increased in importance with the creation of the area's neighborhood action program (NAP). In mid-1970, the Lindsay administration began to set up pilot programs of political decentralization in selected planning districts. Under the terms of the program, which had "neighborhood stabilization" as its aim, a local storefront office would be set up to help residents deal with city bureaucracies. An area executive director, appointed by the mayor, would develop community advisory committees on safety, education, health, housing, and so forth, and draw up proposals to be financed from an annual $525,000 allocation to the district. As in the case of the school board, these funds were paltry from a city perspective; but to the neighborhood, the funds were large enough to produce competing claimants.

By 1973, the NAP had emerged as the executive branch of a developing two-branch neighborhood government, with the community board as the legislative branch. The chairman of the community board was appointed to the executive directorship of NAP. Effectively, the community board and its nexus of local actors came to dominate the new program.

With the election of Mayor Beame, the NAP experiment came to an end. The new mayor, a product of the Brooklyn regular clubhouses, viewed the program as a threat to the remaining Democratic party organizations in the area.

In its brief lifetime, the NAP illustrated that very small sums of money and the form of representative community-level government (even where it lacked mass roots and major substantive powers) were sufficient to engage large numbers of people in busywork (writing grant proposals, lobbying neighborhood officials, and so forth). These activities, requiring much time and effort, complemented the school board's fragmentary impact on widespread city unrest. The politics of neighborhood life were defined distributionally; and the targets of distributional demands were in the neighborhood, not downtown. "We don't have to keep checking with downtown on policy matters," the NAP director told me, "so long as they don't catch flak downtown. That is our job. Flak catcher."[10]

## CONCLUSIONS

The creation of new vehicles for civic participation (or at least the illusion of participation) in the 1960s aimed at shaping the expression and direction of social unrest. To borrow a simile from Sir Lewis Namier, these elite strategies of created participation resemble dams on a river: they permit subordinate social forces to flow on through established channels of the system, but also make it possible to stem the tide, to prevent the flooding of the banks.

But much as a dam's location not only moderates the water's flow but shapes its future direction, so institutional solutions to the problem of civic incorporation establish new bases of politics and social conflict. As Margaret Levi has stated, "social programs are a forum for action as well as a form of social control. Poor people always understood that they were exploited by the rich and the powerful, but only with the expansion of the state have they gained a viable and accessible target of attack." Indeed, she argues, with only a small degree of overstatement, that since the changing political economy of older industrial cities no longer places them at the nodal point of American corporate expansion, for a growing number of city residents "the critical struggle is at the point of state intervention rather than at the point of production."[11]

We have learned the following three lessons from recent local political strategies of black and white working-class transformation:

1. The goals of various proponents of decentralization and strategies of local power are often conflicting. The Lindsay administration was principally interested in reducing citizen alienation and in preserving social stability through school decentralization and the neighborhood action program. This orientation was diametrically opposed to local activist goals seeking to utilize neighborhood democracy and participation as creative tools of social change.

2. Strategies of localism need to be an integral part of a coherent set of urban and national political orientations that seek to overcome precisely those divisions urban elites have sought to perpetuate. Much as in traditional machine cities or in Daley's Chicago, the Lindsay programs in New York were never meant to be substitutes for powerful centralizing tendencies in the regime. Quite the contrary; the administration promoted substantive centralization and symbolic decentralization at the same time.

Dispersed in many localities, neighborhood insurgents were hampered by the absence of overarching strategies and resources. To mount effective challenges to the social order, it is necessary to aggregate, not to disaggregate conflict, and to make distributive politics redistributive in nature.

3. The barriers between workplace and communal politics need to be overcome if local struggles are to produce more than ephemeral victories.

As Marx saw so clearly, the realms of work, community, and politics are part of an organic social whole. Structural transformations depend on addressing the whole as struggles proceed in the parts.

# NOTES

1. Harvey W. Zorbaugh, *The Gold Coast and the Slum* (Chicago: University of Chicago Press, 1929), p. 251.

2. Reinhardt Bendix, *Nation-Building and Citizenship* (New York: Anchor Books, 1969), chapters 1-3.

3. The term is taken from William Gamson, *Power and Discontent* (Homewood, Ill.: Dorsey Press, 1968), p. 2. For a discussion of these issues, see Ira Katznelson, *Black Men, White Cities* (New York: Oxford University Press, 1973), especially chapters 2 and 12.

4. Eric Hobsbawn, *Primitive Rebels* (New York: Beacon Press, 1959), p. 118.

5. Alan Altshuler, *Community Control* (New York: Pegasus Press, 1970), pp. 195, 197.

6. John V. Lindsay, *The City* (New York: New American Library, 1970), pp. 87, 95.

7. Henry C. Wells, "Notes for the Analysis of School Politics in Washington Heights," unpublished ms.

8. David Protess, "Banfield's Chicago Revisited, The Conditions for the Transformation of a Political Machine," unpublished manuscript.

9. That is, in the sense of Lewis Coser's *The Functions of Social Conflict* (New York: The Free Press, 1956).

10. Personal interview, July 1971.

11. Margaret Levi, "Poor People Against the State," *The Review of Radical Political Economics* 6 (spring 1974): 78-79.

# 16

## THE DEATH OF MAXIMUM
## FEASIBLE PARTICIPATION
Paul E. Peterson

Maximum feasible participation is dead, but it was not killed by Nixon. It did not die because of opposition from the right; it was buried by its own friends. Indeed, although maximum feasible participation made a signal contribution to American politics during the 1960s, subsequent social changes justify its demise.

In developing this argument, I shall consider the purposes of citizen participation in the war on poverty, its consequences for both political elites and black Americans, and its meaning in the context of today's politics.

## THE PURPOSES OF CITIZEN PARTICIPATION

"Maximum feasible participation was mandated as part of the Community Action Program (CAP). Community programs were to be designed by local agencies with the "maximum feasible participation of the residents of the areas and members of the groups served."[1] Similar language appeared in other social service legislation of the late 1960s.

According to one view, those social reform initiatives, with their participatory language, were the product of a bureaucratic reform tradition that had institutionalized itself in Washington.[2] The Kennedy administration policy innovators had grand schemes for the revitalization of a wide range of governmental institutions, particularly those in urban areas. They felt that federal funds, if applied with sophisticated political pressure, could restructure local organizations so as to provide more rationalized, more efficient, better coordinated services. At least some felt that through mobilizing citizens and neighborhood groups, local institutions could be pressured into being more responsive. At the moment of transition from Kennedy to Johnson, these change-oriented activists were in a position to promote an anti-poverty program that would carry out their reform philosophy. Accordingly, there was only one passing comment on maximum feasible participation in all the congressional hearings and debates on the Economic Opportunity Act.

A second view, which we find more persuasive, places these events in a much broader social and political context. This interpretation sees the war on poverty, including its citizen participation feature, as part of the civil rights struggle that began with the northern migration of blacks and finally reached a climax in the mid-1960s.[3]

Even in the quiescent 1950s, urban problems were moving towards the front of the political agenda. Congressional Democrats proposed reform legisla-tion in housing, education, health, and youth employment, though the Republican-southern Democratic coalition in Congress, backed by President Eisenhower's veto, precluded their passage. In the early 1960s, the pressure for government response to black needs and desires rapidly intensified. At the very time when poverty legislation was being considered, government leaders were especially concerned about racial change in urban America, with its effects on crime rates and political unrest and its possible impact on the New Deal coalition that formed the backbone of the Democratic party.

What was needed, among other things, was some form of structural linkage between political and governmental elites and a burgeoning black community.

The community action program, widely recognized as the heart of the Economic Opportunity Act, was suited to this purpose. In the first place, it was quite appropriately not civil rights legislation; applying such legislation to the North would not have easily modified that region's more subtle exclusionary practices and would have aroused great opposition from white urban Democrats.

Second, the poverty program was quite deliberately not a major cash trans-fer program handled either by the Social Security Administration or by state welfare agencies. Although such approaches were rejected partly for budgetary reasons, they also had the defect of not establishing any structural ties with an aroused black community.

Third, local communities were expected to form a new governmental structure, called a community action agency (CAA), that would administer and coordinate a new set of social services for the poor. The political advantages to this programmatic arrangement were numerous. As a new agency, it could be established in areas of greatest social and political need. It could recruit personnel with backgrounds and orientations suitable for achieving program goals, thereby giving blacks access to local government employment long denied them. And as a new agency, CAA needed to develop ties to a local constituency, with politically active civil rights and community organizations.

Maximum feasible participation thus legitimated and extended what CAAs in any case would necessarily have strived to achieve: a viable political relationship with local centers of power. Of equal importance, the National Democratic Administration created a political tie to the black community.

## THE BENEFITS OF MAXIMUM FEASIBLE PARTICIPATION

Any evaluation of the political linkage symbolized by maximum feasible participation must consider its benefits. To judge from the demise of maximum feasible participation, one might guess that either Democratic political elites or black community activists did not profit from the subsequent relationship. Quite the contrary, the very success of maximum feasible participation for both sides has made it obsolete.

Among popular commentators, maximum feasible participation was perceived as a disruptive, threatening, rabble-rousing policy without precedent in the administration of federal programs. Certainly, maximum feasible participation did disturb local bureaucrats and politicians in many central cities; but as threatening as these challenges were to certain individuals or interests, they never added up to a challenge to the urban-based Democratic coalition as a whole. Instead, the political support by blacks for the national Democratic party—only marginal in the 1950s—has been overwhelming since 1964. Of course, we have no precise statistical evidence demonstrating that maximum feasible participation decisively tied black voters to the Democratic party. Other forces, including the traditional tie stemming from the New Deal, were certainly important. But community action nonetheless provided many politically active blacks with a previously scarce opportunity to participate at a high level in the formulation of a significant sphere of government policy. Blacks framed general policies for the local community, recruited personnel, determined day-to-day activities, and were held accountable for results.[4]

They had access to government funds and to employment opportunities in community action programs, manpower training centers, neighborhood youth corps, the school system, private welfare agencies, and parks.

More than anything else, CAPs came to resemble political machines that had wedded previous urban migrants to the dominant parties of another generation.[5] No wonder Nixon tried to destroy community action; no wonder a Democratic Congress, at first fearful of maximum feasible participation, later endorsed and tried to sustain it.

Community action was in fact so successful in establishing linkage between urban blacks and Democratic political leaders that a number of analysts have seen it as a pure case of political co-optation by the white power structure.[6] Programs were devised either in Washington or by local bureaucracies before advisory committees were established. Even those committees usually contained majority representation for government, business, and other established interests. Community action programs themselves were, by and large, service-delivery programs, not enterprises that directly expanded the political power of low-income, minority group citizens.

One can only concur with John Strange who summarized his extensive review of analyses of CAPs in the following words: "In some cases the number of groups participating in the pluralistic contest for power and influence has been expanded . . . But it is generally agreed . . . that no radical redistributions of influence, power, services, rewards, or other benefits has occurred."[7]

While maximum feasible participation failed to radically change power distributions in America, it did successfully incorporate blacks within the pluralistic processes of American politics. For the first time, a program, from its inception, regarded itself as having special responsibilities for black Americans. Second, special efforts were made to identify black target areas, thus justifying heavy emphasis on black recruitment to staff positions and black access to government patronage. Third, since representatives of the poor were included on policy-making bodies, blacks, for the first time, were treated as a distinct interest whose stake in policy development needed deferential consideration. Finally, where the black community was particularly strong and militant, poverty resources helped to open political doors. Local boards and commissions replaced retiring white appointees with emergent black leaders; the 1972 national Democratic convention dramatically emphasized participation and representation; both parties subsequently legislated a commitment to a more racially representative national convention; the number of elected mayors grew from hardly any in 1964 to 108 in 1974;[8] and, nationally, the black caucus in the House of Representatives came to play an important role in the internal bargaining processes of the Democratic caucus. In sum, maximum feasible participation opened up new political opportunities for black elites.[9] Public institutions previously closed to them at least provided channels for the articulation of grievances, offices that could be competed for, employment opportunities that could be distributed, a legitimate point of access to policy makers, and concrete locales where blacks' power could be exercised.

## THE MEANING FOR TODAY'S POLITICS

Maximum feasible participation must be assessed by both its achievements and its limitations. The poor did not become a decisive political force through representation of CAP committees. CAPs developed their own bureaucratic empire without removing representatives from existing decision-making bodies. This minimized conflict and gave openings to blacks in a protected environment, separated from power centers where established white interests dominated.

Black leaders in many cities used the experience and contacts gained in poverty politics to build a base of power within the larger political system. Their success in penetrating established power centers has lessened the need for creating separate arenas for political participation. Such programs today could in fact be counterproductive, by misdirecting the attention of black activists now entrenching themselves within the Democratic party and inside numerous government agencies. The very success of maximum feasible participation in establishing black political power now makes its continuation unnecessary.

## NOTES

1. U.S. Congress, *Act to Mobilize the Human and Financial Resources of the Nation to Combat Poverty in the United States*, Public Law 88-452, 88th Cong., 2d Sess., 1964, p. 9.

2. This point has been made most vigorously in Daniel P. Moynihan, *Maximum Feasible Misunderstanding* (New York: Free Press, 1969). On the origins of the war on poverty, also see Sar A. Levitan, *The Great Society's Poor Law* (Baltimore: Johns Hopkins Press, 1969); James L. Sundquist, *Politics and Policy* (Washington, D.C.: The Brookings Institution, 1968), pp. 111-54; John Bibby and Roger Davidson, *On Capital Hill: Studies in the Legislative Process* (New York: Holt, Rinehart and Winston, 1967), pp. 219-351; Daniel P. Moynihan, "What is 'Community Action'?" *The Public Interest* 20 (fall 1966); "The Professionalization of Reform," *The Public Interest* 19 (fall 1965): 6-16; "Participation of the Poor . . .," *Yale Law Journal* 75 (March 1966): 602-05; Roger H. Davidson, "Poverty and the New Federalism," in *Dimensions of Manpower Policy: Research and Programs*, eds. Sar A. Levitan and Irving H. Siegal, pp. 61-80 (Baltimore: The Johns Hopkins Press, 1966).

3. This view of the origins of community action is presented most clearly in Frances Fox Piven and Richard Cloward, *Regulating the Poor* (New York: Pantheon, 1971), chapter 9.

4. See Murray Seidler, "Some Participant Observer Reflections on Detroit's Community Action Program," *Urban Affairs Quarterly* 5 (December 1965), for observations on this point that are particularly interesting.

5. Robert K. Merton, "The Latent Functions of the Machine," *Social Theory and Social Structure* (New York: Free Press, 1957), pp. 71-81.

6. This charge has been made by Theodore Lowi, *The End of Liberalism* (New York: Alfred Knopf, 1966). Examples mentioned in the paragraph that follows are taken from J. David Greenstone and Paul E. Peterson, *Race and Authority in Urban Politics* (New York: Russell Sage Foundation, 1973); Elliott A. Krause, "Functions of a Bureaucratic Ideology: Citizen Participation," *Social Problems* 16 (fall 1968): 129-43; Kenneth J. Pollinger and Annette C. Pollinger, *Community Action and the Poor: Influence vs. Social Control in a New York City Community* (New York: Praeger, 1972); Dale Rogers Marshall, *The Politics of Participation in Poverty: A Case Study of the Board of the Economic and Youth Opportunities Agency of Greater Los Angeles* (Berkeley: University of California Press, 1971).

7. John H. Strange, "Citizen Participation in Community Action and Model Cities Programs," *Public Administration Review* 32 (October 1972): 660.

8. Joint Center for Political Studies, "Telescope," *Focus* 2 (July 1974): 6.

9. With Weber we are distinguishing political from class and status hierarchies. See H. H. Gerth and C. Wright Mills, *From Max Weber: Essays in Sociology* (New York: Oxford University Press, 1958), pp. 180-95.

## CITIZENS AND THE
## NEW RULING COALITION
Clarence Stone

It is political power—embodied in part in citizen participation—and not administrative procedures that determines who gets what from a public policy and how effectively needs are met. Specifically, service programs with provisions for citizen participation—the kinds of programs spawned by the Great Society— provided a base from which urban minorities could develop and maintain a meaningful degree of political influence. If we eliminate service programs en masse and replace them with revenue sharing, block grants, and income supplements, we may undermine the political power of urban minorities. And, if we undermine the political power of urban minorities, social goals may never be properly met. The same danger is present in these new politics if there are not strong rules for citizen participation, but only lip service.

## HISTORICAL BACKGROUND

After the Second World War, almost all large cities saw the emergence of coalitions composed of (1) political executives, including some top-level administrators, (2) business leaders, and (3) technocrats. This coalition represented the "new convergence of power"[1] or the "executive-centered coalition."[2] The objectives were to upgrade the central business district, increase the tax base, and build support among the affluent and the middle class. While concessions were made occasionally to other groups, the planning and implementation of programs centered on the promotion of downtown commercial activity and on making urban life attractive to the affluent.

Older neighborhoods were bulldozed to make way for office buildings, luxury apartments, hotels, and civic centers. Relocation efforts were inadequate or nonexistent. The objective was not just to provide room for commercial activity, but to move the lower class away from the commercial center, away from high-status institutions, away from affluent residents. Businessmen were not interested in serving low-income shoppers, and they felt that too many of that group would lower the prestige of the downtown area. Technocrats and politicians did not want to serve a low-income clientele, which offered no easy opportunity for spectacular successes.

When Robert Salisbury first described the "new convergence of power" of the executive-centered coalition, he said that it was not powerful; it could not do much to solve the urban crisis. Indeed, for much of the post-World War Two period, the conventional wisdom has been that political influence is dispersed among a variety of "veto groups" and that governmental authority is fragmented. Only rare individuals with exceptional skills, in unusually favorable circumstances, could govern effectively. As Theodore Lowi noted, most cities are ungoverned.[3] While they may be managed with a minimum of graft and corruption, they are not truly governed.

To be sure, we have had few outstanding leaders and no ruling elite. Instead we have three separate elements in the executive-centered coalition—executive leadership, bureaucratic expertise, and business—held together by a common commitment to economic growth.

The coalition rested on a number of favorable conditions, but four factors stand out: (1) the decline of traditional politics, (2) the presence of a passive lower-class constituency, (3) a political vacuum that could easily be filled by executive leadership, and (4) the emergence of a "reform" orientation in city politics.

The executive-centered coalition represented a transition from ward politics to bureaucratic politics. It was the system through which the ability to sell a policy—to convince—replaced old-style bossism as a way of getting things done.

With party organizations declining in strength, the news media assumed great importance as a link between chief executives and citizens. Inevitably, good public relations meant the adoption of a good government image, the cultivation of an activist image, and the promotion of projects (such as downtown revitalization) in which the major newspapers were interested. A good government appeal required the appearance of respectability—projects endorsed by blue ribbon committees composed of business leaders and other civic "statesmen." The appearance of respectability meant the utilization of experts (justifications surrounded by the aura of science were more pleasing than those that emerged directly from the smoke-filled room of politics). It meant extensive use of the private sector, since strictly public projects looked too much like patronage politics in operation. The promotion of private sector activity through programs like urban renewal, in fact, provided profit opportunities that were not lost on important business interests, but such projects appeared to be less of a power grab than did strictly public projects.

The executive-centered coalition, as suggested earlier, was not interested in projects just for the sake of program activity. It had a bias toward economic growth. Economic growth met the immediate needs of coalition members but could be sold on the basis of serving the whole community. Expanding the tax base, producing revenues, and providing jobs—in the abstract, at least— were goals of general benefit.

## THE DECLINE OF THE EXECUTIVE-CENTERED COALITION AND THE EMERGENCE OF A POST-REFORM ERA

The executive-centered coalition, however, contained the seeds of its own destruction. Administrative agencies, which in their youth looked to executive leadership, now have asserted their independence; they have cultivated their own constituencies, devised internal procedures for initiating new programs, and developed their own skills in mobilizing support and in generating revenue. The shroud of expertise, the solidarity of occupational groups, and the disapprobation that once accompanied "political intervention" have provided substantial protection against executive control.

Agency autonomy has come at a cost, however—not a cost borne separately by individual agencies, but one borne by the whole establishment. The political consciousness spawned in the 1960s and the widening scope of administrative activity have shown city residents that many programs have hidden costs. Hence, groups look not only at the direct costs of programs, but also at the opportunity costs. What projects are being sacrificed? The tradeoff of projects is thus a political process. Hence, planning and setting priorities have become political exercises; and because there is no overwhelming consensus on priorities, it is difficult to sell any program as something in the interest of the whole community.

Thus, with a mere active and politically savvy constituency, politicians are less comfortable with the old alliances. Further, economic growth is no longer an unchallenged objective. Consequently, what was the new convergence of power or executive-centered coalition is rapidly becoming a new divergence of power as the post-reform era's spirit of conflict and competition by groups over limited resources grows.

## THE STAKES OF URBAN POLITICS AND HOW THEY MIGHT BE DIVIDED

The decline of the executive-centered coalition, however, does not mean that nonaffluent citizens will be better off. The same incentives that motivated the executive-centered coalition still exist. The business community is still well organized and will use its power to protect property and promote economic growth.

Chief executives and public bureaucracies are still eager for large budgets, room for innovation, and a clientele that brings prestige and quick success. On the other hand, a high level of service to nonaffluent clients is likely to evoke controversy but often little visibility or success. Even if a social program succeeds, it is likely to involve mostly intangible results that will take a long time to surface.

Again, the dynamics of the political situation do not assure that the nonaffluent consumers of urban services are any better off than under the executive-centered coalition. While technocrats are no longer surrounded by a mystique of expertise that makes them immune to criticism, technical complexity does limit public oversight of official decision making. Hence, programs may outlive specific protest organizations. Programs are often too complicated to lend to the kind of drama needed to sustain protest, and protests tend to produce ephemeral victories.[4]

The need for organization in the scramble for tangible benefits is evident because it seems that the prime beneficiaries of the post-reform era in city politics have been the employees of public agencies, not the consumers of urban services.[5] Employees in a given program area hold sufficient common interests to form cohesive organizations, and, as a well-organized group, they have a variety of sanctions they can wield.

A politically aware public is not necessarily a politically rewarded one. Consumers of urban services are aware of their needs, and they are aware of the political process as a way of meeting them. However, as long as constituents are not organized as service consumers, they are likely to be politically ineffective. The truth is that any good politician is able to mobilize support on the basis of rhetoric and skillful manipulation of the media without delivering tangible goods or services.

To be sure, mayors have some power to set and meet priorities, but that power is often used to benefit organized groups with power. That a mayor is elected by a predominantly nonaffluent constituency is no guarantee that the tangible needs of that constituency will be met.

To get their needs met, nonaffluent residents need to be organized around tangible concerns. They also need to participate in the low-visibility decisions that characterize city government, for urban politics is a struggle that encompasses subtle decisions and these affect the distribution of services.

It might be argued that a community cannot provide services unless it first has revenues; that is, human needs must necessarily take second place to economic growth. But economic growth may have unforeseen social costs that further exacerbate human needs. Therefore, the policy process should be based on total community involvement.

Business and technocrats will have their interests represented in the process. Public employees will be represented by their unions. The missing element, the group that has had little influence in either the old executive-centered coalition or the current post-reform period, is the service-consuming, non-affluent public.

## MAJOR ALTERNATIVES BEFORE URBAN COMMUNITIES

Since there are multiple and conflicting demands on city hall, policy decisions may arise from one of three approaches. Under some conditions (that is, a relatively noncontentious citizenry), the city officials may try to cater to the executive-centered coalition. The Sam Massell mayoralty in Atlanta (1970-74) provides one example of this strategy.

Massell ran on a platform of expanding the supply of low-income housing and improving services to the poor. Once in office, however, he sought business support, promoted economic growth, and postponed human needs. His political promises to eliminate slums and rehouse the poor lost priority. Ironically, although Massell had been elected with the overwhelming support of the black community, his major concern was the central business district.

The second alternative, political polarization, represents racial cleavage as urban minorities confront the vested interests and already established centers of power. The politics of polarization may come about either through an external attempt to force change on city hall or through an internal attempt to promote change through the mayor's office. The Ivan Allen mayoralty in Atlanta (1962-70) provides a useful example of the former, and the Carl Stokes mayoralty in Cleveland (1967-71) offers a good illustration of the latter.

In Atlanta in the 1960s a series of neighborhood protests and a few relatively minor outbreaks of civil disorder served (temporarily) to reorient official thinking and reorder city hall priorities. Once the protests lost strength and the threat of civil disorder subsided, the city's efforts to rehouse the poor and to improve neighborhood conditions faltered. Mayor Allen accepted the view of the business community that social programs would serve to make Atlanta a magnet for the poor. He therefore advocated policies to maintain a "proper" economic balance.[6]

Allen, of course, came to the mayoralty from the presidency of the Atlanta Chamber of Commerce. He was a longstanding member of the so-called white power structure, and he was thoroughly imbued with a business perspective. What about someone with different predispositions? What about a black mayor who was willing to do battle with the establishment?

When Carl Stokes was inaugurated as mayor of Cleveland, he sought to pursue the coalition strategy and maintain the support of the white business community and news media. This attempt ran into many problems, however, and he began to strengthen his black political base. He appointed blacks to prominent positions in the city and organized the Twenty-first Congressional District Caucus to give blacks a political base independent of the Democratic party. He thus mobilized a cohesive black constituency as well as a scattering of white liberals.

Carl Stokes was able to achieve some tangible results—his administration built more than 5,000 units of low and moderate-income housing whereas the previous administration had built none.[7] Yet Stokes, by his own account, failed to accomplish one of his main objectives—the reform of the police department. Failure was not from lack of effort, but from lack of power.

Even before Carl Stokes became mayor, a Little Hoover Commission had found the police department to be disorganized and inefficient, with poor community relations.[8] As Stokes saw it, the department was "ingrown, defensive, and isolated."[9] But the mayor had difficulty controlling the department's middle level or rank and file. As Stokes observed, the department's "ability to comply with an order and thwart its purpose at the same time was uncanny."[10]

Change required conflict, but the press invariably interpreted this as a clash of personalities—not of issues, of which there were many. At one time or another, the mayor did battle with the city council, his own police commissioners, his own police chief, other commissioners, the Democratic party and its labor allies, the white newspapers, the county prosecutor's office, several members of the business community, and the suburbs in the Cleveland metropolitan area. Some battles he won, others he lost; but, as he himself observed, "fighting on many fronts" became a constant feature of his administration "and that alone took its toll."[11]

The business community proved increasingly uncooperative. From Stokes's perspective, the news media were unable to focus single-mindedly on substantive issues, but instead presented him with a series of challenges in the form of "rumor, conjecture, speculation, insinuation, and indirect charges."[12]

What lesson do we draw from the Cleveland experience? It is that the mayor alone cannot reform a city bureaucracy. If that bureaucracy is well entrenched and has powerful allies, it is almost sure to outlast the mayor.

A third alternative for cities is to develop the kinds of organized constituencies among urban minorities that make them a genuine part of the politics of mutual adjustment. This process constitutes an undramatic way in which the interests of urban minorities might be represented. In it, policy evolves gradually, encompasses multiple objectives, and involves as well as serves many interests. Some observers characterize this process as "disjointed incrementalism." According to Anthony Downs "a process of mutual adjustment ensues. Those who are unduly harmed by each decision supposedly recoup their losses by exercising whatever economic, moral, or political powers are available to them. Those who benefit use their powers to encourage more of the same. Presiding over this melee is a set of mainly reactive governments and other public agencies. They keep altering the rules of the game and their own programs and behavior so as to correct any grievous imbalances that appear."[13]

At this stage, the politics of mutual adjustment is more ideal than reality. Nonaffluent service consumers have to become an established part of the system before it is genuinely one of mutual adjustment. For nonaffluent service consumers to become an effective part of the policy system, they must have a stable base of political power and access to the processes of decision making.

The heart of the politics of mutual adjustment is agency-clientele relation. Since much of the local government impact on the lives of citizens comes out of the day-to-day routines of agency activities, only if the nonaffluent as service consumers become a fixed part of the agency routines and decisions is there any likelihood that policy adjustments will in fact become mutually satisfying.

## THE POLITICS OF MUTUAL ADJUSTMENT: IS IT FEASIBLE?

The main question about the politics of mutual adjustment is not its desirability, but its feasibility. The pitfalls are many. Such a politics requires that nonaffluent service consumers be an organized part of the political system—a requirement that may very well depend on our ability to develop workable mechanisms for citizen participation.

On this point, Douglas Yates's *Neighborhood Democracy* is an especially useful study. Yates found that citizen participation did increase administrative responsiveness and did, in some circumstances, stimulate the development of neighborhood leadership.[14] Norman and Susan Fainstein in their study of the citizen participation movement found that neighborhood groups could help create a climate in which bureaucratic innovation might take place and enable a more client-centered system to evolve.[15] Research has shown that those citizen participation structures that are most viable from the citizen perspective—the ones that are narrowly service-oriented and aimed at producing visible, short-run results[16]—are also the structures that are most acceptable to city officials. The individuals attracted to serve on such citizen boards are themselves similar in some notable respects to the ward heelers of old. Yates described them as "pragmatic, nonideological leaders who like to solve concrete problems."[17]

In part, the problem is one of creating an opening behind which citizen participation can take hold. This, in part, depends on national urban policy. To the extent that the federal government abandons meaningful citizen participation requirements in revenue sharing or block grants, pressure is removed from local governments to make genuine use of citizen boards. The 1974 Housing and Urban Development Act contains a citizen participation provision; but the legislation requires only (1) that citizens be involved in the planning stage (developing the application for a block grant)—not in the actual oversight and direction

# TABLE 17.1

## The Use of General Revenue Sharing Funds
## (January 1, 1972 — June 30, 1974 [in millions of dollars])

| Rank | Category of Use | All Govern- ments | Per- cent | States | Per- cent | Local Govern- ments | Per- cent |
|---|---|---|---|---|---|---|---|
| 1 | Public safety | 2,190 | 23 | 45 | 1 | 2,145 | 36 |
| 2 | Education | 2,068 | 22 | 2,000 | 57 | 68 | 1 |
| 3 | Transportation | 1,405 | 15 | 267 | 8 | 1,138 | 19 |
| 4 | General gov't/multi- pur. | 841 | 9 | 208 | 6 | 633 | 11 |
| 5 | Environmental pro- tection | 674 | 7 | 56 | 2 | 618 | 10 |
| 6 | Health | 645 | 7 | 231 | 7 | 414 | 7 |
| 7 | Recreation and cultural serv. | 425 | 4 | 40 | 1 | 385 | 6 |
| 8 | Other | 355 | 4 | 316 | 9 | 39 | 1 |
| 9 | Social services for the poor or aged | 354 | 4 | 229 | 7 | 125 | 2 |
| 10 | Financial adminis- tration | 188 | 2 | 24 | 7 | 164 | 3 |
| 11 | Housing and comm. development | 104 | 1 | 37 | 1 | 67 | 1 |
| 12 | Libraries | 101 | 1 | 6 | – | 95 | 2 |
| 13 | Economic develop- ment | 51 | 1 | 13 | – | 38 | 1 |
| 14 | Corrections | 43 | – | 43 | 1 | – | – |
| 15 | Social development | 22 | – | – | – | 22 | – |
| | TOTALS | 9,466 | 100 | 3,515 | 100* | 5,951 | 100 |

*Does not total due to rounding.

*Note*: Tax stabilization–82 percent of 34,487 state and local governments responding in September, 1974, indicated that GRS funds had enabled them to reduce taxes, hold tax rates stable or avoid new taxes.

*Source*: Office of Revenue Sharing, Jan. 1975.

of specific programs, and (2) that citizens be involved in the broadly focused work of developing a comprehensive program of community improvements. In short, the act was written in total disregard for everything that could be learned from the 1960s experience with citizen participation. It does not call for citizen involvement in the provision of concrete and specific services and there is no requirement that their decisions be binding.

It should also be pointed out that the move toward revenue sharing as opposed to categorical grants removes an incentive for cities to initiate and support the very kinds of programs most conducive to effective citizen participation. Narrowly defined programs with immediate client benefits (indeed, social programs of all kinds) are likely to be weakened in comparison with programs of physical reconstruction and economic growth.[18] The latter programs tend to involve the kind of long-range planning and the indirect benefits around which it is difficult to sustain citizen participation.

It should also be noted that a shift from the services to the income strategy of combating poverty would have the likely consequence of reducing citizen participation by removing some of the immediate and tangible benefits of service programs upon which citizens may focus. Thus, by failing to provide programs through which meaningful citizen participation can be developed, we may be increasing bureaucratic aloofness and political alienation, precisely at the time when we want to do just the reverse.

## THE NEED TO DEVELOP AND APPLY POLITICAL CRITERIA

Clearly, the trend of federal intergovernmental policy is toward allowing local governments greater freedom in choosing priorities. The arguments for budgetary flexibility are persuasive ones. Yet the greater degree of freedom accorded local governments should carry with it a greater degree of responsibility and accountability.

Thus, as cities make use of revenue sharing and block grants, as they structure programs and designate purposes, there is a need for urban minorities to make their own systematic evaluations of these programs. Clearly some of the criteria for evaluation should be the following: do the programs enhance the influence of and show regard for the interests of nonaffluent service consumers? Do the programs strike a balance between the meeting of human needs and the other demands on local government? Are there means by which service consumers themselves can say which human needs have priority and how they should be met?

Specifically, the following questions might be asked of every proposed program: (1) Does it offer constituents opportunities to organize around tangible concerns? (2) Does it give the nonaffluent access to bureaucratic deliberations and decision making? (3) Does it provide a lever against excessive concern with physical improvements and observable signs of progress?

If the above questions are asked about the specific programs proposed under revenue sharing and under various block grants, and if the answers to these questions are no's, then we must concede that the politics of mutual adjustment is still an unrealized ideal.

## NOTES

1. The term and the concept were developed by Robert H. Salisbury, "Urban Politics: The New Convergence of Power," *Journal of Politics* 246 (November 1964): 775-97.

2. The term comes from Robert A. Dahl, *Who Governs?* (New Haven: Yale University Press, 1961).

3. Theodore Lowi, "Machine Politics–Old and New," *The Public Interest* 9 (fall 1967): 83-92.

4. See, especially, Michael Lipsky, *Protest in City Politics* (Chicago: Rand McNally, 1970).

5. See the argument by Richard A. Cloward and Frances Fox Piven, *The Politics of Turmoil* (New York: Pantheon Books, Random House, 1934), pp. 314-51.

6. A full account of these events may be found in my *Economic Growth and Neighborhood Discontent* (Chapel Hill: University of North Carolina Press, forthcoming).

7. Throughout this section I am relying on Carl Stokes' autobiographical account of his mayoralty, *Promises of Power* (New York: Simon and Schuster, 1973). In this particular point, see p. 124.

8. Ibid., pp. 168-70.

9. Ibid., p. 172.

10. Ibid., p. 177.

11. Ibid., p. 246.

12. Ibid., p. 228. See also pp. 149-66.

13. Anthony Downs, *Urban Problems and Prospects* (Chicago: Markham Publishing Co., 1970), p. 38.

14. Douglas Yates, *Neighborhood Democracy* (Lexington, Mass.: Lexington Books, D.C. Heath, 1973).

15. Norman I. Fainstein and Susan S. Fainstein, *Urban Political Movements* (Englewood Cliffs, N.J.: Prentice-Hall, 1974), p. 213.

16. Much of the argument above is drawn from ibid., especially pp. 209-14. Also, by the same authors, see "Innovation in Urban Bureaucracies: Clients and Change," *American Behavioral Scientist* 15 (March/April 1972): 511-31.

17. Yates, op. cit., pp. 86-88.

18. Fainstein, op. cit., pp. 211-14.

# 18

## CRIME: TRENDS, CAUSES, AND NEEDED REFORMS
### Lee P. Brown

The present system for controlling crime has failed. Long a major problem in all large urban communities, crime has reached a magnitude some observers classify in epidemic terms. Almost without exception, cities with a substantial black population are suffering from an exceptionally high crime rate.

A 1973 Gallup poll showed that one out of every five persons in the United States had been the victim of some type of crime between December 1971 and December 1972. Figures for the central cities were even more alarming, showing a ratio of one to three persons. Respondents to the poll identified crime as the number one problem in their community. Over 50 percent of those responding felt that crime had increased in their area during the past year, and only 10 percent felt that there was less crime.[1]

## THE GOVERNMENTAL RESPONSE

Governmental efforts to reduce crime have not suffered from lack of money. To the contrary, government expenditures for criminal justice activities have been immense—almost $8.6 billion spent at all levels of government for the 1969-70 fiscal year, for instance. Approximately $5 billion—or three-fifths—went to support police activities.[2] In fiscal year 1972, the federal government alone spent $1,968,996,000 for crime reduction activities.[3]

While other federal agencies have been involved, the government's major effort to control crime has been through the Law Enforcement Assistance Administration (LEAA). Presently, LEAA's budget approaches $1 billion.

To date, the official strategy for reducing crime has been to strengthen the criminal justice system. This strategy was spelled out by former President

Richard Nixon on October 12, 1969, in an address to Congress when he requested "more police, more judges, more prosecutors, more courtroom space, a new public defender's office, better penal rehabilitation facilities and reform in the procedures for dealing with juvenile offenders."[4] In fact, LEAA was given the "specific mission of improving the entire criminal justice system through a comprehensive approach of assistance at all levels."[5] The bulk of its funds, however, go to local government through state block grants.

It is interesting to note the fluctuation in the crime rate in light of the expenditure of federal funds to fight the crime problem. According to FBI statistics, from 1960 to 1969 serious crime in the nation increased by 122 percent. In 1968, the FBI reported a 17 percent increase in the crime rate; in 1969, 12 percent; in 1970, 11 percent, and in 1971, 7 percent. In July 1972, the FBI reported that serious crime increased only 1 percent in the first quarter of 1972—the lowest increase in 11 years. During the last quarter of 1972, there was an 8 percent reduction in the crime rate. That decrease dropped to 1 percent through the first half of 1973. During the last three months of 1973, however, reported crimes went up by 16 percent. Figures for the first six months of 1974 also showed a 16 percent increase.[6]

Some criminologists have suggested that the apparent increase in crime after 1968 can, in fact, be attributed to governmental policy. The theory is that cities had to show a "crime problem" in order to receive LEAA funds. Similarly, it is speculated that the decline in the crime rate was also related to LEAA funding. This theory suggests that around 1970, to continue receiving funds, cities had to show progress in controlling the crime problem—hence a reported reduction in crime. This idea, however, is merely speculative, with no empirical research to support it.

The upsurge in reported crime in 1973 is also linked to national policy. As stated by Jerry V. Wilson, recently retired chief of the Washington, D.C. Metropolitan Police Department:

> The disclosures which are generically called "Watergate" began to unfold in the early summer and the administration could no longer speak out with authority on behalf of strong law enforcement. No longer could it convincingly call for stringent penalties for burglars and other law breakers. No longer was it possible to complain about lax plea bargaining and lenient judges.[7]

## QUESTIONING CRIME STATISTICS

Finding reliable data on the volume of crime is not easy. LEAA, recognizing the inequities in the existing system for reporting crime (for example, the FBI's *Uniform Crime Reports*), commissioned the U.S. Bureau of the Census to undertake a criminal victimization study. Among its findings:

Throughout the United States during the first 5 months of 1973, crimes of violence and common theft, including attempts, accounted for approximately 18 million victimizations of persons age 12 and over, households and businesses. Of the total number of victimization, about 57 percent concerned businesses.

The single, most prevalent type of crime was personal larceny, which comprised about 40 percent of all victimizations recorded . . .[8]

Victimization studies confirm the belief that crime is much more prevalent than reported to the police. Like many other aspects of American life, the problem of crime is not evenly distributed, nor is the criminal justice system equitable in its treatment of citizens.

There is ample evidence that blacks, for example, are more likely to be arrested than whites; when arrested, they are more likely to be prosecuted; when prosecuted, they are more likely to be convicted; when convicted, they are more apt to be imprisoned; and when imprisoned, they receive longer sentences.

FBI figures show that of all arrests in 1973, 28.5 percent of the arrestees were black. Blacks constituted 55.7 percent of those arrested for violent crime and 33.3 percent of those arrested for property crime.[9] In viewing these statistics, however, it should be kept in mind that they represent only those who have been arrested, and not necessarily those who committed an offense.

Additional evidence of the inequities of the criminal justice system can be seen in the following examples:

A 1969 study showed judges spent less time on cases involving blacks than those involving whites.

Another study conducted in 1969 revealed blacks are adjudged guilty more often than whites (41.7% vs. 28.3%).

The same study showed blacks accused of a felony are much less likely than whites to be placed on probation, which indicates that race affects penalty.

The above point was further supported by statistics which showed that among offenders sentenced to federal prisons in 1972, the average sentence was 43.3 months for whites and 58.7 months for non-whites.

In 1970, of the 479 condemned men on death row, more than half were black.

In 1970, whites convicted of income tax evasion were committed to federal prisons for an average of 12.8 months, non-whites for 28.6 months.

An LEAA study of local jails' inmates showed that 42 percent of all persons housed in such facilities were black.

A state prison inmate census conducted for LEAA revealed that in 1973 approximately 48 percent of all prisoners were black.[10]

Ironically, as a 1970 LEAA study stated, those "most likely to be victims of violent crimes are males, youths, poor persons and blacks."[11]

In November 1974, LEAA published the first national crime victim survey, which revealed that black males are crime victims at a rate of 85 per 1,000 persons, compared with a rate of 74 per 1,000 for white males. The survey revealed that across the country blacks are also more likely to be victims of assault, robbery, rape, and burglary. It is also noteworthy that black households have a higher burglary rate than do white homes in all income groups, from very poor to quite well-to-do.[12]

Outside of the social and psychological implications of the above, crime also has a disproportionate economic impact on the black community. It was estimated that in 1969 crime cost the black community approximately 10 percent of its aggregate family income as compared to less than 5 percent for whites.

Andrew F. Brimmer, formerly of the Federal Reserve Board, recognized the heavy economic toll exacted in black communities by unchecked crime:

. . . a significant share of the hard-earned income and a sizeable proportion of the wealth that the black community has struggled to accumulate are being dissipated through the wastage of criminal offenses. Moreover, the cost of crime is by no means evenly distributed in the . . . [black] community—just as it is not evenly distributed in the nation at large. Instead, the poorest members are far more likely to be victims—especially in cases of personal violence.[13]

In looking at the crime problem in America, it is essential to recognize that crime is not one-dimensional but rather multifaceted. Including not only violent and property offenses, but also white-collar criminality, organized crime, and the lawlessness of governmental officials, it must be attacked in its entirety.

## CRIME CONTROL MEASURES

That existing methods of controlling crime have failed is evident from its steady rise as reported by the FBI. The number of unsolved offenses cited in those reports attest to the fact that a majority of those who commit crimes are never apprehended. Furthermore, the correctional process has failed to rehabilitate many of those found guilty of criminal activities, as is evident from the high rate of recidivism.

Although the criminal justice system (police, courts, and corrections) has been assigned the role of controlling crime, it cannot do the job alone. Community involvement is not merely desirable, but necessary.[14] What is needed is a fresh approach, an approach which considers the following fact:

> Government programs for the control of crime are unlikely to succeed all alone. Informed private citizens, playing a variety of roles, can make a decisive difference in the prevention, detection and prosecution of crime, the fair administration of justice, and the restoration of offenders to the community.[15]

Prevention of crime, rather than the mere detection, apprehension, conviction and incarceration of offenders, must be the number one priority in the control of crime. More policemen, better equipment, more prosecutors and judges, and larger prisons are not the answer.

To the contrary, as stated by the National Advisory Commission, "the highest attention must be given to preventing juvenile delinquency, to minimizing the involvement of young offenders in the juvenile and criminal justice system, and to reintegrating delinquents and young offenders into the community."[16] If the cycle of recidivism is to be broken, it must begin with young people, since the more involvement a youth has with the formal criminal and juvenile justice systems, the more likely it is that he will be further involved.[17]

A second priority of the National Advisory Commission is that "public agencies should improve the delivery of all social services to citizens, particularly to those groups that contribute higher than average proportions of their numbers to crime statistics.[18] The preponderance of evidence suggests crime is much higher among those groups who are the victims of poverty, racism, illiteracy, discrimination, and unemployment, and where medical, recreation, and mental health resources are inadequate.[19] It is not difficult to make the correlation between crime and jobs when the crime rate is the highest in areas of the city with consistent unemployment rates of almost 40 percent. It is also not difficult to make the correlation between crime and poverty when "46 percent of the black jail inmates had been earning less than $2,000 a year when arrested, and another 12 percent had been earning less than $3,000 a year."[20] Nor is it difficult to make a correlation between crime and education when 64 percent of the blacks in state prisons have failed to complete high school.[21]

A third and most important priority of the National Advisory Commission is that "citizens should actively participate in activities to control crime in their communities."[22] This strongly suggests that government funding of community programs to reduce crime is a must.

Stating that the community must be involved is not to suggest that the agencies of the criminal justice system do not have a significant role to play. Their success in fulfilling that mission, however, is contingent upon the development of new definitions of their tasks and new directions for their operations.

It must first be recognized that the term criminal justice system is in itself an overstatement. In reality, the system represents separate components (police, courts, and corrections) with different and often conflicting goals. This dichotomy was best summed up by the President's Crime Commission when it wrote:

> The police role . . . is focused on deterrence. Most modern correctional thinking, on the other hand, focuses on rehabilitation and argues that placing the offender back into society under a supervised community treatment program provides the best chance for his rehabilitation as a law-abiding citizen. But community treatment may involve some loss of deterrent effect, and the ready arrest of marginal offenders, intended to heighten deterrence, may be affixing a criminal label complicating rehabilitation. The latent conflicts between the parts may not be apparent from the viewpoint of either subsystem, but there is an obvious need to balance and rationalize them so as to achieve optimum over-all effectiveness.[23]

Couple the intramural conflict among the components of the criminal justice system with the exclusion of community agencies from the process, and it is easy to see why the nation has been unsuccessful in mounting a unified attack on the crime problem.

Since the police are the most visible element of the criminal justice system—and its entry port—the bulk of the discussion that follows will be devoted to police problems. It is not too much to say that in the minds of much of the general public the police represent not only the law but "government."

## THE POLICE

Police agencies tend to reflect the attitudes of the community they serve. For example, in homogeneous communities with similar cultures, values, class, race, and social status, the police tend to function as part of the community, with a minimum of conflict. They are supported by the life-style of the community they are serving.

On the other hand, in communities characterized by differences in race, values, cultures, social class, and status, the police are often at odds with certain segments of the community. Problems occur because the police tend to be responsive not to all segments of the community, but rather to its prevailing power structure. Thus, blacks, for example, come to view the police not as their protectors, but as protectors of the status quo and representatives of those forces that they view as the source of their frustrations.

Rather than viewing their role in the narrow context of "crook catchers," police must see themselves as service agencies, with law enforcement only one, though an important, aspect of the services they render. Their first priority, and indeed the first priority of the total community, should be crime prevention, but some traditional assumptions under which the police operate must be questioned. For example, in view of some experiments across the nation, one must ask whether preventive patrol is a worthwhile crime reduction strategy. Is there a real relationship between a response time and apprehension of offenders?

In developing goals for law enforcement, the following statement developed by the Multnomah County (Oregon) Department of Public Safety might prove helpful:

1.  Provide emergency actions and services, not readily available from other agencies, that may save human life.
2.  Provide programs and actions directed at the causes and conditions of delinquency and crime that will result in the prevention of juvenile delinquency, criminal deviancy and crime.
3.  Provide programs and actions to acquire information about criminal behavior and responsibility and expeditiously handle that information in a manner consistent with the best interest of involved persons, the community and society.
4.  Respond by direct involvement, advice or referral to those situations which if left unattended would logically result in serious mental anguish, disorder, injury, property damage or loss of individual rights for people within the jurisdiction.
5.  Provide actions and programs for coordination between support agencies that seek to facilitate social justice and justice processes.
6.  Provide order maintenance programs and actions to reduce danger and facilitate normal community and social operations during periods of unusual disruptive occurrences such as civil protest, natural disaster, riot and war.
7.  Provide programs, procedures and activities that will result in efficient, effective and fair management of the police organization and satisfaction of personnel career needs.[24]

As a second step in redefining their mission, the police must acknowledge that arrest and incarceration of suspects is not always in the best interest of the individual or society. Diverting suspected offenders from the criminal justice system should be recognized as a legitimate alternative available to the police and used accordingly. The youth service bureau concept is one appropriate strategy that should be adopted by the community in support of diversion.

Third, municipal and county policy makers must recognize the importance of competent police leadership. Police executives must be selected for their ability as managers and not solely on such criteria as their success as detectives or investigators. Development in the police profession has occurred faster at the lower levels than at the top. This trend must be reversed.

Fourth, the central theme that should guide all aspects of police reform is the need for citizen involvement. The police must abandon their element of secrecy and allow all segments of the public to contribute to policies and procedures. In our form of government, the police and the military must be accountable to the citizenry.

Fifth, the recruitment and retention of qualified personnel is the key to effective policing. Too often police recruitment efforts emphasize the "spirit of adventure" rather than "the spirit of service." Ideally, the composition of police departments should mirror the composition of the community. It is indeed ironic that blacks comprise over 12 percent of the nation's population but only about 4 percent of the police personnel.

The need for increased minority representation on police departments has been adequately documented by at least two presidential commissions. The 1967 Presidential Commission on Law Enforcement and Administration of Justice pointed out that departments policing minority communities with only white officers leave themselves vulnerable to the charge of being an occupying force. Additionally, the commission noted that minority officers can help overcome racial stereotypes held by white officers and can aid in policing the minority community because of their familiarity with its cultural differences.

More recently, the National Advisory Commission on Criminal Justice Standards and Goals advanced a standard that urges that police agencies "take affirmative action to achieve a ratio of minority group employees in approximate proportion to the makeup of the population."[25] An affirmative action program must include more than mere espousing the position of being "an equal opportunity employer." Rather, it must recognize that the disproportionate representation of blacks in police work is directly related to the total race relations situation in America today.

Young black men and women have read and taken seriously the report of the Kerner Commission, which stated that "what white Americans have never fully understood—but the Negro can never forget—is that white society is deeply implicated in the ghetto. White institutions created it, white institutions maintained it and white society condones it." Young blacks thus see the police selection process as designed to screen them out rather than bring them in. This situation can be corrected if police agencies couple their stated desire for more minority officers with affirmative action. Selection procedures should be thoroughly revised. For example, are the written examinations valid, job related, and culturally unbiased? Do oral examination boards include minorites? Are minor arrest records used to exclude candidates without good cause? Essentially, each police agency should "insure that it presents no artificial or arbitrary barriers—cultural or institutional—to discourage qualified individuals from seeking employment or from being employed as police officers."26

A sixth essential in redefining the mission of police agencies is reexamination of the training program. A veteran police official says that it is at the recruit academy that the umbilical cord binding the rookie to the civilian is clipped.27 What this suggests is that police training programs, by taking away the officers' ties with the community, do not adequately prepare new officers for the realities of the job. For example, study after study has shown that the police spend only 10 to 15 percent of their time in law enforcement activities, although 85 to 90 percent of their training is in this area. Individuals leaving the training program must view themselves as representatives of an agency that is an integral part of and responsive to a society composed of varying cultures and life-styles.

The method by which the police handle citizens' complaints alleging misconduct by officers is probably the sorest point in police and community relationships. Existing procedures, often biased in favor of the police, have led some observers to label the police complaint mechanism the "world's largest washing machine"—everything that goes in dirty comes out clean. Not only conscience, but also good administrative practice calls for establishment of some mechanism to ensure a person who is aggrieved by official action a chance to be heard and the knowledge that his complaint will be handled with respect and the power and willingness to correct wrongful police actions. The attempts to establish civilian review boards are good examples of what happens when large segments of the public distrust the police method of handling citizens' complaints. This problem can be alleviated by establishing a mechanism independent of the police department, but part of city government, to handle all complaints against governmental officials, including the police. This suggestion is consistent with the recommendations made by the President's crime commission.

The importance of effective policies to control the use of firearms by the police is a very critical issue. Recent research revealed that if a person is killed by a stranger in a large city, a great percent of the time the assailant will be a police officer.

What is generally not known by the public and is either unknown or unpublicized by the police and other officials is the alarming trend in deaths of male citizens caused by, in the official terminology, "legal intervention of police." These are the cases recorded on the death certificate as justifiable homicide by legal intervention.28 Of particular concern is the fact that "black men have in fact been killed by police at a rate some nine to ten times that of white men."29

Cities should adopt the National Crime Commission's firearms use policy, which calls for the prohibition of any lethal force except in self-defense or the defense of a citizen after all other means have failed. Police agencies should operate under the policy that lethal force must not only be legally justified, but socially and morally warranted as well, and in keeping with the ideas of rational and humane social control.

Official corruption is acute when the police, society's enforcers of the law, are involved. Only recently has the problem been officially acknowledged by the International Association of Chiefs of Police, the professional body that represents the interests of law enforcement. But more is needed than just the mere acknowledgement that corruption exists. Independent agencies should be established on a statewide basis to investigate and prosecute all forms of official corruption, including that involving the police. Police officials should be required periodically to disclose their financial holdings. Stringent codes of ethics should be developed and institutionalized into the police establishment to bring about peer pressures as a means of dealing with corruption.

Police-community relations programs, as traditionally operated by police departments, have failed. The chief reason is that the functions of police-community relations were viewed as the responsibility of police-community relations officers and separate from the operational aspects of police work. Many such programs amounted to little more than public relations programs designed to improve the police image.

An effective police-community relations program must involve examination of police policies and procedures in light of their negative impact on the community. It must carry with it the willingness and ability to change abrasive policies and procedures. It must be included in the training and retraining of police officers and must include the community as an equal partner. It must address even those conditions that are of concern to the community residents but are traditionally considered to be non-law enforcement issues.

Federal funds designed specifically for improving police and community relationships should be made available to both community groups and the police. No aspect of police reform is more important.


## COURTS AND CORRECTIONS

A full discussion of the problems of the courts and corrections is not possible in this forum. Each is crucial to the sound functioning of the criminal justice system, however, so a few of their weaknesses must be highlighted.

High on any agenda for court reform should be a ban on plea bargaining. This self-defeating practice lures prosecutors into lodging more serious charges than can be justified so that they will have something to trade away when the bargaining begins. Although it is the means by which more than 90 percent of criminal cases are disposed of, it is an overrated method of clearing dockets.

"Elimination of plea bargaining is likely to create less of an increase in the number of trials than many believe. It is virtually certain, however, that it will increase the fairness and rationality of the processing of criminal defendants."[30]

Greater thought also must be given to reducing the discrepancies in sentencing, a failing of the courts that often inflicts harsher penalties on blacks and other minorities than on white defendants. Juries should not be involved in sentencing, but judges, who would then do the job alone, should receive more meaningful training in that critical task. Indeterminate sentences, a major source of frustration for prisoners, must be abolished.

Judges should be just as accountable to the public as other officials, and the way to accomplish this is to make judgeships elective offices. This would doubtless bring more blacks and other minorities to the bench. Of 16,000-plus state judges, only about 325 are black. In federal courts they number fewer than 20 out of 600.

In discussing the American correctional system, the National Advisory Commission on Criminal Justice Standards and Goals stated that it offers "minimum protection for the public and maximum harm to the offender. The system is plainly in need of substantial and rapid change."[31] Such a commentary is indeed sad in view of the awesome responsibility of that system. The nation's recidivism rate, however, leaves little room for arguing the merits of the observation.

Essentially, the correctional system does not correct. Rather, it often generates greater criminality in those it incarcerates. It is costly. It overlaps and duplicates institutions. It is overcrowded. Most of all, it operates under philosophies that at best can be considered antiquated, and at worst, brutal and inhumane. In fact, the deleterious conditions in many prisons have led the entire prison system of some states to be declared unconstitutional through violation of the Eighth Amendment's prohibition against cruel and unusual punishment.[32]

Most progressive individuals in the correctional field believe that the most promising solution to the current dilemma is to abandon the outdated nineteenth-century philosophy of locking offenders up for long periods of time in large prisons. As forcefully stated by the National Advisory Commission: "Our institutions are so large that their operational needs take precedence over the needs of the people they hold. The very scale of these institutions dehumanizes, denies privacy, encourages violence, and defies decent control."[33]

It would seem, based upon the failure of the existing correctional system, that a new approach must be developed. Such an approach should call for a moratorium on construction of any new large correctional facility.[34] Instead, programs should be developed to treat offenders in the community. Treatment of offenders in the environment in which they must eventually function is the most promising direction for effective correction. It represents an extension of what has already proved to be more effective and less costly than incarceration. For example, over two-thirds of those in the correctional system are currently in some type of community-based program such as probation, parole, or work or study release. The one-third that are imprisoned is too many.

Greater utilization must be made of volunteers, of minorites, of women. Citizens should be involved in setting correctional policy. Although many correctional institutions have a majority nonwhite population, only about 8 percent of the nation's correctional employees are nonwhite. At the time Attica exploded, 54 percent of the inmates were black, yet there was only one black on the staff.

Since many offenders are deficient in education and training, improvements must be made in such opportunities for offenders, be they institutionalized or on probation or parole. To do otherwise is to continue the vicious cycle of recidivism.

## IN SUMMARY

The problem of crime in America is pervasive and immense. Its solution calls for a concerted effort on the part of the entire community. All segments of society must join forces to eradicate those socioeconomic conditions that are considered the root causes of crime. These surely include unemployment, inadequate housing, inferior education, overcrowding, discrimination, racism, and inadequate health and recreational resources. Indeed, the community has a responsibility that has yet to be realized. The government has a responsibility to see that funds are made available to community organizations to assist them in the battle against crime. If the nation is sincere about controlling the crime problem, benign neglect is not the answer.

By the same token, the criminal justice system must develop new approaches to the crime problem. The components of the system must deviate from the traditional mode and concern themselves with the social injustices that breed crime, for they are the ones that must handle the problems nurtured by poverty, ignorance, racism, bitterness, and despair. It is not sufficient for the criminal justice system to operate under a philosophy that social and economic problems are the concern of social justice agencies.

The criminal justice system can ill afford to continue to be society's janitor, sweeping society's debris under the rug and thereby making the solutions to the problems even more difficult. Instead, it must realize that the public mandate being voiced in no uncertain terms is "change or be changed."

## NOTES

1. Gallup poll, January 13, 1973 and January 15, 1973.
2. Law Enforcement Assistance Administration (LEAA), *Expenditures and Employment Data for the Criminal Justice System: 1969-70* (Washington, D.C.: U.S. Government Printing Office, 1972).
3. Attorney General's First Annual Report, *Federal Law Enforcement and Criminal Justice Activities* (Washington, D.C.: U.S. Government Printing Office, 1972), p. 4.
4. For the text of that address, see New York *Times*, October 12, 1969, p. 64.
5. Attorney General's First Annual Report, p. 39.
6. Ibid. Also see Jerry V. Wilson, "Government Influence on Crime," Washington *Post*, October 17, 1974, p. A18.

7. Wilson, ibid., p. A18.

8. U.S. Department of Justice, *Criminal Victimization in the United States: January-June 1973*, Vol. 1 (Washington, D.C.: U.S. Government Printing Office, November 1974), pp. 1-2.

9. Clarence M. Kelley, *Federal Bureau of Investigation Report: Crime in the United States* (Washington, D.C.: U.S. Government Printing Office, 1973), p. 142.

10. National Advisory Commission on Criminal Justice Standards and Goals, *A National Strategy to Reduce Crime* (Washington, D.C.: U.S. Government Printing Office), 1973, p. 14.

11. Lee P. Brown, "Crime, Criminal Justice and the Black Community." *The Journal of Afro-American Issues* 2, no. 2 (May 1974): 95.

12. Richard W. Velde, "Blacks and Criminal Justice," an address delivered before the Second Annual Conference on Blacks and the Criminal Justice System, University of Alabama, February 5, 1975.

13. Andrew F. Brimmer, "An Economic Agenda for Black Americans," a speech delivered before the Charter Day Convocation celebrating the one hundred fifth anniversary of Atlanta University, October 16, 1970.

14. National Advisory Commission on Criminal Justice Standards and Goals, *Community Crime Prevention* (Washington, D.C.: U.S. Government Printing Office, 1973), p. 7.

15. Ibid.

16. National Advisory Commission on Criminal Justice Standards and Goals, op. cit., p. 23.

17. Marvin E. Wolfgang, Robert M. Figlio, and Thorsten Sellin, *Delinquency in a Birth Cohort* (Chicago: The University of Chicago Press, 1972).

18. National Advisory Commission on Criminal Justice Standards and Goals, op. cit., p. 25.

19. Ibid.

20. Velde, p. 2.

21. Ibid.

22. Brown, op. cit., p. 27.

23. National Advisory Commission on Criminal Justice Standards and Goals, *Criminal Justice System* (Washington, D.C.: U.S. Government Printing Office, 1973), p. 1.

24. Multnomah County (Oregon) Department of Public Safety, *Neighborhood Team Policing Proposal*, unpublished, p. 20.

25. National Advisory Commission on Criminal Justice Standards and Goals, *Police* (Washington, D.C.: U.S. Government Printing Office, 1973), p. 329.

26. Ibid.

27. Arthur Niederhoffer, *Behind the Shield: The Police in Urban Society* (Garden City, N.Y.: Anchor Books, 1967), p. 43.

28. Phillip Buell and Paul Takagi, "Code 984: Death by Police Intervention," *The Journal of Afro-American Issues* 2, no. 2: 110.

29. Ibid.

30. National Advisory Commission on Criminal Justice Standards and Goals, *Courts* (Washington, D.C.: U.S. Government Printing Office, 1973), p. 46.

31. National Advisory Commission on Criminal Justice Standards and Goals, *Corrections* (Washington, D.C.: U.S. Government Printing Office, 1973), p. 113.

32. Ibid., pp. 113-14.

33. National Advisory Commission on Criminal Justice Standards and Goals, *Corrections* (Washington, D.C.: U.S. Government Printing Office, 1973), p. 12.

34. Ibid.

# 19

## THE DISCRETION
## OF JUDGES
George W. Crockett

If you were driving down the highway and you violated a traffic signal and the state trooper pulled you over and gave you a lecture instead of a ticket, you would say that he was a very understanding policeman. The next day you might be driving down that highway, absentmindedly doing the same thing. The state policeman might pull you over and give you a ticket. I will not undertake to use the language you would use to describe him. In each of these cases, the officer is exercising what lawyers refer to as police discretion.

If you complain that your neighbor attacked you with a stick, the prosecutor has a choice of charging your neighbor with one of about five different criminal offenses, ranging from assault and battery to assault with intent to murder and carrying penalties from 90 days to life imprisonment. In deciding which one of these charges to make against your neighbor, he would be exercising what we call prosecutorial discretion. It is difficult for lawyers to decide where discretion ends and individual compromise begins, so it must be next to impossible for laymen to understand the distinction.

What is judicial discretion? Let me give a few definitions. Discretion in one sense is explained as

> the power exercised in court to determine questions to which no strict rule of law is applicable but which from their nature and the circumstances of the case are controlled by the personal judgement of the court. Discretionary in that sense is said to be final and cannot be set aside on an appeal except when there is an abuse of discretion.

Another comment on what is meant by discretion: "It is that power of decision exercised to the necessary end of awarding justice based upon reason and the law but for which decision there is no special governing statute or rule." To summarize all of this in my own words, judicial discretion is the art of judging, of balancing, competing social considerations, especially in areas that are uncontrolled by statutes, ordinances, judicial precedents, or other fixed rules of law.

Interestingly, the overwhelming bulk of the decisions a trial judge is called upon to make relate to the area of judicial procedure, not substance. Equally interesting is the fact that most judicial procedure is not controlled by statutes, ordinances, or other fixed rules but is left to the discretion of trial court judges. Examples would include motions to change the place of trial, to adjourn, to require disclosure of evidence, to challenge the legality of an arrest or the admissibility or exclusion of evidence. All of these rulings are subject to judicial discretion. It is no wonder, then, that most of the injustices cited by minority groups relate to this broad area of judicial procedure in which the individual judge is authorized by law to exercise his judicial discretion. That discretion, like all discretion, will reflect the background and basic philosophy of the particular judge.

I recall travelling in the Soviet Union and meeting with Soviet professors, judges, and lawyers. The thing that they were most proud of, as far as their judicial system was concerned, was the Soviet citizen's "right to legality." After considerable questioning, I discovered that it meant simply this: every Soviet citizen must be punished in the same way for the same violation of law. In Washington, judicial discretion would probably dictate that a college professor caught driving drunk would not be sentenced to clean the sidewalks as a construction worker might be required to do. In the Soviet Union, both would be out cleaning the sidewalks. There is very little room for judicial discretion under Soviet law.

I mentioned some of the areas in which trial judges exercise judicial discretion and to that extent determine the physical freedom citizens enjoy. Take the whole area of arrest, search, and seizure. Under the law you can be arrested and deprived of freedom whenever a police officer has probable cause to believe that a crime has been committed and that you may have committed it. But what is probable cause? There again, it is left to the discretion of the judge to decide whether or not a given situation was sufficient to constitute probable cause.

Suppose a police officer sees someone getting out of a taxi at night in an area known to be frequented by narcotics users, look in the direction of the uniformed officer, and immediately get back into the car, lean forward, and reach down to the floor. Is the police officer justified in deciding that he has probable cause to believe that the passenger has narcotics or is carrying a pistol in the car? If so, then he may arrest the incriminating evidence. One judge will decide that there was probable cause and a valid arrest in this case. Another judge, perhaps on the same bench, will decide that furtive conduct alone was not enough, that the arrest and search were invalid, that the evidence thus obtained was illegal, and that the case should be dismissed. The difference in the result, then, is the difference in the background and philosophy of the two judges exercising judicial discretion.

Take the whole issue of bail, which is very much in the forefront today. The law is that bail must be reasonable, not excessive; but what is reasonable to one judge may not be reasonable to another. Take the question of jury selection and the extent to which the trial·judge will allow questioning of prospective jurors to uncover latent prejudices. A few years ago I presided at the trial of a rape case. The plaintiff was a 17-year-old white girl and the two defendents were adult black men. I felt that under these circumstances there was a necessity to probe the possible racial or color prejudices of the prospective jurors, and I did so. The law did not require me to do this, and hardly any white judge would have done it—because this was a matter of judicial discretion.

Take the matter of sentencing; one judge gives two years and another ten. The legislature has given the trial judge judicial discretion to decide, within a minimum and a maximum, what a sentence shall be. Take the matter of release on probation; there again you have the operation of judicial discretion. I think I shocked many of my colleagues when I announced I would automatically put a defendent on probation when I was convinced that he was a victim of police brutality. Complaint was made to the chief justice of Michigan, who was compelled to announce publicly that I had discretion to do this if I so decided.

I could go on giving other examples of judicial discretion, but I think I have given you some idea of the sheer power we Americans have vested in our judges. Ever since the famous eyeball-to-eyeball confrontation between Supreme Court Chief Justice John Marshall and President Thomas Jefferson, judges alone have had the right to determine the meaning of the law. We judges tell presidents what they can and cannot do. We tell whole legislatures to disband and to reconstitute themselves.

This leads to my second point. We have in this country approximately 20,000 judges of courts of record who exercise that sheer power I am talking about. Of that number, only 385 are black. Look at any other minority in this country; one of the first things minority groups do as soon as they obtain political consciousness is to recognize where the power is and go to the polls (or use their political influence) to get representation in the judicial branch of the government. One judge and one decision can do more to protect your rights than any elected mayor. But we blacks seem to concentrate on electing mayors; we pride ourselves in saying that we have a black mayor who is taking over some bankrupt metropolitan city. When we go to the polls to vote, we don't even look at the judicial ballot. That, I submit, is where the power is.

Now I get down to my crucial point. Of these 385 black judges, some are engaged in the process of bringing this country back to its constitutional moorings and are catching hell in the process. Bruce Wright of New York insists that, under the constitution, bail is supposed to be an assurance that the accused will be available for trial and not a punishment. He is using his judicial discretion to reform the police department's high bail policy, and the police department of the city of New York is furious. Judge Wright is taken off the criminal docket and put on the civil docket. Evidently neither the black judges in New York nor the black people in Harlem know about it, because none of them are protesting this action.

Somewhat the same thing happened to me a few years ago after I ordered the Detroit police department to release 147 black persons who had been arrested in violation of the federal and state constitutions. The media condemned me out of hand. Both houses of the Michigan legislature passed resolutions to impeach Judge Crockett. The governor called upon the state's Judicial Tenure Commission to investigate Judge Crockett with a view to removing him from office. Ultimately, of course, they realized—some apologetically—that all I had done was to follow the law; but I was not saved because my exercise of judicial discretion was correct. I was saved because the common people came to my rescue, because black and white students at Wayne University printed on the masthead of the school paper, "IF CROCKETT GOES, DETROIT GOES!"

This power of judicial discretion is too great and too meaningful to leave in the hands of others without seeking to share some of it yourself. We black judges, like all judges, are products of our personal experiences. We come up from you; we reflect your thinking. Make this power of judicial discretion work for you also. Go out and get yourselves some black judges—and when you get them, make sure you support them!

# 20

## CITIZENS AND
## CRIME REDUCTION
Gerald Caplan

Recent studies conducted by the Law Enforcement Assistance Administration (LEAA) and its National Institute of Law Enforcement and Criminal Justice have shown that many law-abiding citizens are turned off by a system designed to protect them. Angry or indifferent, they become uncooperative. As victims, they do not report the crimes committed against them; as witnesses, they do not participate in investigations and trials; and as jurors, they display resentments that may sometimes influence their judgment.

Unfortunately, this behavior is quite reasonable. Because the criminal justice system so often operates to serve its own needs at the citizen's expense, it becomes an adversary.

LEAA-sponsored surveys of crime victims indicate that large numbers of citizens fail to report crimes, even the most serious ones.[1] Across the nation, the incidence of rape, robbery, aggravated assault, and burglary is approximately three times higher than that reported to police. Larceny is almost five times higher.

While the phenomenon of unreported crime is not new, few appreciate the magnitude of the problem. Surveys conducted for the President's Crime Commission in the mid-1960s reveal that an overwhelming proportion of crime is never reported to the police.

We do not fully understand the implications of these findings. For some, no doubt, nonreporting makes sense and no unhappy consequences occur; but how many others lack the confidence in our criminal justice agencies to seek assistance? How many are so turned off by the system and its maze of legalisms that silent suffering and permanent loss seem preferable?

The most common reasons cited in the LEAA surveys for not reporting crimes were that the victims felt the police "couldn't do anything" or the incident "wasn't important enough."

## CONCERN FOR THE VICTIM

We can do much to change these feelings. Concern for the crime victim can match concern for the offender. The millions now spent studying the problems of the offenders need not—as they do now—dramatically outweigh the meager sums allocated to the problems of victims, witnesses, and jurors. Some remedies come to mind.

1. Plea bargaining study. Many victims are simply worn out by a certain type of legal maneuvering called plea bargaining. In our system, plea bargaining is the rule, not the exception. It is strictly an affair between counsel for the accused and counsel for the government.

As part of the National Institute's victim studies, it will sponsor research on the feasibility of involving the victim in the plea-bargaining process, perhaps at a pretrial conference presided over by a judge. The victim—possibly through counsel—would be given the opportunity to have a say, to participate. This would be, of course, a radical departure from traditional practice. It may be unwise; certainly its implications are not well understood. But we think it merits examination.

2. Victim ombudsman. Creation of a victim ombudsman is another idea that may have merit. The ombudsman would be there to help victims, to keep them informed of the progress of their cases. He would explain the various steps in the criminal process and provide the victim with a more realistic understanding of the law and of what is expected.

3. Rape victim study. Another study will address the crime of rape, where the attitudes of policemen and prosecutors—and doctors—have such a profound and often negative effect on the victim. The institute will investigate the ways in which rape victims and witnesses are treated in police stations, hospitals, and courtrooms, and suggest improvements. We know little about preventing rapes, but we should be able to develop, quickly, a new set of vastly improved ways of caring for the victims of sexual assaults.

4. Victim compensation. Victim compensation and offender reparation plans are also being explored. Several proposals have been made in this area: public or private insurance; restitution as a condition of probation; fines, part of which go directly to the victim; attachment of prison earnings to be paid as reparation to the victim. These methods, among others, may provide better assistance to those whom we have been unable to protect.

## WITNESS RIGHTS

Neglect is not confined to victims. Witnesses to crimes also experience problems. As a result, many witnesses simply won't help the police or prosecution. They won't come to court.

A National Institute-sponsored study of witnesses in the District of Columbia gives some indication of the scope of the problem.[2] Preliminary data show that, of nearly 8,000 cases presented for prosecution during the first half of 1973, about 3,000 were thrown out by the prosecutor or judge without a trial. The reason in 42 percent of the cases, according to prosecutors, was that witnesses did not cooperate.

Typically, a witness is told to be in court early in the morning, regardless of the time at which the case is likely to be called. Often the case will not be heard that day, and the witness must return to court again—and perhaps again and again and again. Each postponement is time out of that person's life. Because the pay for a witness averages $10 a day, every postponement and recall, every wasted hour of waiting, means money out of his or her pocket.

Frequently, however, witnesses may be labeled uncooperative when they believe they have done their best to cooperate with the prosecution. Many witnesses in the District of Columbia report they were never notified of when or where to appear for the trial. Others do not understand that being a witness involves more than telling the police officer what they have seen.

In the District of Columbia study, witnesses were asked what they thought would improve the system. Forty-nine percent want better pay; 44 percent speedier trials; 38 percent fewer postponements; and 37 percent better protection for witnesses.

The practice of calling jurors and witnesses at 9 or 10 a.m. no matter when they will be needed is standard in most urban courts. It is also thoughtless. Judges seldom address this problem. Either they are unaware of the problem or they don't care.

## JURORS' RIGHTS

A recent news report illustrates the frustration faced by many jurors. After serving only 20 days in a three-month period, a Detroit housewife angrily told the trial judge that jurors were herded around like animals, were never told what was happening, and spent most of their time waiting, not knowing what they were waiting for. She concluded: ". . . if I ever get in trouble, I'll never ask for a jury trial. I don't want to be judged by a group of angry, frustrated people."

Such conditions need not prevail. The institute has just completed a study of jury operations in seven state and local courts.[3] The study concludes that criminal court jury pools can be cut by 20 to 25 percent and still provide enough jurors for trials. If these study results hold true nationally—as we strongly suspect they do—this solution could save as much as $50 million a year.

## COURT DELAYS

Another subject that troubles citizens is excessive court delay, and one approach to reducing it is to remove certain types of minor cases that may not belong in the courts at all.

In June 1970, half of the 150,000 cases pending before the New York City Criminal Courts were traffic cases. Many had been pending for a year or more. New York transferred nonmisdemeanor moving traffic offenses—speeding, disobeying signs or signals, violating rights of way, improper turning and passing—from the criminal courts to the Motor Vehicle Department's Administrative Adjudication Bureau. At the end of the first operational year, department hearing officers had processed more than 560,000 complaints, conducted more than 180,000 hearings, and revoked or suspended some 2,000 driver licenses. Cases were disposed of within four to six weeks.

In addition to streamlining the traffic and criminal adjudication process, the bureau returned more than $4.1 million to the treasuries of the jurisdictions where the traffic offenses took place. Because of its demonstrated effectiveness and economy, the National Institute has designated it an exemplary project and will encourage other communities to adopt similar approaches.

More important, the decriminalization of all but the most serious traffic offenses reflects the view that running a red light is less serious than robbing a bank. It puts minor traffic violations in perspective. Why go out of our way to treat the average citizen like a common criminal?

## ALIENATION AND INDIFFERENCE

Crime prevention depends upon public confidence in criminal justice. Without the commitment of citizens, the criminal justice agencies are crippled; but millions of citizens are estranged from government institutions and are not likely to get over this feeling overnight.

We have learned that the very design of our neighborhoods and homes may contribute to alienation and indifference. The National Institute is sponsoring several experimental projects to test the relationship between architecture and crime.[4] The hope is that in well-designed neighborhoods, crime and the fear of crime will decline.

Crime prevention is a long-term process. But if citizens share the responsibility, the task will not be insurmountable. Each of us must help.

# NOTES

1. U.S. Department of Justice, Law Enforcement Assistance Administration (LEAA), National Criminal Justice Information and Statistics Service, *Criminal Victimization in the U.S.* (Washington, D.C.: U.S. Government Printing Office, 1974); Federal Bureau of Investigation, *Uniform Crime Reports*, first half (Washington, D.C.: U.S. Government Printing Office, 1973).

2. LEAA, National Institute of Law Enforcement and Criminal Justice, *Witness Cooperation Study* (Washington, D.C.: U.S. Government Printing Office, 1976).

3. LEAA, National Institute of Law Enforcement and Criminal Justice, *A Guide to Juror Usage* (Washington, D.C.: U.S. Government Printing Office, 1974).

4. LEAA, National Institute of Law Enforcement and Criminal Justice, *Crime Prevention Through Environmental Design* (Washington, D.C.: U.S. Government Printing Office, 1976).

# 21

## A REACTION TO
## PROFESSIONALIZATION
## AS A REFORM
Jerry Wilson

Should a college education be required for all police officers? This question, which will be asked with increasing frequency in coming years, has already been answered affirmatively by the 1967 President's Commission on Law Enforcement and the Administration of Justice and the 1972 National Advisory Commission on Criminal Justice Standards and Goals. The latter proposed that four years of college be required by 1983 for all entrants into the police service. Within the police craft, however, attitudes are mixed.

Common justifications for the college education requirement are that the broad discretion delegated to patrol officers demands better educated personnel, that college-educated police are reportedly found to be better performers, and that an increasing national level of education behooves us to raise educational requirements for police officers. Personally, I do not think that the justifications hold up well under close scrutiny.

Patrol officers need not have as much discretion as they have traditionally been delegated. The modern trend is for police chiefs or other governing officials to issue comprehensive guidelines that shift most of the discretion from the patrol officer to the agency managers, where the responsibility should rest. Such guidelines may require extensive training, but certainly not a college education, to understand. It is worth interjecting here that a distinction needs to be made between "training" and "college education." Considerably more training is needed within most police agencies, but hiring college graduates only is not going to eliminate that need.

It is unsurprising that college educated police officers are found, on the average, to be better performers than noncollege personnel. After all, the motivation and discipline required for pursuit of several optional years of schooling, reinforced by the selection and retention processes of many colleges, are factors that will cull from the college graduate group most of the disciplinary problems.

What is really being suggested by those who argue for a college require-ment in order to raise average performance is the substitution of an arbitrarily selected educational level for existing selection tests and criteria.

Virtually everyone agrees that the present tests for selecting police officers are unsatisfactory measures of performance on the job. They measure academic ability reasonably well and predict who will score high in a police academy; but they reveal little about subsequent street performance as a police officer.

Do not think that persons who score low on such tests are stupid, for often they are not. Many of those who score low but passing marks have proven to be loyal, persistent, high-performance police officers. What they often lack, of course, is erudition. Erudite or not, they have much to contribute to the job and to the community. The police craft might become more elite by excluding them, but I doubt that it would be much improved.

One group disproportionately excluded by imposing a college requirement is, of course, blacks, who attend and complete college at less than half the rate of whites. I do not think that racial bias is the motivation of those advocating the college requirement, but racial discrimination will clearly be one practical result.

There are two other subtly troubling aspects to the notion that every police officer have a college education.

First, dissatisfaction is already evident among college graduates who want staff jobs but are kept in field operations. With college education as a standard for all police, many college graduates inevitably will spend their entire careers in relatively routine assignments.

Even more troubling is the thought that there appears to be a growing class bias that measures the individual on the basis of mental test scores and academic abilities rather than on citizenship, reliability, productivity, and capacity to do a given job with proper training.

We should encourage all persons to perform at the maximum of their abili-ties rather than succumb to such intellectual snobbishness.

# 22

Leroy Clark

Much of the scholarly literature[1] and the popular writing on prisons focuses on inmate rights. These matters are peripheral to the question of whether the prisons can be made to have an impact on the prime concern of the public, namely recidivism.

Yet we are aware that the commission of a first criminal offense and recidivism after release from prison go hand in hand with a weak or non-existent employment history.[2] Outside of white-collar crime, organized crime, and certain victimless crimes (prostitution, drug use, and so forth), the overwhelming number of offenses creating the most hysteria in our cities—muggings and burglaries—seem directly related to the inability of an offender to get and maintain a job, especially if he has been incarcerated. This explains why the poor and minorities comprise the vast majority of the prison population—their employment possibilities are depressed by poor schooling and racial discrimination.

It is the thesis of this chapter that if we could find ways to integrate the prisoner into the work world, all the psychotherapy and all the sophisticated programs designed to treat him as if he were a deviate would be largely unnecessary.*

---

*About the only category of nonprofit criminal offenders who might very well benefit from some kind of personalized, individualized psychotherapy are aggressive or exploitative sex offenders such as rapists or child molesters. But the ordinary prison is hardly the place to begin their rehabilitation, especially since it is a place where we are artificially creating sexual problems for the rest of the prison population by depriving them of their usual heterosexual contacts.

201

Despite the wealth of data indicating that the prisoner has experienced a disconnection between himself and work, the bulk of prisoners today are not productively employed while incarcerated, or being trained for such employment. One would think we should be attempting to introduce the work relationship into prisons, for the simple reason that work may be the best deterrent to a continued life of crime.

It becomes even more surprising that we fail to do wo when correctional officials say that idleness in prison seriously erodes their capacity to maintain discipline.

## THE WORK TRADITION IN PRISONS

The idle prisoner is of recent origin. The exclusion of prisoners from work was the exception and not the rule in the early days when prisons were first constructed. Indeed, prisons were initially built in response to two impulses: first, a desire to avoid the death penalty and the mutilation and branding of prisoners that carried over into the American colonies from England; and second, to have prisoners work and pray in a solitary situation that would be morally regenerative. Thus, work as punishment and penance had its first currency in the early stages of prison development. When the interest in producing a religious conversion in prisoners began to wane, a concept began to develop that prisoners should work to recompense the state for the costs of running the prison.[3]

A number of abuses developed from this use of the prisoner, and since the "paying his own keep" notion still survives, some of the same problems exist today. Prisoners were forced to work for the state with no wages for their labor, and the most flagrant abuses occurred when prisoners were literally leased to private employers. Any payment went to the state. It was easy for private employers to exploit this powerless, despised group, and thus prisoners worked for long hours in unsanitary and unsafe conditions. If by chance a prisoner happened to be a skilled, diligent worker, his reward was often that he was denied parole and kept in prison longer for the benefit of the private entrepreneur.

The leasing out of prisoners soon ended, not only because of the scandalous way in which they were used, but more importantly because private employers who had no access to this form of cheap labor began to complain. The final blow to this system came from the labor unions who complained that since jobs were scarce, they should not go to the unworthy (read convicts).

It was during the depression of the late 1920s and early 1930s that the labor unions were most vocal in trying to bar the prisoners from work they desperately needed and thought rightfully belonged to them. Then a very different view of the prisoner and work developed. The prisoner was no longer to be forced to work as punishment—his punishment was not being allowed to work.

Against this background the so-called state-use system was developed, in which prison-made goods were barred by federal legislation from the private sector; such goods could be sold only to government agencies.[4] This might not have been so bad if it only meant that prisoners were being pushed into government work, since the civil servants were not well-organized enough at that time to complain that prisoners were poaching on their work. However, this development, which characterizes prison work today, had a number of failings that made it inadequate to meet the test of truly building a work capacity in prisoners.

First, the actual impact of introducing the state-use system was to reduce the number of prisoners productively employed from 75 percent in 1885, to 50 percent, in 1926.[5] In the federal system in 1974, only 25 percent of the inmates were employed in prison industries.[6]

Second, the prime goal of the state-use system was to profit from the prison labor; thus unskilled prisoners were not given extensive training, but were put to low-level, repetitive tasks or to janitorial-maintenance work. The prisoner gained no skills transferable to the private sector, and to some extent the prison maintained a monopoly on the only kind of work prisoners were allowed to do (for example, making license plates).

## A CONTEMPORARY PRISON WORK PROGRAM

What should be the goals for prison work, and what legislation might we have to change in order to achieve a greater capacity to draw prisoners into lawful occupations and away from criminal activity? I would posit that the goal of prison work ought to be, as much as possible within the confines of the security needs of the prison, to reproduce a vocational training and employment situation comparable to the one free laborers outside the prisons experience, including the job benefits and rights that free laborers enjoy.

1. Minimum wage. As of 1968, 33 states indicated that they paid their prisoners wages ranging from 4 cents a day to a high of $1.30 a day. In five states, only 10 percent of the inmates earned any money at all.[7] This is hardly likely to contribute to a prisoner taking seriously the notion of labor efficiency and incentives, and indeed, it has always been a major complaint of prisoners when they have rioted.[8] Prisoners should be paid whatever minimum wage is mandated by state or federal legislation, and above the minimum wage, the going wage prevailing in the area for work of that nature.[9] The prisoners should probably be required to contribute to the support of their families, if they are paid a going wage. There is no reason for that obligation to end simply because they are in prison. Further, it would enhance the possibility that the prisoner might re-enter his family upon his release, because he has at least contributed to their support. Some persons have objected to paying prisoners the prevailing wage on

the grounds that the cost of their upkeep should be deducted from their wages. However, if one truly began to deduct the full cost of conviction and incarceration, this should entail seeking reimbursement for the entire criminal justice system, because the salaries of prosecutors, legal aid societies, probation officers, and so forth, are all part of the surveillance, apprehension, defense, and conviction mechanism. If we included the capital invested in building the prisons, we would be back at zero wage for all prisoners. A prison is in no sense a hotel in which a prisoner is receiving free room and board. And the notion that free laborers will feel cheated because they do not have the free ride that the prisoner is getting is hard to take seriously. No free laborer would change places with the prisoner, given the other deprivations that go along with incarceration.

2. Workmen's compensation, pensions, unemployment compensation. Prisoners do not, in most states, receive compensation as other laborers do when they sustain an injury due to employment. This is true even in the states where prisoners are required to work—and even where a prisoner can show that the injury was occasioned by the negligence of supervisors. This is a particularly destructive and inhuman policy (lamented even by some of the courts that have been forced to deny a prisoner relief),[10] especially for prisoners who have lost limbs and become permanently disabled, and who then have another major obstacle to securing employment upon leaving the prison. Workmen's compensation statutes should be amended to accord the same benefits to prisoners as to other workers.

3. Pension rights. A right to certain pensions can be lost if one is convicted of a felony. Legislation that conditions pension payment upon the satisfactory completion of duties while employed is probably reasonable and an added incentive for honest and trustworthy performance. However, some statutes do not have such a causal nexus, and a conviction, unrelated to any breach of trust in one's employment, can cause a divestment of pension rights. There is again no reason for this special lifetime punishment, especially when it falls on the elderly prisoner with special problems securing work.

4. Unemployment compensation. Prisoners are now given a small sum of money ($10-$25) upon leaving the prison, ostensibly to ease their way back into normal life. This obviously is inadequate, especially since a prisoner may have a more difficult time than the average person in finding employment. This could be remedied if prisoners were entitled to unemployment compensation based on their having worked while in prison.

5. Unionization. Prisoners in a few states have recently demanded the right to form unions to engage in collective bargaining about their working conditions. The right to organize and bargain collectively with the correction officials should be accorded to prisoners. Prison officials have tended to resist the development of prisoners' unions, for fear that they may disrupt the power relationships in the prison and be a base for prisoner rebellion. While unions obviously would enhance the power of the prisoners, there is no reason to presuppose that it

would of necessity be exercised irresponsibly. Indeed, there is some reason to believe that the covert, unorganized, and individualized bargaining that the tougher, more vicious prisoners now engage in to secure privileges for themselves is a contributor to prison disorder.[11]

6. Ending the state-use system. The federal legislation and any state legislation that restricts prisoners to producing products and services for governmental agencies should be repealed. Indeed, private industry ought to be actively encouraged to set up employment opportunities within the prison, which could continue once the prisoner left the prison. There ought to be some government subsidy for private employers as an incentive for their participation, and also to underwrite any necessary training or education for the prisoners.

One reality that encourages subsidization is that the prison population is apt to need basic remedial education before being able to benefit from specific job training. This need has often been ignored, and prisoners have been utilized instead as unskilled labor, making their employment upon release spotty or low-paid in an automating economy. A private company must be paid to undertake remedial education in addition to vocational training.

## WOMEN IN PRISON

It is very rare for female prisoners to be accorded any training or meaningful work. A number of reasons are frequently put forward in explanation: female adults comprise a small fraction of the total offender population, and their prisons are not large enough to accommodate vocational training and a developed industry. They are also usually short-termers, and there is little success in rehabilitating persons who commit the kinds of offenses for which many are incarcerated (for example, drug use and prostitution). I think this latter group probably ought not to be in prison at all. Further, the female offender population is rapidly on the increase, and is being charged with many of the same crimes as men. If their present places of incarceration are not appropriate for job training and rehabilitation programs, they simply ought to be transferred to the male prisons, where they can avail themselves of such opportunities.

## CONCLUSION

To be effective, the in-prison reforms suggested in this paper should be combined with other measures. One would be to eliminate much of the legislation that bars convicts from employment in various government positions. Another would be legislation to place the burden of proof on private employers to justify their rejection of a person with a criminal record. They would have to show that, given the nature of the job sought by the ex-convict and the nature of his offense, it would be reasonable to disfavor him (for example, a serious reckless driving offense might disqualify an ex-convict for a taxi driver's job).

The major obstacle, however, to all of the suggestions for fully integrating the prisoner into regular work is the failure of our economy to generate full employment. As long as jobs are scarce, and becoming increasingly so, there will continue to be strong resistance to giving jobs to prisoners when others are unemployed. We probably recognize, however, that alarm about the rising urban crime is wasted energy unless we are willing to implement policies to bring about full employment. If the private economy cannot fully absorb all the able-bodied persons around, then clearly it is time for the government to institute supplementary public employment so that everybody in the society who wants to work is given the opportunity to do so.

## NOTES

1. *Nolan* v. *Fitzpatrick*, 451 F. 2d 345 (1st Cir., 1971); *Long* v. *Parker*, 390 F. 2d 816 (3rd Cir. 1968); *Lee* v. *Washington*, 390 U.S. 333 (1968).

2. See Daniel Glasser, *The Effectiveness of a Prison and Parole System* (New York: Bobbs Merrill, 1969).

3. George G. Killinger and Paul F. Cromwell, Jr., *Penology—The Evolution of Corrections in America* (St. Paul, Minn.: Nest Publishing Co., 1973), pp. 12-73.

4. Hawes-Cooper legislation, 49 U.S.C. sec. 60 (1970); Ashurst-Sumners Act, 49 Stat. 494 (1935).

5. Luis N. Robinson, *Should Prisoners Work* (Philadelphia: John C. Winston, 1931).

6. Richard G. Singer and William P. Statsky, *The Rights of the Imprisoned* (New York: Bobbs-Merrill, 1974), p. 890.

7. Elmer Johnson, "Prison Industry," in *Crime, Correction and Society*, ed. Elmer Johnson (Homewood, Ill.: The Dorsey Press, 1968), p. 568.

8. New York State Special Commission, official report, *Attica* (New York: Bantam Books, 1973), p. 253.

9. Lawrence S. Root, "Work Release Legislation," *Federal Probation* 36 (March 10, 1972): 38.

10. *Warren* v. *Booneville*, 151 Miss. 457, 118 So. 290 (1928).

11. See Note, "Bargaining in Correctional Institutions: Restructuring the Relation between the Inmate and the Prison Authority," *Yale Law Journal* 81 (1972): 725.

# 23

## CIVIL SERVANTS, UNIONISM, AND THE STATE OF CITIES
Wilbur C. Rich

Wilbur Thompson, an economist, once asserted, "No nation is so affluent that it can afford to throw away a major city."[1] Cities must be reclaimed. Growth-oriented policy analysts have managed to suggest formulas that are simultaneously altruistic, humane, logical, positivistic, incremental, and pluralistic. But many of the models proffered pose serious problems. Are there limits to the growth of cities? What is the fate of cities with a declining tax base? Why do persons stay in cities once it becomes clear that they will never find jobs? Why do urban politicians commit their cities to obligations for which there is little hope of finding revenue?

## THE FORRESTER MODEL

In these times of dwindling financial and environmental resources, J. W. Forrester, an M.I.T. systems engineer, offers an instructive model.[2] Forrester finds that present urban policy choices that seem humanitarian—welfare, low-income housing, job training—are deleterious to the internal revival capacity of cities. The present policies, for example, promote the growth of low-income housing at the expense of middle-income taxpayers. The present corporation tax system makes corporations nomadic in the sense that they must move (usually outside the city) in order to get tax advantages. This is also true for the zoning policies that promote residential dwellings instead of industrial or a mix of the two.

Business, housing, and population are the three basic elements in the Forrester model. Whether or not urban systems become stagnant depends on how the system regulates its mix of the three. Severe population loss, housing structure decay, and nomadic industries can rob a city of its economic base and thus its vitality. The aging of cities results from short-range, politically self-serving, unscientific policies.

To Forrester, economic recovery requires retrenchment of city welfare policy so as to discourage the underemployed (working and nonworking poor) from coming to the city. He would do this by not providing them with a place to live. An urban removal policy like the Chicago lakeside redevelopment project is one way to accomplish this. A rent control policy like New York's could achieve the same end by leading to the decay of housing and forcing the poor out. Forrester would lure industry back and make remaining industry comfortable through tax incentives and changes in zoning laws.

Forrester rejects piecemeal, superficial approaches to city problems, but he has been criticized for his prescription. Urban historians do not treat his work seriously because Forrester does not seem to know much about urban history.

The Forrester model also reveals a glaring conceptual gap—the role of the urban bureaucracies and unions. This writer believes that a modification of the Forrester model might make it more relevant to the urban condition.

## THE BUREAUCRATIC-NEOSYNDICALISM MODEL

The growth of the public sector in cities is no less than phenomenal. There are several million civil servants in urban bureaucracies today. The rising cost of municipal personnel threatens to bankrupt the city, fiscally and politically, but unionization has made public employment secure and strengthened the civil servants' ability to resist changes. It is no longer responsible to argue that unions are simply wage and benefit hustlers, for they have influenced public policy beyond their own expectations.

The unions resemble the old syndicalists in their stress on worker primacy and their seeming disregard for the economic survival of the cities. Modern city civil servants see themselves as members of the working class. They must strike not only to gain the respect of their private sector brethren, but, more importantly, to gain a sense of personal dignity. The strike has a cleansing effect on the poor image of the bureaucrats.

The antiintellectual tone of the union leadership also supports the syndicalist analogy. Leaders do not blush for having nothing to say except that workers need more pay and benefits; and they do not seem to have thought about the city as a long-term enterprise and how they will fit into its future. Norton Long observes:

> The scoring system of union leaders and their union audience is how
> well they do for their members in competition with other unions
> for such gains as are to be made. They are concerned about wages,
> working conditions, and the maintenance and increase in the number

of jobs and the size of the union membership on which their own prestige and power depend. They have little concern about how costs are to be met; that is someone else's business. The unions are also in many cases able to halt vital services on which the city's functioning depends. Teachers' strikes, garbage collectors' strikes, blue flu, and a growing number of other "labor actions" show just how vulnerable the large city has become to the blackmail of its employees.[3]

## THE WELFARE BUREAUCRACY

Cities are welfare bureaucracies, with human-problem agencies that do nothing to augment the tax base. These agencies recruit a certain type of marginal middle-class work force. The caseworkers, rehabilitation workers, public school teachers, child care workers, and health workers all make their living servicing the poor. The politics is analogous to an urban leapfrog game: one class using the backs of the other for social mobility. Their economic position is fragile, and the transparency of their social position generates a sense of powerlessness and anger. The anger expresses itself in the militancy of their unions and associations.

The human-servicing bureaucracies grow as the city remains a magnet for the poor. The unskilled workers Forrester wishes to regulate and manipulate have become a sort of industry in themselves. The problems generated by citizens have become jobs for other citizens.

Indeed, the overproduction of people is the building block of great bureaucratic empires. In a sense the city is creating two welfare groups, working and nonworking. A visit to an income maintenance center or recertification center of the New York City Human Resources Administration provides an opportunity to observe these two groups. Former welfare recipients are serving welfare recipients. The working welfare recipients often assume the behavior patterns of the next level of the bureaucracy. These new paraprofessionals are barely assigned to the centers before the unions recruit them.

The revival of the cities cannot be done without according a major role to unions and bureaucracies. Any rational public policy must include input from these new interest groups. There is a series of questions city managers must ask themselves in dealing with unions: What are the implications for cities without resident laws for their civil servants? What effects will disruptive strikes have on public policy planning and implementation? In what kinds of cities are unions most effective? What are the political and fiscal implications of cities that turn over their labor negotiations to arbitration? What kind of laws accelerate or retard union development? What types of politicians are most open to union co-optation? What sort of linkages do public employee unions develop with industrial unions? What role does union leadership envision for itself in partisan politics? What types of coalitions can unions establish with other public associations and constituencies? Will unions co-opt efforts to increase citizen participation? Can the city afford to invest so much of its energies and resources in costly agencies and their personnel? Unless a city has undertaken some long-range analysis of these questions, it runs the risk of becoming a bureaucratic city-state.

The unionization of civil servants has made them less neutral toward the direction of public policy. Where they once had only an organization to protect, they now have a union to nurture. Any city using a simulation model to make choices must include bureaucratic sabotage as a real threat to planning. Unfortunately, unions will follow the edict of the Bible: they will be fruitful and multiply, regardless of public choice.

## IS THERE ANY REASON TO BE HOPEFUL?

If the bureaucratic-neosyndicalism model does anything, it raises questions about how government solves problems. The agency-service approach to problem solving is a legacy of the New Deal. It is doubtful whether this strategy is appropriate for today's urban problems. Why do we need a city agency once we have identified a problem? We must define limits to urban government growth to save urban government.

But it is easy to attack the normative solutions of others, and much more difficult to come up with ideas on one's own. This writer is very much attracted to solutions of Norton Long and Peter Drucker. Long envisons the city's function as an upgrader of the disadvantaged. In order to do this, the city must reassert its sense of community. Citizens who agree on "shared purpose can sustain a legitimate leadership and an acceptable normative order."[4] Long, like most optimists, tells us a grim tale (agreeing with the many ideas of neosyndicalist bureaucratic model) but ends up exhorting us not to despair—we can do it. We, meaning fair-minded liberal whites and hard-working blacks, can revive the city. The problem with this thinking is that it ignores the constituency interest groups with a stake in the status quo.

Drucker believes that government must "decentralize" its functions to other institutions in order to do less and achieve more. Like Forrester, be believes in using economic incentives to preserve a capitalist society. Drucker tells government to release its grip on certain functions so it can get back to governing and planning.[5] If Drucker and Long have more in mind than organizing housing cooperatives, returning the charity functions to private philanthropic organizations, or making the city into a tourist attraction, then a system pessimist can be hopeful. The idea of allowing the disadvantaged the freedom to organize public service corporations is interesting, but is it practical? Can Harlem residents create a mini-sanitation department for their community? Will the use of vouchers to select schools create the competition necessary for good education? Could Harlem residents operate the twenty-sixth precinct? Should Harlem, South Side Chicago, Watts, and so on, be granted special local corporation status? There are many kinds of urban experiments, which are not sandbox oriented, that may be worth investing time and resources, but the major problem is a lack of a conceptual breakthrough about what we want cities to be in the future.

## NOTES

1. Wilbur R. Thompson, *A Preface to Urban Economics* (Washington, D.C.: Resources for the Future, Inc., 1963), p. 10.

2. Jay W. Forrester, *Urban Dynamics* (Cambridge, Mass.: M.I.T. Press, 1969).

3. Norton Long, *The Unwalled City* (New York: Basic Books, 1972), p. 115.

4. Long, op. cit., p. 184.

5. Peter Drucker, *The Age of Discontinuity* (New York: Harper and Row, 1969), p. 226.

# 24

## PLANNING AND THE FUTURE OF CITIES
Bette Woody
Lawrence D. Mann

Planning has a long tradition in local government in the United States, but until the 1960s it had limited impact. Moreover, it was isolated from the citizens. Today and in the future, the limited focus of planners in serving economic interests or in designing ideal patterns of land distribution, which was never realized, has been largely abandoned and will continue to be replaced with a concern for integration of community goals into the decision-making process of local government.

Planning as a tool for modernization of urban environments is often overlooked by local government officials. However, with recent changes in the basic concepts of planning roles, including a strong shift to policy, problem solving, environmental monitoring, and implementation, planning has emerged as a powerful tool to help communities move towards balance and economic and social health.

Planning identifies the problems and questions for the future of communities. It provides data to support choices about public and private actions. Two necessities for translating planning into action are resources—particularly fiscal resources for capital investment—and design. The public economy of local government is increasingly constrained in its abilities to finance projects, but careful planning can help spread limited resources. Design is a means for organizing activities spatially in ways that assist the activities of citizens. Design that takes account of the interaction between people and space will increase the livability of urban environments.

## Public Policy Program
### Advisory Board

Andrew Billingsley
Morgan State University
Baltimore, Maryland

Frank de Leeuw
Congressional Budget Office
Washington, D.C.

Harvey A. Garn
The Urban Institute
Washington, D.C.

Charles V. Hamilton
Department of Political Science
Columbia University
New York City, New York

Charles Harris
Political Science Department
Howard University
Washington, D.C.

Thomas A. Hart
Westinghouse Electric Corporation
Washington, D.C.

Matthew Holden
Public Service Commission of
    Wisconsin
Madison, Wisconsin

S. M. Miller
Department of Sociology
Boston University
Boston, Massachusetts

Gilbert Steiner
Brookings Institution
Washington, D.C.

Charles Taylor
Academy for Contemporary Problems
Columbus, Ohio

Ronald Walters
Political Science Department
Howard University
Washington, D.C.

HERRINGTON J. BRYCE, a graduate of the Maxwell School, Syracuse University, Syracuse, New York, is Director of Research and Director of the Public Policy Fellows Program, Joint Center for Political Studies, Washington, D.C. Dr. Bryce is a 1970-71 Brookings Economic Policy Fellow, Brookings Institution, Washington, D.C., and a senior staff member of the Urban Institute. He was also on the faculty of the Massachusetts Institute of Technology. He is the coeditor of *Population Policy and Urban Conservation*, and author of "On Identifying the Maximum Socio-economic Gaps between Regions of Different Levels of Per Capita Income," "Toward Full Employment: A Minority Perspective," in *A Full Employment Program for the 1970s*, eds. Alan Gartner, William Lynch, Frank Riessman, and "Problems of Policy Management and Implementation by Local Government." He is a member of the American Economic Association, American Political Science Association, American Society of Public Administrators, and American Society of Planning Officials.

MARCUS ALEXIS is Professor of Economics and Urban Affairs, Northwestern University. He is a co-author of *Organizational Decision Making* and *Empirical Foundations of Marketing: Research Findings in the Behavioral and Applied Sciences.*

ROY W. BAHL is Professor of Economics and Director of the Metropolitan Studies Programs, Maxwell School, Syracuse University. He has authored *Metropolitan City Expenditures* and co-authored *Taxes, Expenditures and the Economic Base: A Case Study of New York City.*

LEE P. BROWN is Director of Public Safety, Multnomah County, Portland, Oregon. He is the author of *Crime, Criminal Justice and the Black Community* and *The Death of Police-Community Relations.*

LEE CALHOUN is a lecturer in Political Science, Howard University and is the author of *The Problem of Human Experimentation from a Black Perspective* and *Social Research and the Black Community: Selected Issues and Priorities*, Lawrence E. Gary, editor.

ALAN CAMPBELL is Dean, Maxwell School of Citizenship and Public Affairs, Syracuse University. He has authored *The Political Economy of State and Local Government Reform* (co-ed. Roy W. Bahl) and *Metropolitan American: Fiscal Patterns and Government Systems* (with S. Sacks).

GERALD CAPLAN, Director of The National Institute of Law Enforcement and Criminal Justice, U.S. Department of Justice, Washington, D.C., has authored "The Police Legal Advisor," *The Journal of Criminal Law, Criminology and Police Science*. It has been published as an appendix to the Task Force Report of Police for the President's Commission on Law Enforcement and Criminal Justice. He also has written "Reflections on the Nationalization of Crime," *Law and the Social Order*.

LEROY CLARK is Professor of Law, New York University School of Law. Among his publications are *The Grand Jury—The Use and Abuse of Political Power* and "The Labor Law Problems of the Prisoner," *Rutgers Law Review*.

PHILLIP CLAY is Assistant Professor of Urban Studies, Massachusetts Institute of Technology. He has contributed to *America: Housing Needs*, Joint Center for Urban Studies, M.I.T./Harvard University and authored a monograph entitled *A Safe Place to Live/Design for Security in Multifamily Housing*.

GEORGE W. CROCKETT, JR. is Judge, Recorder's Court, Detroit, Michigan. His publications include "Justice, the Courts, and Change," *The Journal of the National Institute of Applied Behavioral Science* 10, no. 3 (1934) and "Criminal Justice in China," *Judicature, the Journal of the American Judicature Society*, 59, no. 5 (1975).

ERNEST ERBER is Director of Research and Program Planning, National Committee Against Discrimination in Housing, Inc. His publications include a volume of professional papers, *Urban Planning in Transition*, which is widely used as a textbook in planning courses. He also has authored "The Inner City in the Post-Industrial Era—A Study of Its Changing Social Fabric and Economic Function," published in *The Inner City* (Declan Kennedy and Margrit I. Kennedy, editors; Elek Books, Ltd. 1974).

HARVEY GARN, a 1958 Rhodes Scholar, is Program Director, Urban Development, Processes and Indicator Research, The Urban Institute. He has authored "The Integration of Equity and Efficiency Criteria in Public Project Selection," with Martin C. McGuire, *Economic Journal*, 1969.

THE HONORABLE KENNETH A. GIBSON is the Mayor of Newark, New Jersey and President-Elect of the United States Conference of Mayors. Mayor Gibson has authored "The Black Community and Cooperative Ventures," three series of articles in *The Black Economy* magazine, 1973.

CHARLES HAMILTON is President, Metropolitan Applied Research Center. His publications include *The Bench and the Ballot: Southern Federal Judges and Black Voters*, Oxford University Press, 1973 and *The Black Experience in American Politics*, G.P. Putnam Press, 1973.

IRA KATZNELSON is Associate Professor of Political Science, University of Chicago. He has authored *Black Men, White Cities*, Oxford University Press, 1973; and co-authored *The Politics of Power*, Harcourt, Brace, Jovanovich, 1975.

MILTON KOTLER is a Resident Fellow, Institute for Policy Studies, Washington, D.C. His publications include *Neighborhood Government*, Bobbs Merrill, 1969 and "The Ethics of Neighborhood Government," *Social Research*, Summer 1975.

HOWARD N. LEE is the Ex-Mayor of Chapel Hill, North Carolina. He is now the Director, Office of Human Development, Duke University. His publications include "The Southern Political Revolution," *The Black Politician*, edited by Mervyn Dymally, 1970 and "Political Trends in the South," *Law Review*, North Carolina Central University Law School Press, 1971.

LAWRENCE MANN is Professor of City Planning, Harvard Graduate School of Design, Cambridge, Massachusetts. He has authored "Community Decision Making," *Readings in Community Organization Practice*, Ralph Kramer and Harry Spect (editors), Prentice Hall, 2nd edition, 1975 and "One More Truth to Teach About Population Biology," *Social Implications of Biological Education*, Arnold Grobman (editor), National Association of Biology Teachers, 1970.

ERIC MARTIN is an undergraduate student at Dartmouth College.

RICARDO A. MILLETT is Associate Professor, School of Social Work, Atlanta University, Atlanta, Georgia. His publications include "The Concept of Intelligence in Four Villages in Guatemala," report for the Institute of Nutrition of Central America and Panama, 1970 and *The Educational Manpower Needs of Developing Black Colleges: An Analysis of the Constraints of Resource Allocation (Manpower and Budget) on the Planning and Staffing Needs of Shaw University in Raleigh, North Carolina and Federal City College in Washington, D.C.*, published in a study of the Education Professions Development Act Training Programs for Higher Education Personnel, 1973, Abt Associates, Inc.

PAUL E. PETERSON, Professor of Political Science, University of Chicago has authored *Race and Authority in Urban Politics*, Russell Sage Foundation, 1973 and co-authored with David Greenston *School Politics Chicago Style*, University of Chicago Press, 1976.

THOMAS F. PETTIGREW is a Professor of Social Psychology, Harvard University, Cambridge, Massachusetts. He has published *Racially Separate or Together?*, McGraw Hill, 1971 and he has edited *Racial Discrimination in the United States*, Harper and Row, 1975.

WILBUR RICH is an Assistant Professor of Political Science, Columbia University. He has written *Who Runs New York City: Bureaucratic Power in New York City Politics* (forthcoming) and "Accountability Indices: The Search for the Philosopher's Touchstone," *Administration and Mental Health Journal*, Fall 1973.

SEYMOUR SACKS is Professor of Economics, Maxwell School, Syracuse University, Syracuse, New York. He has authored *City Schools/Suburban Schools: A History of Fiscal Conflict*, Sacks et al., Syracuse University Press, 1972 and has co-authored *Metropolitan America: Fiscal Patterns and Governmental Systems*, with Alan K. Campbell, Free Press, 1967.

CLARENCE STONE is Associate Professor of Government and Politics and Urban Studies at the University of Maryland, College Park, Maryland, where he is also Research Associate, Bureau of Governmental Research. His publications include *Law and Justice*, Duke University Press (Stone et al.), 1973 and *Economic Growth and Neighborhood Discontent*, University of North Carolina Press, 1976.

NANCY TEVIS is a Research Associate, The Urban Institute, Washington, D.C. She has authored "Costs: Estimation and Use in the Value of CDC," Urban Institute Working Paper 0719-01-4, August 1974 and "Evaluating Community Development Corporations: A Summary Report," The Urban Institute, March 1976.

DAVID WALKER is the Assistant Director for Governmental Structure and Function, Advisory Commission on Intergovernmental Relations, Washington, D.C. His publications include "How Fares Federalism in the Mid-70's," *The Annals of the American Association of Political and Social Science*, November 1974 and "New England and the Federal System," *Publius, Journal of Federalism*, Fall 1972.

JERRY WILSON is the former Chief of Police, Washington, D.C. He is now Chairman of Task Force on Disorders and Terrorism. His publications include *Police Report, Boston*, Little, Brown and Company, 1975 and *Police and the Media* (co-authored with Paul Q. Fuqua), Little, Brown and Company, 1975.

BETTE WOODY is Commissioner of the Department of Environmental Management for the Commonwealth of Massachusetts. Her publications include "Transportation and the Poor," Issues for the New York and New Jersey Metropolitan Regions, Regional Plan Association Committee on Minority Affairs, 1972 and "Southern Corridor Land Development," M.I.T. Urban Systems Laboratories, 1972 (co-authored with Elbert Bishop).

COMMUNITY DEVELOPMENT STRATEGIES: Case Studies of Major Model
Cities
George J. Washnis

THE EFFECTS OF URBAN GROWTH: A Population Impact Analysis
Richard P. Appelbaum, Jennifer A.
Bigelow, Henry P. Kramer, Harvey L.
Molotch, and Paul Relis

INNOVATIONS FOR FUTURE CITIES
Gideon Golany

POLITICIZING THE POOR: The Legacy of the War on Poverty in
a Mexican-American Community
Biliana C. S. Ambrecht

THE POLITICS OF HOUSING IN OLDER URBAN AREAS
edited by Robert E. Mendelson and
Michael A. Quinn

PROBLEM TENANTS IN PUBLIC HOUSING: Who, Where, and
Why Are They?
Richard S. Scobie

PUBLIC HOUSING AND URBAN RENEWAL: An Analysis of
Federal-Local Relations
Richard D. Bingham

URBAN PROBLEMS AND PUBLIC POLICY CHOICES
edited by Joel Bergsman and
Howard L. Wiener